In this century psychiatric hospitals have often come to be seen as places of incarceration rather than of true asylum for the mentally ill. At the same time there is a belief that community care policies have brought about a decline in the provision of asylum for some of the patients whose needs were previously met by the psychiatric hospital. This book opens up the debate about how far these views are accurate.

Based on an empirical examination of psychiatric care in the past and the present with an international focus, *Asylum in the Community* critically assesses the concept of asylum and shows how it can be operationalised for services outside the hospital. Drawing on work in the USA, Belgium, Spain, Ireland and England, contributors analyse such services from both user and provider perspectives. From these analyses the editors establish the key elements of asylum that should be considered in developing contemporary community services for the mentally ill.

Asylum in the Community offers a multidisciplinary approach to new directions in psychiatric care. It provides a balanced assessment of a controversial, topical issue for managers and providers of mental health services and those teaching or training in the mental health services.

Dylan Tomlinson is Senior Lecturer in the Sociology of Health and Illness at South Bank University, London, and **John Carrier** is Senior Lecturer in Social Policy at the London School of Economics.

 WITHDRAWN

Contributors: Mark Finnane; Rosalind Furlong; Geraldine Huka; Oscar Martínez Azumendi; James Oerton; Lindsay Prior; James Raftery; Andrew Scull; Jan Wallcraft.

Asylum in the community

Edited by
Dylan Tomlinson and John Carrier

London and New York

This book is dedicated to the memories of
Geoff Bromley, whose main concerns were those
contained here, and whose contribution to
the field was immense, and to Joanne Snooks, desk
editor at Routledge, whose commitment saw the
book through to publication.

First published 1996
by Routledge
11 New Fetter Lane, London EC4P 4EE

Simultaneously published in the USA and Canada
by Routledge
29 West 35th Street, New York, NY 10001

Routledge is an International Thomson Publishing company I(T)P

© 1996 Dylan Tomlinson and John Carrier

Typeset in Times by
Florencetype Limited, Stoodleigh, Devon
Printed and Bound in Great Britain by
T.J. Press Ltd, Padstow, Cornwall

British Library Cataloguing in Publication Data
A catalogue record for this book is available from the British Library

Library of Congress Cataloguing in Publication Data
A catalogue record for this book has been requested

ISBN 0–415–10742–3
ISBN 0–415–10743–1 (pbk)

Contents

Illustrations

TABLES

Contributors

Oscar Martínez Azumendi is a community psychiatrist who has studied the development of mental health centres in England and Spain, and has published in both his own country and the UK on this topic. He has a special concern with the social circumstances of people using mental health centres and their expectations with regard to service possibilities.

Mark Finnane is Professor of History at Griffith University, Brisbane, Australia. His books include *Insanity and the Insane in Post-Famine Ireland* (1981) and *Police and Government: Histories of Policing in Australia*. He is currently researching issues in the history of punishment and the history of violence.

Rosalind Furlong is Consultant Psychiatrist for the Haringey Healthcare NHS. She was previously a Consultant at the former Friern Hospital, where she was Chair of the Medical Committee. She has a special concern with the development of services for those suffering long-term mental illness, both in relation to her own patients and in relation to her being an exponent of the Haven concept of care in professional journals.

Geraldine Huka trained as a lawyer and has had a long-standing concern with the over-representation and forcible detention of black people in mental institutions. She acted as Adviser to the African Caribbean Mental Health Association and subsequently held the post of Director for this organisation, where she had reponsibility for the development of the Sanctuary project which is described in this book.

James Oerton is a clinical psychologist with a particular interest in deinstitutionalisation. As a member of the Team for the Assessment of Psychiatric Services (TAPS), in its study of hospital closure, he interviewed a large number of ex-mental hospital residents in community settings and his contribution to this book draws on the results of that work.

Lindsay Prior is Senior Lecturer in Sociology at the University of Ulster and has undertaken a range of substantial mental health research projects, covering both institutional and community care. He has published many scholarly papers on the sociology of mental health and is the author of *The Social Organisation of Mental Illness.*

James Raftery is a Senior Health Economist with the Wessex Institute of Public Health Medicine. He was previously Health Economist and Honorary Lecturer at St Georges Hospital, London. His PhD challenges the notion that asylum care is in significant decline and he sets out the basis of that challenge in his contribution to this book.

Andrew Scull is Professor of Sociology at the University of California. He has carried out extensive research on the development of asylums, and is an internationally acclaimed authority in this field. He is perhaps best known for his book *Museums of Madness*, which has been recently revised and republished as *The Most Solitary of Afflictions: Madness and Society in Britain 1700–1900.*

Jan Wallcraft is a Survivor of Mental Health Services who has extensive experience of acting as a user consultant, facilitator and speaker. She has specialised for MIND and other campaigning organisations in surveying users' views of services on a national level and working with them to communicate those views. She is currently undertaking a PhD study of asylum in the community.

Acknowledgements

The editors would like to acknowledge the help of Dr Darra Phelan, who made it possible for them to gain access to the records kept in the Ballinasloe Asylum, County Galway, and who gave us some insight into the Irish refuge context.

Thanks are also due to Maggie Wallace, formerly of the Team for the Assessment of Psychiatric Services, who assisted the editors and James Oerton to obtain medical case notes for patients resident at Friern and Claybury Hospitals.

Finally the editors would like to record their gratitude to the Leverhulme Trust who awarded them a small grant in 1991 to enable the study of patients' case notes reported in Chapter Six to take place.

Introduction

Dylan Tomlinson and John Carrier

Few would defend the mass-produced care of the large mental hospital, and it is government policy in Europe and America for residential care to be provided on a smaller scale in community care settings. Community care, however, has, of late, been subjected to ever more critical scrutiny. This has led to 'Scull's dilemma' being posed (Jones, 1982). This is the dilemma of those who see institutional neglect being succeeded by community neglect and who thus look in vain for an alternative. Scull suggests in this volume that the dilemma is the dilemma of society at large rather than of mental health care analysts. But whoever it is that faces the dilemma, its existence calls for a reappraisal of the role of the mental hospital in giving asylum, in its truest sense. This book attempts such a reappraisal, from a variety of perspectives, and assesses whether 'true' asylum can be provided in the community.

True asylum as retreat or refuge is a concept that is surprisingly ill-defined. Reparation and even relief from poverty have been argued to lie within its compass. The rather general and often sweeping definitions of true asylum that have been offered in relation to the functions of the mental hospital have tended to lack evidence to support them. To some extent it has been taken as an unquestioned assumption that there has always been, and continues to be, provision of asylum in the psychiatric hospital. A major concern we share with our contributors is therefore to address the lack of evidence to support this claim.

The book begins with an examination of the objectives of asylum for nineteenth-century founders of the 'asylum movement'. It moves on to analysis of case notes and archival material to assess the ways in which the founders' objectives were met, if at all, during succeeding historical periods. In focusing on true asylum we are not primarily concerned with the issues of violence, unpredictability and dangerousness in relation to mental illness. These issues, and their significance for mental health, have been thoroughly debated in both popular and academic forums elsewhere. We are raising several key questions in this appraisal of mental hospitals and asylum. Is the gift of asylum disappearing as mental hospitals close down? If so, can asylum be given in non-hospital settings without the institutionalism, neglect and abuse of patients that have tended to occur in mental hospitals? Do users/survivors believe that the concept of asylum has any relevance to their care and well-being?

At the risk of some crudeness in interpreting the chapters of the contributors concerned, we can highlight a very significant debate presented in the book at this point about the perceived loss of asylum presented by mental hospital closures.

REAL OR ARTEFACTUAL LOSS OF ASYLUM?

In Chapter One, Scull provides a succinct account of the decline of the 'retreat' as the form of asylum which early mental hospitals found themselves unable to sustain, under pressure of large numbers of apparently incurable cases. Where humane intentions underpinned the development of these retreats, with benevolence towards the mad a key element in their treatment, such intentions, in Scull's view, do not underpin the contemporary shift of mental hospital care to community care. He considers that community care fails the sufferers of chronic psychosis in particular. This is on account of the social indifference and political liberalism which are associated with a poor development of community care infrastructure.

Scull's account has a familiar feel in its focus on the shortcomings of community care. Raftery's account, on the other hand, has no such familiarity about it. In his view, the idea that there has been any radical shift away from institutional care, and therefore from asylum in that sense, is quite mistaken. Whether social indifference or political liberalism has been responsible for the promotion of community care or not, the situation is quite to the contrary of that suggested by Scull. At least in the British context, the gift of asylum is being used to an unparalleled extent to offer hospital-based shelter and care to the mentally ill, including those with long-term or recurrent disabilities. This has been made possible by continued real increases in the level of funding of mental health services. Scull's argument in this respect, of a community care era having replaced an asylum era, creates a false impression. Historically, in relation to hospital beds, our contemporary governors are being as generous in their provision and at least as humane as their Victorian forebears. For Raftery, what needs to be explained instead is the rise in asylum provision which took place in the first half of the twentieth century, with provision falling back to more 'natural' levels thereafter, when the rush to community care is popularly held to have taken place. Scull and others have created an artificial polarity between institutional and community care, and this needs to be addressed.

Up to this point, as the reader may be aware, we have assumed that true asylum is synonymous with the retreat aspect of mental hospital care, or the care given in the discrete psychiatric units of general hospitals. But is it? In our own research we could find no commonly accepted definition of asylum. The frequent association of the concept with the mental hospital has of course led to it having taken on very negative connotations in the contemporary period. So often analysts of the mental hospital, especially social scientists, have seen it to be performing a primarily social control function, with retreat being of little, if any consequence. Those who suggest, as we do, that the hospitals provided relief from suffering and a place of safety for some of their residents run the risk of ridicule from such quarters.

The closures of mental hospitals taking place on an international scale have led some psychiatrists and prominent voluntary organisations to argue that true asylum is being lost in the process of large institutions being removed from the mental health care landscape. They argue, as Furlong does in her contribution to this book, that there are beneficial aspects of mental hospital care which can only be provided in discrete campus facilities. Mindful of this argument we asked our contributors to consider whether true asylum, where those experiencing acute mental distress had appealed to physicians, policemen, Justices of the Peace and others for relief by admission to the mental hospital, had been a significant phenomenon in the history of these hospitals, and if so to consider its nature.

In relation to this question we are presenting in this book some instructive contrasts in relation to the history of mental hospitals in Spain, where true asylum does not appear to have been significant, and the history of mental hospitals in Ireland and England, where such asylum does appear to have been so. Martínez Azumendi shows the way in which the religious and political injunctions placed upon the family to care for the chronically sick in Spain have led to mental hospitals being seen less commonly as places for asylum to be sought. The moral treatment associated with the 'retreat' movement did not affect the Spanish hospitals and families in Spain have tended to experience extreme feelings of guilt if they did not care for relatives suffering long-term illnesses at home. In the post Civil War period, the Franquist dictatorship maintained this pressure on the family to care for their chronically sick at home, and in some respects Spain is an extreme example of this familialism in a western context.

Finnane and Prior, in examining the Irish institutions, which, if only in respect of religious injunctions on the family to care, one would expect to show a relative lack of true asylum giving, find that, quite to the contrary, mental hospitals in Ireland seem to have been popular places of relief-seeking for the mentally ill and their families. Finnane illuminates processes hidden from us by the development of Irish asylums as institutions ostensibly for the compulsory admission and care of what were termed 'Dangerous Lunatics' for the period from the mid-nineteenth to the mid-twentieth century. This legal framework for admitting patients in Ireland indicates that, in theory, most mental hospital residents were placed there because they were dangerous. The framework would thus seem to have ruled out any significant degree of true asylum being given. In practice the law relating to Dangerous Lunatics was subverted to enable the admission of large numbers of the not-so-dangerous. The relationships between society, administrative processes for hospital admissions, and the legal framework for committal allowed for a negotiated refuge to be sought which confounds the received wisdom of Irish patients being primarily 'put away'. Prior's contribution provides some support for Finanne's views. He considers that the social control thesis does not work when applied to the Irish context, where patients appeared to have been entering hospital from a cross-section of society rather than being drawn from a stratum of social undesirables or failures.

In examining the English case we also find case notes evidence of true asylum being a feature of mental hospitals (Chapter Six).

We suggest that there were plenty of reasons why terrified and traumatised people who were experiencing severe mental distress would want to be placed in a mental hospital. As Hobbs notes, the East End of London, where most of the patients whose notes we studied came from, had become a metaphor for crime and depravity by the beginning of the twentieth century, with fighting and stealing for bread, work or property commonplace (Hobbs, 1989: 105–108). This may go some way towards explaining why a minority of patients requested to be admitted to hospital while others felt 'fatuously happy' at an early stage in their admission.

We also discuss the issue of whether true asylum is something specific to the mental hospital in our analysis. We suggest that perhaps the key distinguishing feature of mental hospital asylum is that patients are able to remain 'unaccounted for' for extended periods of time. The reason for our using this phrase will be apparent from reading Chapter Six. By it we mean that mental hospital staff allowed patients to remain under their care for as long as they could not present themselves as coherent individuals having some volition in life. In our view this attribute of asylum can be provided outside the mental hospital, and we explore the possibilities of such provision in the conclusion to the book.

The question of whether the concept of asylum can have any meaning or relevance to contemporary users or survivors of services is addressed by Wallcraft. She suggests that users are seeking to reclaim the concept from the clutches of psychiatry so that its 'general meaning' of a place of safety may be reinstated. She argues that the concept can be decoupled from hospital or hospital-like care and be applied constructively to the development of community asylum. Such asylum would not only offer places of safety but also offer a significant degree of control over the administration and evaluation of such places to their users.

Wallcraft's vision is very much at odds with the proposals of Furlong for the provision of asylum in 'havens' – complexes of sheltered accommodation and day care. The Haven concept, first mooted in 1986, has been widely debated. In Chapter Seven, Furlong has re-evaluated the need for such complexes in the light of detailed study of individual long-stay patients' clinical needs for asylum in Friern Hospital. She argues that the placement outcomes for a group of patients who were to have been placed in Haven homes suited to their particular clinical needs, but who were instead resettled in a variety of alternative forms of care not designed for their particular needs, support her original view that provision of separate greenfield care facilities for such patients is required.

While we have made much of Ireland in this introduction, we have not so far mentioned colonialism or racism, which are of obvious importance in relation to mental health issues. The African Caribbean Mental Health Association (ACMHA) has established a sanctuary for those experiencing not only profound emotional crises but also, as a result of their skin pigmentation, being vulnerable to racist treatment and lack of social support. Huka's chapter reviews the development of this project as a form of asylum in the community intended to counter the racism and isolation which have been well documented as a feature of the mental health experience of African-Caribbean people. Like Wallcraft's community asylum the ACMHA sanctuary is not intended to provide indefinite asylum. This is an issue to which we return in the conclusion.

In that our contributors include not only psychiatrists and sociologists but a survivor of psychiatric services, a health economist, a legal historian, and a psychologist, we feel that this book offers a thorough inspection of the possibilities for asylum in the community. By deploying this interdisciplinary range of contributions we have also been able to take an international view of this issue, through our focus on Ireland, Spain and England. We hope, with our contributors, to have made a modest contribution to the securing of asylum in the community.

REFERENCES

Hobbs, D. (1989) *Doing the Business*, Oxford: Oxford University Press.
Jones, K. (1982) 'Scull's Dilemma', *British Journal of Psychiatry*, 141: 221–226.

Chapter 1

Asylums
Utopias and realities

Andrew Scull

INTRODUCTION

This chapter provides a series of historically informed reflections
on the vicissitudes of the term 'asylum'. The concept has, it turns
out, undergone striking changes in meaning over the course of
the past two centuries. Originally associated at the outset of the
nineteenth-century lunacy reform movement with utopian visions
of institutions that would serve as humane and creative retreats,
to which the mad would repair for rehabilitation, the concept
acquired darker overtones in the Victorian age, as initial expectations met with disappointment, and what were intended as
philanthropic foundations degenerated into more or less well-
tended cemeteries for the still breathing. In the second half of
our own century, such 'loony bins' have come under sustained
ideological assault, and the once positive associations of the term
asylum have been transformed, via the writing of the sociologist
Erving Goffman and others, into something with sinister overtones of the concentration camp. Most recently of all, however,
the failure of community neglect masquerading as community
care has created renewed interest in the relevance of the more
positive meanings that can be attached to the notion of 'asylum'.

IMAGES OF THE ASYLUM

For much of the twentieth-century, institutional psychiatrists have
shied away from the term 'asylum'. Even a hundred years ago,
the concept's associations with what Ernest Jones called the
'Chubb lock era' in psychiatry were an embarrassment for professionals desperate to escape their public image as little more than

custodians of the degenerate and defective, and concerned to emphasise their links with the more respectable sectors of the medical profession. Hence the eagerness with which alienists sought in those years to relabel their establishments as mental hospitals and themselves as expert practitioners of psychological medicine. In the half century since the Second World War, the reluctance to make use of the older terminology has become even more pronounced. A generation of sociological studies critical of the mental hospital's therapeutic pretensions culminated in Goffman's (1961) denunciation of such places as fundamentally and irremediably flawed. *Asylums*, his book of that title, proclaimed, stigmatised, dehumanised, and systematically *dis*abled the inmates they purported to cure. They were 'total institutions' that, in crucial respects, resembled nothing so much as concentration camps. With institutional care for the mentally ill rapidly falling into disfavour in political circles during the same period, as policy-makers rushed to embrace the mythical vision of a community anxious to re-embrace the mentally ill, the asylum's fate seemed sealed on still another front. Its paymasters increasingly dismissed it as a well-meaning experiment gone wrong, an expensive irrelevance now thankfully to be relegated to the dustbin of history.

In view of its ignominious end, it is difficult to recall how differently the founders of the asylum era expected their creation to turn out. The lunacy reform movement of the early nineteenth century was driven forward, in substantial measure, by a utopian vision of the possibilities of asylum life. So, far from being 'a moral lazar house' (Coombe, 1950: 376) wherein the deranged were hidden and hope and humanity abandoned, the asylum in the imagination of its proponents was transmuted into the 'moral machinery' through which the mind was to be strengthened and reason restored.

To be sure, the moral outrage that gave energy and urgency to the reformers' efforts was periodically refuelled by trade in lunacy. A series of parliamentary inquiries appeared to provide lurid confirmation of the public's worst gothic nightmares about what transpired behind the high walls and barred windows of the madhouse. The reports of the Select Committees themselves, and the books and pamphlets produced by those agitating for lunacy reform, contained a compelling amalgam of sex, madness, maltreatment, and murder, mixed together in a fashion guaranteed at once to titillate and repel: patients bled and drugged into insensibility; their public display, 'like animals in a menagerie';

unregarded deaths from botched force-feeding and the brutality
of uncaring attendants; the corrupt confinement of the sane,
amidst the shrieks and raving of the mad; the placing of even
those madwomen who retained some semblance of 'innate' female
purity and modesty at the disposal of the lascivious ruffians who
served as madhouse attendants; and the ingenious array of 'bolts,
bars, chains, muffs, collars, and strait-jackets' madhouse propri-
etors had devised to coerce a measure of order from recalcitrant
raw materials.

At least as vital to the achievement of lunacy reform, however,
was the construction of a positive image for the reformed asylum.
Here, if its proponents were to be believed, were 'miniature
worlds, whence all the disagreeable alloys of modern life are as
much as possible excluded, and the more pleasing portions carefully cultivated' (Anon., 1836–1837: 697). Most famously realised
by Tuke and Jepson at a Quaker institution, the York Retreat,
this novel version of a haven for the mentally ill presented a very
different scene to those with occasion to view it.

The asylum was now to be a home, where the patient was to
be known and treated as an individual, where his/her mind was
to be constantly stimulated and encouraged to return to its natural
state. Mental patients required dedicated and unremitting care,
which could not be administered on a mass basis, but, rather, must
be flexible and adopted to the needs and progress of each case.
Such a regime demanded kindness and an unusual degree of
forbearance on the part of the staff. If the ideal were to be successfully realised, the attendants would have to be taught to keep
constantly in mind the idea that 'the patient is really under the
influence of a disease, which deprives him of responsibility, and
frequently leads him into expressions and conduct the most
opposite to his character and natural dispositions' (Tuke, 1813:
175). Crucial, too, was the moral influence of the asylum's
governor. By paying 'minute attention' to all aspects of the day-
to-day conduct of the institution, by always setting, through his
own example, a high standard for subordinates to emulate in their
dealings with the inmates, by observing the patients daily, sometimes hourly, he could foster the kind of intimate and benevolent
familial environment in which acts of violence would become rare.
Indeed, as the autocratic guiding spirit of the whole curative apparatus, the superior moral and intellectual character of the medical
superintendent was an essential precondition for success.

Classification, separation, and employment, all central features
of Tuke's version of moral treatment, were to be combined with
careful attention to the architecture and physical setting of the
asylum. Since it was recognised that the insane were very sensi-
tive to their surroundings, buildings ought to emphasise as little
as possible the idea of imprisonment or confinement. Indeed,
spacious and attractive accommodation could make its own contribution to the inmates' 'moral training', and to replacing 'their
morbid feelings . . . [with] healthy trains of thought' (Browne,
1837: 191). Treatment could thus be individualised and adapted
to the peculiarities of the particular case, and interaction managed
and controlled within carefully constructed communities of the
mad.

Here was an ideological vision of extraordinary resonance and
surpassing attractiveness, of a social universe constituting an
organic, harmonious whole wherein even the rage of madness
could be reigned in without whips, chains, or corporal punishment,
amidst the comforts of domesticity and the invisible yet infinitely
potent fetters of 'the desire for esteem' (Tuke, 1837: 157). Men
like William Tuke, William Alexander Francis Browne, and John
Conolly insisted, moreover, that theirs was a 'description . . . not
. . . of a theorist, or of an enthusiast, but of . . . practical [men]
long accustomed to the management of lunatics' (Conolly, 1838:
74). It was, said Browne (1837: 231), 'a faithful picture of what
may be seen in many institutions, and of what might be seen
in all, were asylums conducted as they ought to be'. Within the
controlled confines of the institution, even the irrational and the
raving could be reduced to docility and cured of their madness,
and by moral suasion and self-sacrifice, rather than by force. With
all the fervour of a new convert, John Conolly (1847: 143) deliv-
ered a panegyric to the new asylum, the place where

> calmness will come; hope will revive; satisfaction will prevail.
> Some unmanageable tempers, some violent or sullen patients,
> there must always be; but much of the violence, much of the
> ill-humour, almost all the disposition to meditate mischievous
> or fatal revenge, or self-destruction will disappear . . .
> Cleanliness and decency will be maintained or restored; and
> despair itself will sometimes be found to give place to cheer-
> fulness or secure tranquillity. [The asylum is the place] where
> humanity, if anywhere on earth, shall reign supreme.

VICTORIAN MUSEUMS OF MADNESS

The small, intimate institution which allowed even a remote approximation to this idyll did not survive for long. The influx of a horde of pauper lunatics brought the demise of the notion that the asylum should be a substitute household. Instead, local magistrates insisted on taking advantage of presumed economies of scale, and until well into the twentieth century, the average size of county asylums grew almost yearly. The degree of regimentation needed to administer institutions of 500, 1,000, and more ensured that such asylums would be the virtual antithesis of their supposed inspiration, the York Retreat. To Tuke, moral treatment had meant the creation of a stimulating environment where routine could be sacrificed to the needs of the individual. Here the same term disguised a monotonous reality in which the needs of the patients were necessarily subordinated to those of the institution; indeed, where a patient's needs were unlikely even to find expression. Hence John Arlidge's trenchant conclusion (1859: 102) that 'a gigantic asylum is a gigantic evil'.

At the margin, among those newly admitted to an asylum, turnover remained reasonably rapid, with between a quarter and two-fifths being discharged within a year or so of their arrival. Each year, however, a very substantial fraction remained behind to swell the population of chronic, long-stay patients, and as the size of county asylums grew remorselessly, annual admissions formed a smaller and smaller fraction of the whole. An overwhelming and growing proportion of the asylum population thus came to be composed of patients who lingered year after year; and it was this spectre of chronicity, this horde of the hopeless, which was to haunt the popular imagination, to constitute the public identity of the asylums, and to dominate Victorian and Edwardian psychiatric theorising and practice. Despairingly, W.A.F. Browne viewed the collapse of the vision he had once propagated of the asylum as a curative establishment under the weight of 'a vast assemblage of incurable cases' (Crighton Royal Asylum, 1857: 8). Their numbers ensured, he said, that

> The community becomes unwieldy; the cares are beyond the capacity of the medical officers; personal intimacy is impossible; recent cases are lost, and overlooked in the mass; and patients are treated in groups and classes. An unhealthy moral atmosphere is created; a mental epidemic arises, where delusion, and

debility, and extravagance are propagated from individual to individual, and the intellect is dwarfed and enfeebled by monotony, routine, and subjection.

(ibid.)

As asylums silted up with the chronically crazy, those Browne dubbed 'the waifs and strays, the weak and wayward of our race',[1] so Victorian psychiatry moved steadily towards a grim determinism, a view of madness as the irreversible product of a process of mental degeneration and decay. The madman, as Maudsley put it, 'is the necessary organic consequent of certain organic antecedents: and it is impossible he should escape the tyranny of his organization' (Maudsley, 1879: 88). Insanity constituted nothing less than a form of phylogenetic regression – which accounted, of course, for its social location and for the lunatic's loss of civilised standards of behaviour and regression to the status of a brute. Maudsley rhetorically asked,

Whence came the savage snarl, the destructive disposition, the obscene language, the wild howl, the offensive habits displayed by some of the sane? Why should a human being deprived of his reason ever become so brutal in character as some do, unless he has the brute nature within him?

(Maudsley, 1870: 53)

Employing ever harsher language which combined a physiological account of madness with 'the look and tone of moral condemnation', (Turner, 1988: 179) psychiatric discourse now exhibited a barely disguised contempt for those 'tainted persons' (Straham, 1890: 337) whom it sequestered on society's behalf. And within such a world-view, given that the notion of mass sterilisation never acquired the status of a serious option in Britain,[2] the asylum was naturally accorded a wholly new significance in the battle to contain social pathology and to defend the social order.

Local authorities were always reluctant to spend 'extravagant' sums of money on the poor, and the funds for a predominantly custodial operation were predictably scarce, rarely more than what was needed to supply a bare minimum of care. Occasionally, indeed, the cheeseparing went too far, as in Buckinghamshire between 1916 and 1918, when the official dietary tables for St John's Hospital suggest that a male patient's daily food allowance provided only 40 grams of protein and 750 calories a day (which may be compared with what is now estimated to be a minimum requirement for a sedentary man of 60 grams of protein and 2,100 calories). Female patients received even less. With a deliberate policy of semi-starvation carried to this extreme, the result (as J.L. Crammer, 1991: 76–77, 113, 126–127, has noted) was a very sharp increase in asylum mortality rates, till in 1918, a third of the asylum population died in the space of twelve months, a denouement which finally shamed the authorities into action and led to limited improvements in the patients' diet.

Recent work has shown that even in small, richly endowed private facilities – the Crichton Royal Asylum in Dumfries, the Ticehurst Asylum (the favourite resort for deranged English aristocrats), and the York Retreat itself [3] – the quality of care provided by an essentially custodial operation tended to diminish steadily over time. Although, as Anne Digby (1985: 199, 56) summarises in her findings for the York Retreat, 'individuality was not crushed into helpless anonymity' (as in the county asylums), still by the last third of the nineteenth century, control and discipline were the paramount goals of the institution, and 'patients were no longer subjects to be treated but objects to be managed'. All of which serves, I think, to re-emphasise just how difficult it is to sustain staff and patient morale and to maintain the quality of care in the absence of some prospect of therapeutic success.

COMMUNITY CARE OR COMMUNITY NEGLECT?

Victorians, who observed the often shocking contrast between the utopian visions of the first generation of reformers and the realities of asylum operations as they turned out to be, consoled themselves with the reflection that 'the worst asylum that can at this day by possibility be conceived, will still afford great protection' to the lunatic compared to his treatment in the community (Thurnam, 1845: 104). From the mid-1950s onwards, our own generation has embraced with equal foolishness the contrary proposition, the contention, in Elaine and John Cumming's (1957: 55) words, that 'the worst home is better than the best mental hospital'. It is difficult to decide which delusion has proved the more harmful to the seriously handicapped and chronically disabled who once thronged the back wards of our institutions.

With sociologists lending the mantle of academic respectability to what was once the hyperbole of muck-raking journalists – the chilling equation of the mental hospital and the concentration camp – and psychiatrists joining in the chorus in a minor key, lamenting the role of mental hospitals in producing 'institutionalism' or 'institutional neurosis',[4] the rush to abandon the asylum in favour of 'community treatment' was effectively legitimised, not by a careful demonstration of its merits and requirements, but by rendering the alternative simply unthinkable. Without the necessary infrastructure and financial support to build alternative systems of care, the results have been predictably catastrophic – particularly, as the late Peter Sedgwick (1982: 213) noted more than a decade ago, 'for those mental patients who need something rather more than short-term therapy for an acute phase of their illness'.

It should be starkly apparent, from the history I have reviewed here, that our collective reluctance to make a serious and sustained effort to provide a humane and caring environment for those manifesting grave and persistent mental disturbance has far deeper roots than the callousness of our contemporary political leadership. Still, recent changes in our political culture – in Britain just as clearly as in the United States – have scarcely improved the prospects for a satisfactory resolution of what one recent Maudsley lecturer called 'Scull's dilemma' (Jones, 1982: 221–226): the difficulty that confronts someone simultaneously critical of traditional mental hospitals and of so-called community care. The idea that we bear a collective moral responsibility to provide for the unfortunate – indeed, that one of the marks of a civilised society is its determination to provide *as of right* certain minimum standards of living for all its citizens – has been steadily eroded over the past two decades. In its place, we have seen the resurgence of an ideology far more congenial and comforting to the privileged: the myth of the benevolent 'Invisible Hand' of the marketplace, and its corollary, an unabashed amoral individualism. There is little place (and less sympathy) within such a world-view for those who are excluded from the race for material well-being by chronic disabilities and handicaps – whether these derive from physical or mental disease, or from the more diffuse but cumulatively devastating penalties accruing to those who belong to racial minorities or live in dire poverty.

The punitive sentiments directed against those who must feed from the public trough extend only too easily, of course, to embrace those who suffer from the most severe forms of psychiatric misery. Those who seek to protect the long-term mental patient from the opprobrium visited upon those dependent on state charity may do so by arguing that the patient is both dependent and sick. But I fear that this approach has only a limited chance of success. After all, despite two centuries of propaganda, the public still resist the straightforward equation of mental and physical illness. Moreover, the long-term mental patient in most instances will not get better, and often fails to collaborate with his or her therapist to seek recovery. Such blatant violations of the norms governing access to the sick role in our societies (cf. Parsons, 1951) make it unlikely that chronic schizophrenics will be extended the courtesies and exemptions accorded to the conventionally sick. Instead, even those incapacitated by psychiatric disability all too often find themselves the targets of those who would abolish social programmes because they consider any social dependency immoral.

CONCLUSION

Few of us, I suspect, would welcome the reincarnation of an unreconstructed psychiatric Victorianism, and there seems in any event little prospect of its rebirth, if only on the grounds of its cost. And yet we can feel no more confident than our Victorian forebears that we have devised a satisfactory system of humane and continuous care for those grossly disabled by what we call psychosis. Clearly, for some substantial sub-set of this population, one vital component of the needed array of services is a form of sheltered care – asylum, if you please – that will satisfy the basic human need for a roof over one's head and enough to eat, for occupation, for the embrace of a community that cares. How we are to reach such a Utopia, when the alternatives history presents us with are inadequate, often inhumane, and always underfunded mental hospitals or a grossly underdeveloped and frequently non-existent system of community care, is dare I say it, not Scull's dilemma but yours – and that of the all-too-indifferent larger society in which we both reside.

NOTES

1   Quoted in the *Journal of Mental Science* 4, 1857, p. 201.
2   For an apparently serious suggestion that one might 'adopt the old Scotch custom of castration and spaying, Mr. Lawson Tait would

willingly spay the females for a limited sum, and we could work the
males ourselves' see Strahan, op. cit., p. 462.
3 See Scull, A. (1991) *The Asylum as Utopia; W.A.F. Browne and the
   Mid-Nineteenth Century Consolidation of Psychiatry*, London:
   Routledge; C. MacKenzie, 'A family asylum: a history of the private
   madhouse at Ticehurst in Sussex, 1792–1917', unpublished Ph.D.
   dissertation, London University, 1987; Digby, A. (1985) *Madness,
   Morality and Medicine: A Study of the York Retreat 1796–1914*,
   Cambridge: Cambridge University Press.
4 Wing, J.K. (1962) 'Institutionalism in mental hospitals', *British Journal
   of Social and Clinical Psychology* 1, pp. 38–51; Wing, J.K. and Brown,
   G.W. (1970) *Institutionalism and Schizophrenia*, Cambridge:
   Cambridge University Press; Barton, R. (1965) *Institutional Neurosis*.
   2nd edition, Bristol: Wright.

REFERENCES

Anon., 'Review of *What Asylums Were, Are, and Ought to Be*',
   (1836–1837) *Phrenological Journal*, 10, no. 53, p. 697.
Arlidge, J.T. (1859) *On the State of Lunacy and the Legal Provision for
   the Insane*, London: Churchill.
Browne, W.A.F. (1837) *What Asylums Were, Are and Ought to Be*,
   Edinburgh: Black.
Combe, G. (1950) *The Life and Correspondence of Andrew Combe, M.D.*
   Edinburgh: Maclachlan and Stewart.
Conolly, J. (1838) 'Review of *What Asylums Were, Are and Ought to Be*',
   British and Foreign Medical Review 5, no. 9, p. 74.
Conolly, J. (1847) *On the Construction and Government of Lunatic
   Asylums*, London: Churchill.
Crammer, J.L. (1991) *Asylum History: Buckinghamshire County Pauper
   Lunatic Asylum – St. John's*, London: Gaskell.
Crichton Royal Asylum (1857) *18th Annual Report*.
Cumming, E. and Cumming, J. (1957) *Closed Ranks: An Experiment in
   Mental Health Education*, Cambridge, Mass.: Harvard University
   Press.
Digby, A. (1985).
Goffman, E. (1961) *Asylums: Essays on the Social Situation of Mental
   Patients and Other Inmates*, Garden City, New York: Doubleday.
Jones, K. (1982) 'Scull's dilemma', *British Journal of Psychiatry* 141, pp.
   221–226.
Maudsley, H. (1870) *Body and Mind*, London: Macmillan.
Maudsley, H. (1879) *The Pathology of Mind*, London: Macmillan.
Cf. Parsons, T. (1951) *The Social System*, New York: Free Press.
Sedgwick, P. (1982) *Psychopolitics*, London: Pluto Press/New York:
   Harper and Row.
Strahan, S.A.K. (1890) 'The propagation of insanity and other neuroses',
   Journal of Mental Science 36.
Thurnam, J. (1845) *Observations and Essays on the Statistics of Insanity*,
   London: Simpkin Marshall.

Tuke, S. (1813) *Description of the Retreat*, York: Alexander.
Turner, T. (1988) 'Henry Maudsley: Psychiatrist, philosopher, entrepreneur', in W.F. Bynum, R. Porter, and M. Shepherd (eds) *The Anatomy of Madness*, vol. 3, London: Routledge.

Chapter 2

The decline of asylum or the poverty of the concept?

James Raftery

INTRODUCTION AND SUMMARY

This chapter suggests that the conventional wisdom to do with the decline in the availability of asylum for the mentally ill in the United Kingdom is largely a myth. The definition of asylum[1] is taken to apply to places designated for the reception, care and treatment of the mentally ill (variously defined as mentally disordered, lunatics or insane). A myth is a 'fictitious or unproven person or thing'. I argue that the myth has arisen because of the failure to distinguish between the different meanings that asylum might have, in particular between the total number of places available (the stock) and the number of persons using those facilities over any period (the flow). Two types of asylum are distinguished in this chapter:

- Asylum 1 – referring to the stock of patients (or places) at any point in time, and
- Asylum 2 – referring to the number of persons admitted to asylum each year.

In summary, the mental hospital sector in England and Wales has witnessed two conflicting trends in the period 1945–1990 – a well-known decline in the stock of inpatient places (Asylum 1) and a much less remarked upon but dramatic increase in first and total admission rates (Asylum 2). The cost of mental health services, which are almost entirely publicly funded, has also risen dramatically. This chapter[2] explores trends in these two types of asylum, argues that conclusions based on Asylum 1 are misleading at best, and shows how trends in Asylum 2 indicate opposite conclusions from those to be drawn from Asylum 1.

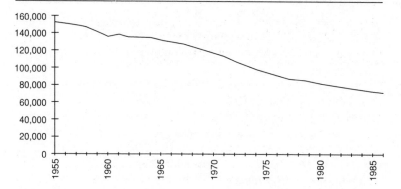

Figure 2.1 Total mental hospital places, public and private, England and Wales, 1955–1986

ASYLUM 1 – MENTAL HOSPITAL PLACES IN ENGLAND AND WALES

The conventional picture of the decline of 'asylum' as defined by Asylum 1 or the stock of places is as shown in Figure 2.1, which shows a fall in the number of mental hospital places from 155,000 in 1955 to around 60,000 by 1986, with a further fall to 47,000 places by 1993 (Hirsch, 1993). However, this picture is misleading both in terms of the timescale covered and by not being set in terms of places per 1,000 population.

When a longer-term picture, expressed in terms of places per 1,000 population, is examined as in Figure 2.2, a somewhat different pattern emerges, which can be captured in six main points. First, although the pattern of decline in total provision is striking, so is its rise, as shown in Figure 2.2 which includes places occupied by all lunatics, whether in public asylums, private hospitals or workhouses. The total number of places per 1,000 population rose throughout the period 1860 to 1914, fell with the onset of war and recovered slowly to peak again before war in 1939. The well-known 1955 peak is best described as a minor peak in a downsloping plateau, after the higher peaks of 1939 and 1914. The 1955 peak is more noticeable in retrospect because of the subsequent long-term decline. Places rose from around 1.5 per 1,000 in 1855 to a peak of over 3.5 in 1914 and a second lower peak in 1955 before falling back to around 1.5 per 1,000 by 1986.

Second, England and Wales had over 3 places per 1,000 population for a relatively short period between 1900 and 1960 – the 'golden age' of Asylum 1. Although the decline after 1955 was sharp, the rise in that ratio had been equally sharp. Nostalgia for the golden age of asylum can really only apply to the first half of the twentieth century.

Third, within that period of relatively high provision of places, some dramatic declines occurred, notably around 1918, when deaths due to influenza reduced the inpatient population. The decline during the Second World War was due more to discharges as mental hospitals were used for other purposes. All through the period from 1871 to 1981, the psychiatric inpatient population had a significantly raised mortality with standardised mortality ratios around three times what one might expect.[3]

Fourth, the age pattern of inmates shifted, from the bulk of the inmates being in the young to middle age groups up to 1955, and with a shift to the over-65s thereafter. Although the lunatic asylums always had a considerable level of inflows and outflows, the bulk of places were occupied by long-stay patients. The accretion in the number of long-stay patients, who entered at a relatively young age, accounted for the increase in Asylum 1 and it was the run-down in this category of patients that accounted for the bulk of the decline after 1955.

Fifth, the compulsory nature of Asylum 1 has to be remarked upon. Over 80 per cent of psychiatric inpatients were certified in England and Wales up to 1959. Certification involved an extreme removal of citizens' normal legal rights (Unsworth, 1987). Once certified and admitted, patients had no right to discharge themselves. Since admission involved legal processes, discharge also tended to be cumbersome. The term 'inmates' which also applies to prisons, seems more appropriate than patients. The abolition of certification after 1959 may have had more influence on patients' abilities to discharge themselves than has generally been noted. It is curious that nostalgia for Asylum 1 ignores the extreme degree of paternalism involved.

Finally, since the above data exclude all places not located in psychiatric hospitals or units, a full picture requires inclusion of the range of types of accommodation which have proliferated in recent years. A 1993 survey (Davidge et al.) of all types of accommodation catering for the mentally ill showed that between 1982 and 1992, the decline in NHS psychiatric beds had been compensated for almost in full by a rise in other forms of provision, mainly in privately owned hospitals and hostels. Although these data

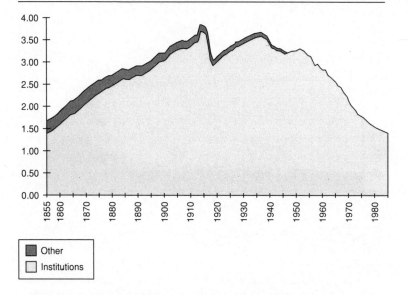

Figure 2.2 Lunatics/mentally ill in care per 1,000 population, by institutional and other care, 1855–1986

failed to separate out patients by age or diagnosis, making comparison difficult, they none the less suggest caution in generalising from the decline in NHS psychiatric beds to an overall fall in Asylum 1.

Overall, then, to the degree that the population in mental hospitals can be considered to be in receipt of asylum, the level of provision exceeded 3 per 1,000 only for a relatively short period, that is the first half of the twentieth century. That population was subject to raised mortality and was detained compulsorily. Both the rise and the decline in Asylum 1 seem to have been due to long-stay patients, the net recruitment of whom stopped around 1950. In more recent years, there is evidence to suggest that the decline in NHS psychiatric beds has been offset by a rise in other forms of accommodation, mainly in privately provided hospitals and hostels.

ASYLUM 2 – MENTAL HOSPITAL ADMISSION RATES IN ENGLAND AND WALES

What of Asylum 2, the number of patients admitted to psychiatric asylum? Figure 2.3 shows the first and total admission rates

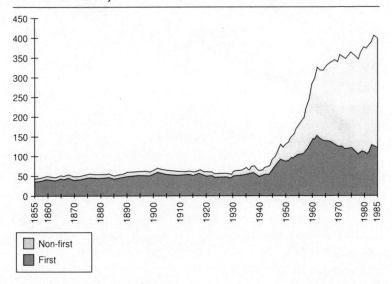

Figure 2.3 First and other admissions per 100,000, England and Wales, 1855–1986

(per 100,000 population) to the institutions covered in Figure 2.2. Rather than a pattern of decline, an extraordinary growth occurred after 1945, with the total admission rate rising by a factor of almost ten (from around 50 to 450 per 100,000) and the first admission rate by a factor of three between 1945 and 1965.

Several points are worth emphasising in relation to Figure 2.3. First, the growth in the total admission was highly specific to the period after 1945. Admission rates in the previous 90 years had shown little change, remaining at around 50 per 100,000 population between 1855 and 1945, with first admissions accounting for the bulk of all admissions.

Second, the expansion was largely due to the non-first admission rate. The first admission rate, which is often taken as a proxy for the incidence of the more serious forms of mental illness, showed a roughly threefold rise to around 1965 after which it fell. The non-first admission rate rose by a factor of 5 between 1945 and 1968. After 1965, all of the increase was due to the non-first admission rate.

In the third place, when first admission rates are examined by diagnosis, the admission rate for some of the more serious diagnoses such as schizophrenia showed a slight fall, leading to suggestions that the incidence might be falling (Der *et al.*, 1990). Much of the expansion in first admission rates was due to depression, and to some diagnoses which did not exist previously, such as personality disorders, and drug and alcohol abuse. While it is impossible to know how patients admitted under these diagnoses might have been diagnosed or treated in earlier periods, it seems very likely that patients who would not have been admitted in previous periods have been admitted in recent decades.

Finally, much of the expansion in admissions was of voluntary patients. Well before the abolition of certification in 1959, patients were being admitted as voluntary patients. Indeed, in Scotland, where very similar trends can be observed in both types of asylum, voluntary admission had been introduced in 1932, and an increasing proportion of first admissions were so classified from the 1930s, providing an example which England and Wales followed in 1959.

The conclusion to be drawn from the history of Asylum 2 must be that there has been a dramatic increase in the proportion of the population being admitted to psychiatric inpatient care each year in the period 1945 to 1986 to levels much above those in any previous period.

THE DECLINE IN ASYLUM 1 (THE STOCK OF ASYLUM PLACES)

Since the decline in Asylum 1 as measured by the stock of inpatients has provided most cause for concern to do with asylum, it is worth exploring that trend in greater detail, specifically in relation to duration of stay and mode of discharge. Figure 2.4 profiles the decline in Asylum 1 by duration of stay. The decline in Asylum 1 was almost entirely in the very long-stay sector, specifically those patients with a stay of more than five years. Remarkable consistency applied to the number of places per 1,000 for shorter-stay places – either one to five years or those with a stay of less than one year. No less than 80 per cent of the decline was due to the long-stay patients.

DEINSTITUTIONALISED – DEAD OR ALIVE?

Figure 2.5 shows how these long-stay patients who accounted for the decline in Asylum 1 were discharged, distinguishing live and dead discharges. For the group with a length of stay of over five

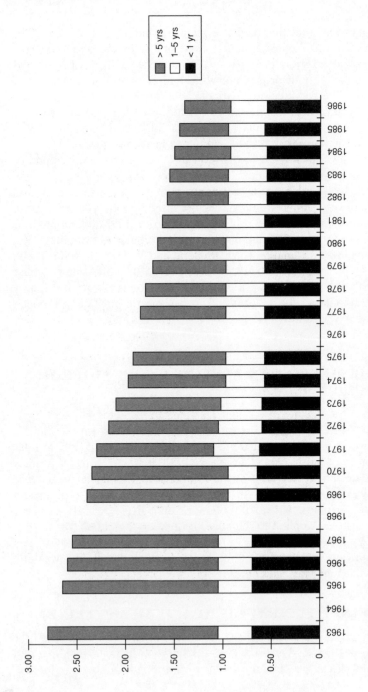

Figure 2.4 Inpatients per 1,000 population by duration of stay, England, 1963–1986

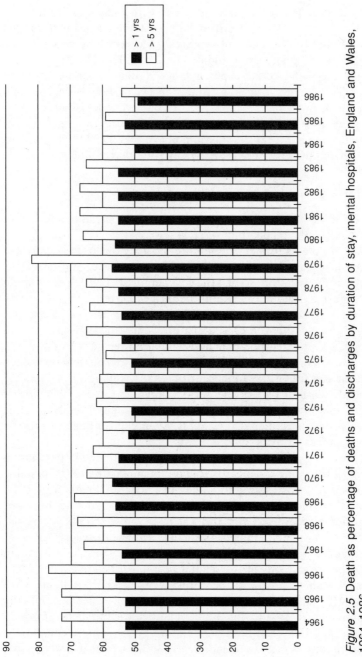

Figure 2.5 Death as percentage of deaths and discharges by duration of stay, mental hospitals, England and Wales, 1964–1986

years, some 70 per cent died. For those with a stay of over one year, around 50 per cent died. Given that these long-stay patients tended to be elderly, often having been admitted very long ago, the high proportions dying is not unduly surprising. However, by contrast with the fears often expressed about deinstitutionalisation of helpless patients on to the street, the experience in England and Wales suggests that live discharges accounted for less than one third of decline in the long-stay inpatient population. It seems clear that the decline in the stock of asylum places was due very largely to a decline in the provision for long-stay patients, most of whom died.

COSTS

Part of the myth is that costs played a major part in the decline of 'asylum' (undefined, but referring to Asylum 1). This section explores the pattern of expenditure, showing that as the number of inpatient places (Asylum 1) has declined, the level of total spending has risen sharply, so that the cost per inpatient week has soared.

Figure 2.6 shows the overall pattern of current expenditure on psychiatric services between 1870 and 1986, expressed in constant 1985 prices using the GDP deflator (Feinstein, 1972). Aggregate spending was clearly dominated by that on pauper lunatics in the institutions covered by the Lunacy Commissioners, which accounted for over 90 per cent of total spending throughout all but the earliest part of the period. Aggregate spending followed the trend in inpatient numbers up to the advent of the NHS, after which this pattern ceased to apply. Spending continued to rise as the number of inpatients fell after 1955.

Spending (in 1985 prices) ran at around £60 million per annum from 1870, rising steadily to around £150 million by 1900. Spending continued to rise slowly to a peak of under £200 million by 1914, but then fell sharply to around £100 million during the war. Spending recovered after the war to its pre-war level of around £200 million and resumed its steady increase to reach a peak of around £300 million by 1940. With the 1939 war and a fall in number of patients in the mental hospitals, spending again fell – but less sharply than in the earlier war – to £250 million. After the war and with the initiation of the NHS, spending initially continued at around the £250 million level but then began to increase rapidly, reaching £500 million by 1960 and continuing to rise despite the drop in inpatient numbers to reach some £700

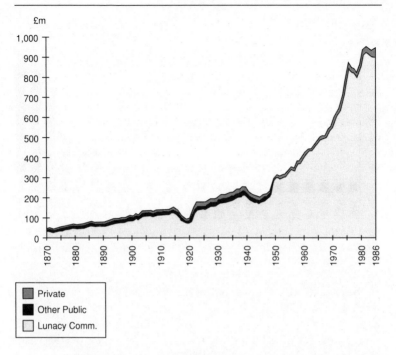

Figure 2.6 Expenditure on psychiatric services in 1985 prices, England and Wales, 1870–1985

million by 1970 and over £1,300 million by 1985. As shown in Figure 2.6, spending on non-NHS facilities became noticeable again by the mid-1980s, so that by 1985, such (estimated) spending accounted for some 9 per cent of the total.

Average cost per patient

The combination of fewer inpatient places and rising expenditure combined to push up the cost per inpatient per week as shown in Figure 2.7. The average cost of maintaining a patient in County Lunatic Asylums remained remarkably unchanged from 1875 to 1920. Expressed in constant 1985 prices using GDP deflator, the cost of maintaining a pauper lunatic remained around £20 per week from 1870 through to 1920. Unit costs began to increase after the 1914–1918 war, however, reaching £23 per week in 1925 and £31 in 1935. No data are available for 1940 and 1945.

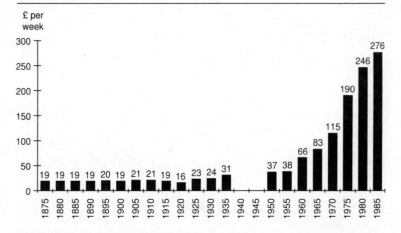

Figure 2.7 Cost per inmate per week, 1985 prices, England and Wales, 1875–1985

The weekly cost (somewhat more widely defined) was £37 per week in 1950, and £38 by 1955. However, as inpatient numbers began to fall, unit costs rose rapidly: doubling in each of the succeeding decades. Unit costs rose to £66 per week by 1960, £83 in 1965, £115 in 1970 and £190 by 1975. Further rises continued to take place, to around £246 in 1980 and £276 in 1985.

Taking the period 1950 to 1985, unit costs rose by a factor of seven, while inpatient numbers fell to around one third of their 1955 level: *ceteris paribus*, such a drop in inpatient numbers would have pushed up unit costs by a factor of three. The sevenfold rise suggests that while the failure to adjust spending on inputs in line with inpatient numbers was responsible for much of the rise in unit costs, it does not explain the entire rise. The other key component was the increase in staffing which paradoxically increased as the number of inpatient places fell.

OTHER COUNTRIES

These findings are supported by the analysis of several other countries, notably Scotland and Ireland, each of which shared the following features:

● substantial declines in Asylum 1 after around 1955, but at a slower rate than England and Wales, with evidence of a similar ageing and depletion by death of the long-stay population;

- rapid increases in Asylum 2, as measured by both first and repeat admission rates;
- a rapid rise in expenditure on mental health services in the past three decades, despite the fall in Asylum 1 in each country.

CONCLUSIONS

The above review of the historical data suggests that the concept of asylum requires 'unpacking' to distinguish Asylum 1 from Asylum 2. Distinguishing stocks from flows introduces a temporal element into the concept of asylum. Analysis of Asylum 1 by duration of stay, age group and modes of admission and discharge casts light on trends, particularly showing that its rise and fall were due almost entirely to the accretion and depletion of very long-stay inpatients who have been dying off in recent decades. Debates on the 'decline' of the asylum, by failing to make the distinction between Asylum 1 and 2, and by generalising from the decline on the long-stay group, have mythologised an overall decline in asylum. By contrast, a focus on Asylum 2 suggests that never in recent history have so many people been admitted to inpatient psychiatric care. The key issue, then, relates to what has happened to those persons who might in the golden age have found long-term asylum in the mental hospitals.

Several possible alternatives exist to do with demand and supply. The demand for long-term care of 1 to 2 persons per 1,000 may have been specific to a cohort of persons, such as those born between 1880 and around 1920. Changes in the epidemiology of mental illness so severe as to require very long inpatient care are little understood. It is possible, as Hare (1983) has argued, that an epidemic of such illnesses occurred around that time. The similarity of trends in both Asylum 1 and 2 in Scotland and Ireland could be seen as supporting such a hypothesis. Whatever the truth, those born before or after that period were very much less likely to receive such long-term institutional care, whatever their needs might have been. The degree to which those born later have benefited from more recent treatments, notably drug treatments as well as ambulatory health service contacts is also unclear, but some effect seems likely.

A supply-side explanation is also worth considering. The period 1900 to 1960 in which England had 3 inpatient places per 1,000 people included the decline of the British empire and two major

wars as well as other social upheavals. The similarity of the pattern
of rise and fall of mental hospital places in many industrialised
countries could be seen as suggesting links to the forms of organisation of those societies. Further, changes in the organisation of
housing, of income support and in forms of social control and
mores are likely to have had large but difficult to quantify effects
on both the demand for and supply of psychiatric care. However,
such large questions cannot be answered here.

What can be concluded, however, is that the concept of asylum
is more complex than many have made it. Simple disaggregation
of Asylum 1 and Asylum 2 reveals very different patterns and
perhaps more optimistic conclusions that an emphasis on Asylum
1 alone might suggest.

NOTES

1 The best definition is that of the Kings Fund Consensus 1987
   conference: 'a safe place of refuge or shelter providing protection
   and support which may or may not involve partial withdrawal or
   removal from the rest of society. It may or may not involve treatment'.
2 Based on the author's unpublished Ph.D. thesis, 'Economics of psychiatric services in England and Wales, Scotland and Ireland, 1850–1985',
   University of London (1993).
3 See my unpublished Ph.D. thesis, which estimates standardised
   mortality ratios (SMRs) for the population detained as lunatics for
   various years.

REFERENCES

Der, G., Gupta, S. and Murray, R. M. (1990) 'Is schizophrenia disap-
    pearing?', *Lancet* 335: 513–516.
Davidge, M., Elias, S., Jayes, B., Wood, K., Yates, J. (1993) *Survey of
    English Mental Illness Hospitals*, Birmingham: Health Service's Man-
    agement Centre.
Feinstein, C. H. (1972) *National Income, Expenditure and Output of the
    UK 1855–1965*, Cambridge: Cambridge University Press.
Hare, E. (1983) 'Was insanity on the increase?', *British Journal of
    Psychiatry*, 142: 439–455.
Hirsch, S. (1993) *Bed Availability in England and Wales, 1992–3*,
    Department of Health, London: HMSO.
Kings Fund (1987) *The Need for Asylum in Society for the Mentally Ill
    or Infirm*, The Third Kings Fund Forum Consensus Statement,
    London: Kings Fund.
Unsworth, C. (1987) *The Politics of Mental Health Legislation*, Oxford:
    Clarendon Press.

Chapter 3

Asylum and the community in Spain

Oscar Martínez Azumendi

In this chapter I am going to trace the history of asylums in Spain, examine some of the religious and political influences which have shaped their development, and consider the prospects for asylum in the community. A Spanish curiosity in relation to psychiatry is the constancy of popular belief in the power of piety, love, duty and redemption to cure the sufferer of mental illness. This is one of the main reasons why hospitals developed in Spain largely due to the efforts of religious foundations, as places affording charitable shelter, places where the mad who had no other place to go could be taken in until their godlessness passed.

This curious feature of Spanish history places the country both in the rear and in the van of community psychiatry. On the one hand, half-way houses and other forms of rehabilitation facilities for the resettlement of patients have not developed, owing to the lack of a strong belief in medical rehabilitation as a means of cure. On the other, families have played a critical role in the care of those with chronic mental health problems, and Spain has managed with a low number of psychiatric hospital beds compared with other countries in Western Europe (Secretaría Federal de Acción Social P.S.O.E., 1982; Mangen, 1986: 21). The conditions in Spain for the creation of asylum in the community supported by the family are thus, arguably, some of the best in Europe.

The chapter is divided into two parts. The first part deals with the origins of Spanish asylums, and examines salient political and religious influences upon their development. It concludes with an account of recent efforts to develop community mental health services which highlights the role psychiatrists have played in promoting the shift of care away from institutions.

The second part of the chapter outlines the prospects for asylum in the community, examining a range of factors bearing on these prospects, from household size and family formation, through attitudes to the chronically mentally ill among families caring at home for them, to the wider scene of voluntary organisations at work in the mental health field. It is concluded that family asylum in Spain is somewhat distinctive in a European context but that the increasing secularisation and individualism of Spanish society are likely to lead to it becoming less extensive in the near future. Respite care and home care are urgently required for the support of families currently experiencing considerable burdens, particularly to sustain the efforts of women within them. At the same time, alternative residential and day care facilities need to be developed so that more independence among people with chronic mental illness, many of whom would prefer not to be domiciled within the family household, can be encouraged.

PART ONE: THE SPANISH CASE OF ASYLUM IN HOSPITALS

The origin of asylums

Spain saw the establishment of what could be considered the first Western psychiatric hospital in Valencia in 1409. After witnessing a scene in which a mentally ill person was mocked and mistreated in the street, and strongly affected by the cruelty of the situation, Father Gilabert Jofré (1350–1417), of the Merced religious order, decided to request the aid of his parishioners in building 'an establishment or hospital where the mad and the innocent could be accepted and cared for in a Christian manner and not walk through the streets causing and receiving harm' (Alonso-Fernández, 1989). The completion of this hospital, which was built within a year, was to be followed by the establishment of others in Spain at Zaragoza (1425); Seville (1436); Valladolid (1436); Palma de Mallorca (1456); Barcelona (1481); Toledo (1483) and in the New World in Mexico (1567).

There is also some evidence that an Arab psychiatric hospital or 'Maristan' may have been established at an even earlier date, 1367, in the south of Spain at Granada, a city at the centre of Arab influence in the Iberian peninsula. In the opinion of some scholars the Granadan 'Maristan' might well have been the first

Western psychiatric hospital (García Granados *et al.*, 1989). And it is also highly probable that this hospital had the dubious honour of being the first to be emptied of its mental patients for purely economic reasons at the end of the fifteenth century. This early instance of 'deinstitutionalisation' was carried out by order of King Ferdinand and Queen Isabella, the 'Catholic Monarchs', so as to convert the hospital into a mint, arousing protests from Granadan nobles over the helpless state of its madmen, forced to wander the streets through the lack of any institution that would take them in.

It was also in Granada, in Lucena Street in 1537, that San Juan de Dios (1495–1550) opened the doors of his hospital to receive 'all illnesses and type of person . . . cripples, disabled, lepers, the dumb, madmen, the shaking palsied, the scabious, and some others very old and many children; and apart from these many other pilgrims and travellers who arrive here . . .'. The hospital order that he founded underwent a rapid development (O.M., 1942) spreading across the different continents of the globe. This order has now reached a position where, together with the order of the Hermanas Hospitalarias del Sagrado Corazón de Jesús, it is responsible for most of the beds in the private sector in Spain, on which a significant proportion of the country's population depends.

This first period, which has come to be called the Golden Age of Spanish psychiatry, saw the introduction of rational methods in the treatment of madness, with the mad being considered ill rather than possessed, as was predominantly the case in the West. The Spanish case is therefore instructive in relation to asylum being provided out of pious and charitable motives from the beginning, with protection of the insane from abuse and from lack of rudimentary care being the chief objective.

Just as Christian piety had played a role in the development of these early forms of asylum, however, so Christian zealotry, as much as the need for the governors of Spain to confine those threatening the social order, was to play a role in the deterioration of care and protection afforded within the hospitals. The mad were condemned occasionally during the period of the Inquisition, though in general their cases were passed over, with the religious authorities more concerned with converted Arabs and Jews, 'the new Christians' (Blázquez, 1986). González Duro (1994) reports that there were real epidemics of 'possessions', mainly among women, during the early seventeenth century. However, such possession was not so strongly censured by this period of Spanish history, being rather a disgrace that could happen to anybody.

There is some evidence of a further tentative movement towards the implementation of rational methods for the treatment of madness in psychiatric hospitals at the end of the seventeenth century. The *Ordinaciones* of the General Hospital of Saragossa, of 1681, for example, set out regulations providing for the humane treatment of the mad. These regulations restored the mad once more to the status of being 'unwell like the rest of patients', a status which warranted their being given care for the purpose of cure and any necessary clinical remedies for their malady. For the 'furious ones', separated, closed infirmaries were to be provided within which medicines would be dispensed. Given such regulations as these, and the fact that in the seventeenth and eighteenth centuries the majority of lunatic asylums were attached to general hospitals, with the obligation for doctors to attend the mentally ill, it could easily be imagined that the conditions existed for the Spanish authorities to take advantage of the movement towards reform that was taking place in various parts of Europe at the end of the eighteenth century (i.e. the moral treatments of Chiarugi, Tuke and Pinel). However, in Spain, in spite of the essentially clinical and therapeutic spirit being in the ascendance, socio-economic and politically repressive factors in the wake of the Independence War ruined the country's charitable institutions, including the psychiatric hospitals (Espinosa, 1980).

With the social advancement of medicine in the nineteenth century, mental illness came to be viewed as a symptomatic dysfunction of the organism, the treatment of which presented great difficulties. Thus, even though science came to occupy the place of religion and the mentally ill were no longer liable to be seen as possessed, the psychiatric hospitals can only be considered to have acted as a depository and place for the exclusion from society of the mentally ill. With doctors being very thin on the ground, the Spanish asylums retained their pre-eminently charitable character, especially since the majority were still dependent on religious orders. With successful treatment a remote hope, the functions of protection and care which had inspired the founding of the psychiatric hospitals, even though the quality of care had fallen to such low levels, remained dominant. In this period, pitiful conditions of economic shortage were reached that produced distressing situations of genuine hunger (Espinosa, 1980) and even motivated some of the charitable institutions to threaten the local administration with opening their doors if they did not receive sufficient resources for their inmates (Gil and Boadas, 1987).

With time, social and environmental factors acquired progressive importance in the understanding of the genesis of illness, whether this was mental or physical. The first studies appeared that focused on social phenomena, such as industrialisation and emigration, in relation to their significance for mental health. With the advent of the twentieth century and the appearance of 'modern' socio-cultural values, mainly those underpinning the social and political rights associated with democracy, together with other economic and therapeutic determinants, one of the most radical changes in the care of the mentally ill took place. This was through the movement for mental hygiene, which was concerned with individual learning and developmental processes. This movement, while contributing to the gradual abandonment of the asylum model in Europe, had limited consequences in Spain, as did the movement for community psychiatry. The slowness of the response in Spain, where reform did not get underway until well into the second half of the century, was mainly due to the continued pre-eminence of the charitable spirit that I have already referred to as dominating Spain's psychiatric institutions, though the conservative forces ruling the country were also important. Within the charitable framework, mental illness, despite being acknowledged as a proper illness, was still considered a trial of the moral strength of the sufferer rather than something amenable to care for the purpose of cure. The mentally ill person was considered as an afflicted brother or sister who should be the subject of love and pity. Mental illness, in this framework, was associated with concepts such as temptation, sin, evil, concupiscence, shame, guilt, etc., and as something for which penitence and strength of will could be a much more effective help than that offered, for example, by a misdirected psychoanalysis or by other psychological approaches that differed from a traditional medicine-based form of clinical treatment.

All this can be seen as a kind of crusade for the quixotic Spanish Catholic who felt it his duty to face the mistakes, threats and risks of new ideas and ways of living coming from abroad (Palacios de Borao, 1954).

It was not until the last few decades that the reformist ideas of community psychiatry were cautiously recognised in Spain, forcing the religious hospitals of the private sector, without going so far as to abandon their traditional spiritual framework, to begin timid experiments with services outside hospitals (such as supported flats and day hospitals). This was in an effort to improve the social prestige of the Church and to guarantee its income, partly by contracting with local state authorities for the support of some of its services. The necessity to maintain its income has become of increasing importance to the Church with its separation from the state, and the increasing secularisation of Spanish society leading to a fall in the level of donations being received.

The legislative background

In order to understand the framework for the recent development of the ancient psychiatric institutions and their gradual re-orientation towards community care, it is necessary to gain at least a cursory knowledge of Spain's mental health legislation from the late nineteenth century.

Although a royal decree was issued in 1885 which, for the first time in Spanish history legislated for the internment of the mentally ill, this legislation was more concerned with the defence of personal freedom than with the social danger of the mad. The decree drew a distinction between two types of admissions: 'observation' cases, which required judicial authorisation (or the obligation to communicate this within three hours to the Mayor or Governor if it had to be carried out urgently), and cases of 'definitive' confinement, for which judicial authorisation was always required.

Two years later, a further decree was issued which made it the responsibility of the *Diputaciones* – the local authorities – to maintain the twenty-six asylums then existing and construct others where necessary. At this stage asylums came to be administered separately from the rest of the health care institutions of the country, which were subject to central control. This separation was maintained until very recently.

A decree of 1931 abolished the previous law relating to 'definitive' confinement, and introduced new procedures for the admission and discharge from hospital of the mentally ill. While the new law sought to give precedence to the medical point of view, it neglected the juridical aspects of protection of the individual against inappropriate hospitalisation, providing no legal safeguards for such situations (except for cases in tutelage), or for any kind of review of them. The decree, because of the liberal ideology underpinning it, was less concerned with the protection of the individual than with the protection of his or her property (Gobierno Vasco, 1984).

Following the Civil War in Spain, the institutional model was consolidated under the dictatorship, which was hardly favourable to changes and innovations, but, rather, was concerned with placing limitations on individual freedom. One significant change which was introduced in this period was the passing of the law of Compulsory Illness Insurance in 1942, which provided for the establishment of out-patient neuro-psychiatric clinics not dependent on psychiatric hospitals.

The democratic constitution of 1978 gave rise to what has come to be called the 'State of the Autonomous Communities'. The Spanish government was decentralised and many of its responsibilities were transferred to the regional governments, which have since attained differing degrees of autonomy. Among these responsibilities are those for developing psychiatric services. This autonomy explains the great differences that can be observed within contemporary Spain in terms of deinstitutionalisation and the degree of community care achieved.

In relation to the juridical regime presently in effect (Xunta de Galicia, 1993), the provisions of Article 211 of the new civil code of 1983 are of great importance. In order better to uphold individual liberties, this code abolished the decree of 1931 and provided safeguards against involuntary confinement, for which judicial authorisation is required prior to any hospitalisation (unless it is considered an emergency and then twenty-four hours can be granted before a physician has to inform the judge). In the same way, every patient stay of more than six months has to be reviewed by a judge.

Since its passing, however, this law has been shown to be ineffective in some respects, and the practical impossibility of guaranteeing judicial assistance in all cases of involuntary confinement has become apparent (Defensor del Pueblo, 1991; Ararteko, 1992).

Another significant landmark in 1983 was the creation of the Ministerial Commission for Psychiatric Reform, which issued its report in 1985 (Informe de la Comisión Ministerial para la reforma psiquiátrica, 1985). This report recommended the strengthening of community mental health services not strategically dependent on the hospital, while special reference was made to the important role that had to be played by the primary health care teams in the field of mental health. Activity would have to be integral (bio-psycho-social) and mental health would be incorporated into the other aspects of health; the report endorsed the role of general hospitals as better suited to the admission of those suffering mental illness than psychiatric hospitals and recommended that alternative facilities for rehabilitation and 're-insertion' of those resident in institutions be developed. Finally, the report drew attention to the need to develop specific programmes directed at specific populations such as children and adolescents, the elderly, and drug abusers, as well as advising on other issues such as forensic psychiatry and evaluation.

One further significant development which is important for an appreciation of the Spanish legislative context was the introduction of legislation for a National Health Service in 1986. In Spain at present, health care coverage is almost universal and free, under the aegis of the Ministry of Health and Consumption. The 1986 law (Ley General de Sanidad) put the care of the mentally ill on the same footing as the care of those suffering from other illnesses, and set out four key principles for its provision:

1 Care in the community at the out-patient level, with the strengthening of systems of partial hospitalisation and home care as a way of maximising the role of prevention.
2 Hospital admissions to be made to general hospital psychiatric units.
3 The development of services of social rehabilitation and re-insertion (into society) in coordination with social services.
4 Attention to primary prevention as well as to psycho-social problems in the population associated with poor levels of general health.

This brief history indicates the following:

1 The importance of recent legislation and ministerial guidance in providing the framework for asylum in the community to be supported by the state.

2 The significance attached in Spain to the integration of mental health services with general health services, following the long period in which the *Diputaciones* (the local authorities) were responsible for psychiatric hospitals.

3 The central role given to the Autonomous Communities in developing mental health services.

The movement towards reform

It was at the beginning of the 1970s that the greatest number of beds in Spanish psychiatric hospitals were available. From that point onwards, under the influence of a significant number of young psychiatrists, some of whom would later assume responsibility for the Spanish Association of Neuropsychiatry (Angosto, 1992), criticism of the hospital-centred model became widespread and attempts at reform began to crystallise. This association has played an important role as a protagonist in the process of reforming mental health care, on numerous occasions making its critical voice heard before the administration and public opinion.

Timidly at first, but spreading rapidly and without interruption, the above-mentioned principles of community psychiatry have been enunciated throughout the country, a process giving rise to numerous confrontations between professionals and the local administrations. Why psychiatrists rather than patients or their families played a leading role in pushing for reform is another interesting feature of the Spanish context which I discuss below.

Just as in other aspects of Spanish social life, the movement for deinstitutionalisation arose not only from purely health care arguments, but was associated with positions that confronted the conservative ideology dominant since the years of the dictatorship. It thus appeared at first as a strongly politicised movement with a strong ideological content. One can detect this radicalism, for example, in the large number of presentations to psychiatric congresses and symposia which discussed the role of political parties, trade unions, feminism, and other citizens' movements as an instrument for psychiatric reform (González de Chávez, 1980). Some of these arguments have even cast the problems of the mentally ill in the guise of political problems, being no different in that sense from the problems of other marginalised social groups – the product of oppression (López Linage, 1977). Under this impetus, it is not surprising to find that some of the first mental health centres were developed hand in hand with centres for family planning (Rubi, 1988).

It must be remembered that the family planning centres were of some historical significance in the context of the devout state-supported Catholicism underpinning Spanish institutions. The movement in favour of their establishment had a strong ideological component (feminism) which was pitted against the old conservative model of orthodox Church teachings. Deinstitutionalisation carried the threat to the Church of the secularising of treatment for the mentally ill.

More recently these positions against the conservative bloc have lost some of their impetus and their supporters have lost some of their optimism about the possibilities for change. This has not only been because of the difficulties and limitations of the objectives and of realising them within the available resources, causing some demoralisation of enthusiasts for reform, but also because of the tempering of the underlying ideological driving force. At the same time, a progressive change in the theoretical and professional profile of Spanish psychiatrists is taking place, with their increasing adherence to a biological model, and this to an even greater extent than that of their counterparts in other Western countries. Nevertheless, few of those Spanish psychiatrists surveyed by Guimón (1990) showed radical postures with respect to any of the possible models (medical, psychological or social), showing instead a certain eclectic orientation.

Threatening the limited reform that is occurring, some have voiced concern about the risks involved in deinstitutionalisation movements, and, at the same time, bitter criticisms have been made about the performance of those young professionals, now matured, who brought about the reform, and who have since attained the very positions of power in the administration which were formerly held by their foes in the conservative bloc (Mediavilla, 1992).

Whatever the merits of these criticisms, it is undeniable that in recent years Spanish society has taken a gigantic stride towards 'normalising' the care of the mentally ill, and bringing it within a broader framework of social protection (Montalvo, 1990). To show the full extent of the changes which can be observed, as well as the distance yet to be travelled in normalising, I would like briefly to refer to a series of conventional indicators of aspects of the reform process.

Table 3.1 Trends in number of long-stay psychiatric hospitals and beds

Year	Number of long stay psychiatric hospitals	Number of beds	Variation in number of beds
1978	114	41942	100
1979	111	41469	98.87
1980	109	40364	96.23
1981	109	38739	92.36
1982	113	37725	89.94
1983	111	35273	84.09
1984	101	33817	80.62
1985	103	32683	77.92
1986	98	30084	71.72
1987	98	29018	69.18
1991	97	23282	55.51

Source: Constructed from data from Defensor del Pueblo, 1991

The extent of reform in Spain

(a) The number of psychiatric beds

This is an obvious, if not ideal starting point in Spain, owing to the absence of any national system for coordinating the 'case registers' which monitor the nature of hospital admissions.

In itself of course, the existence of more or less beds does not tell us much about the type of care available for the mentally ill. However, the increase or decrease in the provision of beds which can be observed over periods of time can tell us something about the kind of health care model which the society in question is moving towards. And, as one might expect, though again Spain lags behind other European countries in this respect, a gradual reduction in the number of psychiatric hospital beds during the last twenty years can be observed (Table 3.1). In 1975, there were 117 psychiatric hospitals (123 beds per 100,000 inhabitants) (Secretaría Federal de Acción Social P.S.O.E., 1982). Provision was by no means uniform across the country, with some provinces having no beds at all, and others having an excessive amount which their administrators sub-contracted to neighbouring authorities (see Table 3.2(a) and 3.2(b)). By the mid-1970s a progressive reduction of the number of beds provided in traditional psychiatric hospitals had begun, and this reduction has since led to the closure of some of them. This reduction has been taking place at

Table 3.2(a)   Short-stay beds and rate per 100,000 population

Autonomous community	Population	Beds in general hospital (1) (Number and rate per 100,000)	Short stay beds in public psychiatric hospitals (Number and rate per 100,000)	Total of short-stay beds (2) (Number and rate per 100,000)
Andalucía	6963116	467/6.71	26/0.37	493/7.08
Aragón	1212025	89/7.34	5/0.41	94/7.76
Asturias	1096155	75/6.84	0/0.00	75/6.84
Baleares	739501	28/3.79	90/12.17	118/15.96
Canarias	1601812	24/1.50	95/5.93	119/7.43
Cantabria	526886	48/9.11	0/0.00	48/9.11
Cast.-La Mancha	1644401	147/8.94	0/0.00	147/8.94
Cast. y León	2556316	262/10.25	51/2.00	313/12.24
Cataluña	6008245	393/6.54	273/4.54	666/11.08
Extremadura	1045201	41/3.92	190/18.18	231/22.10
Galicia	2700288	75/2.78	136/5.04	211/7.81
Madrid	4935642	289/5.86	209/4.23	498/10.09
Murcia	1046561	23/2.20	54/5.16	77/7.36
Navarra	521940	54/10.35	0/0.00	54/10.35
País Vasco	2099978	162/7.71	141/6.71	303/14.43
La Rioja	265823	22/8.28	0/0.00	22/8.28
C. Valenciana	3898241	141/3.62	180/4.62	321/8.23
Ceuta/Melilla	137070	39/28.45	0/0.00	39/28.45
Total	38999181	2379/6.10	1450/3.72	3829/9.82

a slightly increased rate following the judgements of the Ministerial Commission of 1985 discussed earlier.

Whereas there were 41,942 beds for long-stay residents of psychiatric hospitals in 1978, by 1991 there were only 23,282, for a population of nearly 39 million inhabitants. A very large reduction of 55 per cent was thus achieved in the space of thirteen years. Again, one should note that the picture of change is not a homogenous one across the Spanish Autonomous Communities. In the Balearic Islands, the Canary Islands, Extremadura and the Basque Country, the number of hospital beds available has barely changed, and in Cantabria the number has actually increased.

The private beds provided mainly through the religious foundations whose influence has been so strong in Spain have not decreased in number to the same extent as the beds available in

Table 3.2(b)   Medium- and long-stay beds, and totals of all beds, per 100,000 population

Autonomous community	Medium and long-stay beds in private and public psychiatric hospitals (3)	Total of beds in private and public psychiatric hospitals	Total of beds psychiatric and general hospitals
Andalucía	1370/19.68	1396/20.05	1863/26.76
Aragón	1506/124.25	1511/124.67	1600/132.01
Asturias	330/30.11	330/30.11	405/36.95
Baleares	460/62.20	550/74.37	578/78.16
Canarias	942/58.81	1037/64.74	1061/66.24
Cantabria	649/123.18	649/123.18	697/132.29
Cast.-La Mancha	690/41.96	690/41.96	837/50.90
Cast. y León	3406/133.24	3457/135.23	3719/145.48
Cataluña	4241/70.59	4514/45.13	4907/81.67
Extremadura	1139/108.97	1329/127.15	1370/131.08
Galicia	1170/43.33	1306/48.37	1381/51.14
Madrid	2285/46.30	2494/50.53	2783/56.39
Murcia	105/10.03	159/15.19	182/17.39
Navarra	571/109.40	571/109.40	625/119.75
País Vasco	1701/81.00	1842/87.72	2004/95.43
La Rioja	324/121.89	324/121.89	346/130.16
C. Valenciana	540/13.85	720/18.47	861/22.09
Ceuta/Melilla	0/0.00	0/0.00	39/28.46
Penitentiary Hos		403/1.03	403/1.03
Total	21832/55.98	23282/59.70	25661/65.80

Source: Constructed from data from Defensor del Pueblo, 1991

Notes: 1 Some of them for drug detoxification or long-stay. 2 Number of short-stay beds in private hospitals not known. 3 Some of them are short-stay beds from private hospitals

the hospitals administered directly by local authorities. This has meant that the proportion of beds provided by the foundations has increased slightly from nearly 38.7 per cent in 1975 to 42.5 per cent in 1991.

The large-scale reduction which appears to have taken place in provision of psychiatric hospital beds may be a rather artificial one. Some beds have simply been transferred to the responsibility of social services departments, which means that they do not appear in the statistics for long-term patients dependent on the health services, in spite of remaining in the same place and in a similar situation. However, it remains the case that in theory the available number of beds is relatively low for the population for which they must be available (59.7:100,000).

Historically, as in other parts of Europe, these beds were primarily occupied by a large number of patients diagnosed as schizophrenic, possessing little money, being of advanced age, and having undergone long-term hospitalisations (Espinosa, 1986), a profile which is in fact quite similar to that which can be observed at present (Defensor del Pueblo, 1991).

That the reduction in psychiatric hospital beds has been a true indicator of reform is supported by the fact that the number of general hospital beds for psychiatry has been increasing, even though it had reached only the relatively low figure of just over 6 beds per 100,000 inhabitants in 1991. This low figure may, in addition, be an over-estimate, given that some beds dedicated to long-stay patients, or some others for those with drug dependency problems were included within it. By 1991, none the less, there were eighty-five general hospital units in Spain, and the trend towards their integration with the rest of medical services is evident. Thus the contemporary situation is in marked contrast to that of the late 1970s when budgets for community psychiatry were demanded, with proposals often originating from the ideas of progressive 'left-wing' professionals. These proposals were based on sectorisation, deinstitutionalisation, the dismantling of the asylum, the avoidance of chronicity, and teamwork, among other principles.

Even so, examination of the mental health experience of other countries such as the USA, led some in Spain, as early as 1980, to warn of the risks arising from a massive deinstitutional-isation policy whose motives were purely those of saving money (González de Chávez, 1980).

(b) Community mental health teams

With the emphasis placed on community treatment in mental health, the 1980s saw the gradual development of new mental health care teams (Bellot, 1980). In 1991, there were 387 such community-based teams dedicated to the care of adults. These were in addition to a small number of teams working from clinics associated with hospitals, and 216 community neuro-psychiatrists who were not integrated into the community team networks. Deficiencies could be observed in relation to the composition of

Table 3.3 Community support structures

Autonomous community	Number of day hospitals and centres	Beds in hostels and sheltered accommodation	Number of therapeutic communities	Number of occupational workshops
Andalucía	11	132	2	–
Aragón	2	18	1	–
Asturias	5	± 45	3	–
Baleares	–	12	–	–
Canarias	2	49	–	–
Cantabria	–	–	–	–
Cast.-La Mancha	2	–	–	–
Cast. y León	4	± 90	–	–
Cataluña	8	195	–	
Extremadura	–	–	–	–
Galicia	3	20	–	1
Madrid	9	105	–	3
Murcia	2	20	–	–
Navarra	4	54	–	–
País Vasco	6	180	–	–
La Rioja	–	–	–	–
C. Valenciana	3	± 30?	–	2
Total	61	± 950	6	6

Source: Constructed from data from Defensor del Pueblo, 1991

some of the community teams and the numbers of professionals working within them. In the case of 122 teams there was clearly an insufficient minimum of one psychiatrist, one psychologist and one nurse, with some of these posts not even being filled. There were also manifest differences between the regions, as well as in the size of the population covered by each team.

(c) The present situation

As is clear from the above, the degree of psychiatric reform achieved in Spain is far from homogenous, and so one must examine the different kinds of development observable in each of the Autonomous Communities to get a true picture (see Table 3.3). Adopting Aparicio's lucid method (Aparicio, 1993) it is possible to consider the Autonomous Communities as falling into five groups, each illustrative of a distinct model of mental health services development:

1 The institutional model

This model obtains in the Balearic Islands, the Canary Islands, Extremadura, Galicia and Murcia (almost 20 per cent of Spain's population). These communities maintain a model of care that is founded on the traditional psychiatric hospital, with few beds provided in the general hospital, and scarcely any development of mental health teams based in the community or of programmes for the rehabilitation of long-stay patients. Definite plans for mental health services development are virtually non-existent.

2 Mixed model

This model characterises the situation of the Basque Country and Catalonia (21 per cent of the population). Mental health plans are in existence and there is a certain level to which they have been put into practice evident in the existence of community health centres and beds in general hospitals, but there are still acute units based in psychiatric hospitals and a high number of long-stay patients for whom there are no programmes. The lack of coordination between the hospital and the community teams is noteworthy in this model.

3 Reform model with certain inconsistencies

This model applies to Aragón, Madrid, La Rioja and Valencia (just over a quarter of the population). The reform process of developing community services is taking place but in a rather inconsistent way in these provinces. Thus, in some places acute beds in psychiatric hospitals continue to be maintained, rather than being replaced by units in general hospitals, there are large numbers of 'unreformed' long-term beds, and the coverage given by community teams is often very limited.

4 Integrated model with deficits in deinstitutionalisation

This model describes the scene in Castilla-La Mancha and Castilla-León (10 per cent of the population). There are well-defined plans and resources dedicated to the objectives of the reform. In some places there are large numbers of long-stay patients resident in institutions even though programmes for their rehabilitation have been drawn up. In others, such programmes do not exist.

5 Integrated model

This describes the group of Communities with the highest level of reform in place, Andalucía, Asturias and Navarre (22 per cent of the population). Though higher levels of community mental health services remain to be achieved, adequate development has taken place, with programmes of deinstitutionalisation having been set up.

PART TWO: THE SPANISH CASE OF ASYLUM IN THE COMMUNITY

Does Spanish society provide asylum in the community in any sense? When it comes to understanding the full extent of the achievements and weak points of Spanish society in the specific field we are dealing with, it is also necessary to examine in depth not only the results that are numerically quantifiable, such as hospital beds, which were presented in part one of this chapter, but also the evaluations of the detectable trends and the opinions of sufferers and carers themselves. In addition, it is necessary to take into account in a little more depth the cultural context, especially in relation to demographic and household trends, in which mental health services are experienced. The obvious starting point for such an approach is the family itself.

Burden upon the family

There is a certain belief, both within and beyond the frontiers of Spain, concerning Spanish culture, which assumes that there is more tolerance within the family towards eccentric behaviour caused by mental illness or old age. While it is not possible to address this belief and its correspondence or otherwise with reality fully in the compass of this chapter, there is little doubt that it has much to do with the deep-rooted Catholic morality which dominates the country. This morality strongly endorses the family, and more particularly women inside it, as being responsible for securing the welfare of its members and supporting the conceal-ment and negation of possible stresses that could happen in its midst. Domestic duties such as the care of those with disabilities, or the aged, have been sanctified by the Church as the responsi-bility of women, who were discriminated against in law and socially subjected under the Franquist regime that held sway so long over Spain in the twentieth century. All this, in addition to the exalting of maternity by the forces of Franco and by those advocating nationalist ideologies within Spain, have meant that gender differences have been more marked in Spain than in the European countries with post-war histories of a more liberal nature. Equally, the family has occupied a more dominant place in social affairs here than in other countries.

This dominance of the family, together with the gender imbalance within it (Aguado *et al.*, 1994), and the deep-rooted sense of charity, piety and fate, have obviously been of great importance in the development of community care. Spain, in this sense, whatever one's ideological concerns about the situation, provides some of the best conditions in Europe for asylum in the community. Spain is a country where it is possible to visualise that sufferers of mental illness can be realistically provided with support in their own homes to see them through times of crisis, even where emotional disturbance is experienced for long periods.

The family has had to fill the vacuum in intermediate care, for which facilities are lacking in Spain, between hospital and the home. It has, in this respect, already occupied the social space where asylum in the community might be provided in other countries.

These factors even led one of Spain's most well-known psychiatrists, not long after the post-war period began, to advise *against* a modernisation of mental health services, considering the coverage provided by the family to be sufficient (González Duro, 1987). On the other hand, until recent times, there was a certain tendency in professional circles, mainly from the more psychological tendencies in the field, such as those of psychoanalysis or family therapy which are more concerned with understanding and changing internal family dynamics rather than changing external factors affecting the sufferer, to 'blame' the family as a basic aetiological factor in the genesis of mental illness. For the same reason, consciously or unconsciously, such circles have ultimately condemned the family to 'support' the deviant member in its midst, with severe negative judgements made about those family units which, for whatever reason, are held to have evaded their 'responsibilities'.

Just as important though is the absence of a tradition in Spain of shared living patterns outside the family home, such as takes place in the formation of peer group households among the young in other countries. It is unusual for Spanish people to live in single person households, though the trend towards this minority style of living is increasing. Thus, housing patterns provide some explanation also for the lack of development of intermediate structures between family households and the hospital. Though one should never forget, of course, the fact that there are very limited economic resources to support the development of such structures in Spain, a shortage which is common for mental health authorities in Europe.

With only 4.5 per cent of the permanently housed, non-institutionalised population living in one person households (mainly widows), the household with two or three generations of the family living within it remains the preferred type in Spain. There are on average 3.28 persons in each home. Nearly 13 per cent of the population living in households formed of more than one person are living with relatives from three generations (Instituto Nacional de Estadística, 1993). This is a strikingly high figure when compared with that of 1 per cent for such households in the United Kingdom (Central Statistical Office, 1995). This level of co-residence between the generations in family households has even been increasing during the last decade as economic conditions have been stringent, and there has continued to be a scarcity of dwellings.

At the same time the process of family formation has been changing dramatically in just a few years (Durán, 1988b). The popularity of marriage has been falling. Whereas there were 7.63 marriages per 1,000 population in 1972, this ratio fell to 5.5 per 1,000 in 1989. The mean age for marriage has also been increasing. This has meant that the rate of procreation has slowed and that there has been some impact on family size, since marriage is an institution which still normally precedes procreation in Spain, with the country having one of the lowest rates in Europe of children being born to single women. Common law marriages are not increasing as they are in neighbouring countries and cohabitation is very rare. Women have been staying in full-time education for longer periods and have increased their level of participation in the labour force, with their domestic role thus reducing correspondingly (Delgado, 1993). The passing of legislation for contraception, abortion and divorce is another factor involved in this process of change. In this respect, it is not so easy to generalise about archetypal family patterns or behaviour. Nevertheless, households in Spain then are still primarily family households and the family thus marks out the potential territory for help-seeking, and circumscribes likely sources of support for most of those who seek asylum outside the hospital context. This important fact about Spanish life therefore provides some support for the hypothesis I set out earlier that the family is indeed providing such asylum. But one needs of course to ask families and sufferers about their experiences to see if this is indeed the case.

A possible starting point for such questioning is to consider how those patients returned from hospitals to the bosom of their families have fared in the community setting. In fact few rigorous works have been carried out in the field of deinstitutionalisation in Spain which have considered the 'burden' imposed by the process on the family. One of them (Gómez Beneyto et al., 1986) studied a group of 494 patients transferred in 1974 to the hospital of Betera (Valencia) for their social rehabilitation and 're-insertion' into the community. After twelve years of the programme it was found that 129 (26 per cent) had died and that 167 (34 per cent) were living outside hospital. Of the total number in the group still alive (resident both in and out of hospital), a majority were judged to have an impaired quality of life, particularly in relation to poverty and social and work contacts, and a tendency to use nursing homes. Complaints about the burden of their care were common from the relatives who looked after the ones at home and who were receiving little or no therapeutic or social support in that task. The concept of burden in the Betera study was measured in terms of the type of problems that the relatives looking after the patient attributed to their presence in the family home. Essentially, the families studied showed first and foremost problems relative to their own mental health, second, problems in having to alter established patterns of work, family, social and leisure activities, and third, problems in relation to their physical health and in gaining sufficient income, which were perceived as the areas of the families' lives least affected.

The Betera re-insertion programme thus supports the idea that families in Spain are able to provide care for those who have lived in institutions for many years, but that such care imposes a felt burden upon them. The dearth of social contacts among patients 're-inserted' could indicate that the family is probably providing, in some instances, a form of asylum, in terms of a place in which the person can continue to withdraw from society and receive care. This is in contrast to the situation in England and Northern Ireland, where various forms of sheltered living have been most commonly provided as part of hospital closure programmes and where few patients have returned to their families for this kind of asylum type care (Tomlinson, 1991; Health and Health Care Research Unit, 1991).

Regardless of the difficulties inherent in measuring the level of family suffering, it is of capital importance when it comes to studying the effects of policies of deinstitutionalisation and the prospects of developing asylum in the community (Guimón and Sota, 1993). In this respect, one cannot overlook the fact that resistance is developing among families to taking on their traditional care roles. For example, in a study now some ten years old which was carried out in a long-stay hospital, 87.5 per cent of families interviewed rejected the idea of a test period of return to the family homes for the relative resident in hospital. The reason for such rejection most commonly given was fear about the patient's reactions (Hernanz, 1982). This resistance may also be reflected in less favourable outcomes for those patients who do return to home compared with those for whom alternative accommodation and forms of support are arranged. Thus a further study of Betera showed that more significant progress in terms of social interaction was recorded for patients resettled into flats and boarding houses than for patients returned to the family home, where higher levels of withdrawal and anti-social behaviour were accompanied by less favourable attitudes being expressed by carers towards the ex-patients (Jordá et al., 1993).

It is difficult to determine the significance of such findings. On one level they may indicate that the family is ill-equipped to support 're-insertion', but on another they may indicate that it is only the family that can tolerate withdrawal and anti-social behaviour.

Community attitudes

While we have referred to the family, we cannot overlook the community itself that has, in an overall sense, to take in or reject the patient in its midst, and that has the gift of asylum in this sense. Writers such as Baca (1992) point to the risk of trusting too much in the capacity of the population for collaborating with the community model of assistance, and of underestimating the existence of stereotypes of the majority of mental patients, such as their dangerousness, their incurability and their unpredictable behaviour.

To what degree, then, does the wider community provide a tolerant environment and protection from persecution in Spain? In a recent study of attitudes to the mentally ill in Andalucía, a sample of both the general public and of professionals serving the mentally ill was surveyed (IASAM, 1989). Its authors concluded that the majority of both the general population and the health care workers placed the mentally ill on the same level as those with other illnesses. The majority also think that confinement and isolation of patients are not suitable, in spite of there being certain contradictions when an important minority believe in the need for high fences and guardians in the psychiatric hospital. In general the population is in favour of the advantages of community assistance, although it is not sure about mental patients being cared for in general hospitals. With respect to supposed dangerousness, a majority does not consider this an attribute of mental illness as such, although there is an important minority that holds to such a belief.

If these attitudes can in general be considered as positive, one cannot, however, overlook the fact that an important percentage of the population, though not a majority, express their agreement with important restrictions being placed on the mentally ill, specifically on their right to get married and on their right to defend themselves in divorce suits. The percentage in agreement reaches a majority with respect to the sterilisation of the seriously ill and the denial to them of the right to vote. Other indications of certain contradictions in public attitudes surveyed can be seen in that, on the one hand, it is commonly asserted to be more important for patients to receive the support and understanding of friends and relatives than any other treatment, while, on the other, there is widespread acknowledgement of the discomfort and unease for the friends and relatives caused by the presence of the mentally ill among them. Likewise, most respondents recognise that the majority of the mentally ill would prefer to live in their village or neighbourhood, and have the right to choose their place of residence, but, on the other, hand the right of neighbours to oppose this is also upheld.

As was noted above, overall, a favourable attitude towards the mentally ill can be observed, even though the average scores achieved are only situated at the lower levels of what begins to be a positive attitude. The authors of the Andalucía report point out that those who are older, female, living in a rural setting or who possess a low level of educational or professional qualifications tend to be more unfavourable in their attitudes to the mentally ill. Moreover, and in contrast to what one might expect within various sub-groups of the population relative to civil status, religious beliefs and experience relative to mental illness, it is people who live within their family of origin, Catholics and those who have relatives suffering from mental illness who display the most unfavourable attitudes. Similar studies have been carried out among the Basque and Galician populations (Ozámiz, 1985; Rodríguez *et al.*, 1982), areas with very different socio-cultural characteristics but where attitudes were found to be very similar to those expressed in Andalucía. Yllá *et al.* (1982) propose that the levels of knowledge of the population be improved as a strategy to have a positive effect on the prevalent attitudes.

Although one should be very careful in assessing whether the mass media exerts influence on public opinion, clearly the information presented within it is important to consider in relation to attitudes to the mentally ill. Analysis of the contents of mass media information about mental health could give some indication of the extent to which a more humane and benign picture of the mentally ill is emerging.

Three recent studies are worth drawing attention to in this respect, one concerning the Madrid press (Gamo, 1992), one the press in Andalucía (IASAM, 1987), and a third the Galician press (Xunta de Galicia, 1991). All three studies indicate that items featuring violent situations and crimes are prevalent, rather than situations of success or achievements in relation to the mentally ill. However, there were important differences between the press coverages of the three areas. Whereas in Madrid there were scarcely any references to strictly health care subjects, while news about the lunatic asylum was common, in Andalucía, references to political and administrative measures taken to reform psychiatric services were not infrequent and in this type of news an essentially positive evaluation of the mentally ill emerged. The author of the Andalucian study cautions that this evaluation may simply reflect reproduction of information given by those making the reforms but it is interesting that the difference between Madrid and Andalucía in these analyses corresponds to the difference in the degree of reform achieved in the respective Autonomous Communities. The Galician study, on the other hand, highlights the way in which the local press contained news giving more emphasis on the achievements of health reform than the national press. The authors conclude that a health policy aimed at the integration of the mentally ill has more journalistic credibility and beneficial potential when it proceeds from administrative levels that are more accessible and closer to the citizens.

Voluntary associations in the mental health field

Leaving aside the tensions in caring families and the ambivalence of public opinion towards the mentally ill, it is possible that another measure of the level of acceptance and tolerance of any community can be derived from the level of voluntarism in its midst. Contrary to what one might expect when considering the principles of Catholic charity so deeply rooted in Spanish society, it is important to note that hardly any charitable or voluntary associations (non-governmental organisations) for the mentally ill have been formed. The absence of such associations is quite striking and is almost total, barring a few poorly resourced organisations made up of small numbers of the mentally ill and their families and having a negligible impact on the wider society. In the same way, voluntary assistance is limited in the field of mental health and is of quite recent origin (Durán, 1990; Fernández Zapico, 1993).

The lack of voluntary organisations in mental health can be seen as part of a much wider social malaise which some historians have interpreted as a reflection of Franco's legacy. One account thus suggests that:

> maintained in an endless adolescence [Spanish] society has been manipulated to respond to the shake of politicians, with nobody concerned about helping her to mature, or trusting to the community any of the public activities that have been monopolized by the state. This is one of the important tasks for Spain in the twenty-first century, to revive the civil society destroyed by war and dictatorship, and to incorporate within it the performance of the daily tasks of the nation.
>
> (García de Cortázar and González Vesga, 1994: 56)

Social tolerance towards the disabled in Spain

In spite of what has been said in the previous section, if one takes account of the relatively low level of psychiatric beds available in Spain by European standards, and of the predominant role accorded to the family in all social affairs, it is very possible that even today, Spanish society is relatively tolerant towards the mentally ill and that a certain protective role may be assumed by the family. Thus although they express attitudes that are in general less favourable, families in rural areas, because of their main-taining a more traditional type of culture and not being limited in space as families are in an urban environment, tend not to seek to cast out those who fall prey to mental illness among them. Families in urban situations are of course more confined in terms of space. The high proportion of the mentally ill living in family surroundings in urban areas may be due to the shortage of alter-native sources of housing and care, with the result being resentment at the burden of care of the kind found in the Betera study cited earlier.

In the case of the elderly, another of the social groups that has traditionally depended for its survival on the family, even where there is a high level of disability, there are long waiting lists for residential care. Until more residential places are provided, the elderly must survive as best they can, which must either mean remaining alone in their homes or being received, in a rather forced way and without any choice, by some relative. This situa-tion is even worse in the case of the mentally ill, who face the very difficult task of finding another alternative between their family and the psychiatric hospital.

Taking account of all this then, professionals in the service must avoid the error of advising the passage – moving from one extreme to the other – from the traditional family-centred model to the opposite situation where the family is left disconnected from all responsibility. Looking at the family attitudes expressed in the surveys referred to earlier, one can hypothesise the existence of a great deal of tension, suffering and feelings of guilt derived from the contradiction observed between social expectations and individual attitudes. These are very important feelings to consider and to address, rather than take as an indication of the family's inappropriateness to provide refuge and protection within the community, if this is a desired goal for some sufferers. It is known that the family environment has a series of characteristics such as its capacity for adaptation and sacrifice, tolerance, reliability, company, permanence etc., which it will be difficult to provide elsewhere. Not to work with its potentially therapeutic and rehabilitative aspects would seem perverse. But it would be just as perverse to demand the commitment of the family without the professionals supplying a minimum of care and social support (economic aid, home care assistants, day care, crisis intervention teams, facilities for urgent admission, respite homes, etc.) to make the burden upon the family more tolerable for its 'well' members.

In a recent and extensive report about the chronically ill belonging to an association of relatives and sufferers of mental illness in the Basque Country, Igartua et al. (1994) found that three-quarters of those with chronic conditions who were surveyed lived with their family of origin. A further 7 per cent (mostly women) lived with a partner, and another 11 per cent who were generally older and who enjoyed greater economic independence, lived alone. In relation to the attitude of the 'well' relatives in these families, more than 93 per cent rejected the long-stay hospital as a desirable place for care. Just over half of the sufferers themselves and about half of the relatives interviewed stated that the family home was the most adequate location for care, with supervised hostels being the next most adequate location in the relatives' opinion and independent living being the next most adequate location in the view of sufferers.

Igartua and his colleagues found that it was the older relatives living with a relative having a certain awareness of his or her illness who chose the family as the best place for care. Relatives not living with the person suffering the illness, in situations where the latter does not show awareness of his or her condition opt, on the other hand, for care residences external to the family as most appropriate.

This survey suggests two distinct possibilities. First, it suggests that people with chronic illnesses can only be maintained in a family situation where the burden is manageable on account of the awareness and cooperation with advice of the person affected. Second, it suggests that some families may be only too willing to suggest residence outside the family home once separation has been experienced for any length of time and once, in that process, the initial fears or guilt over separation have been overcome. My own research into psychiatric hospital admissions carried out with colleagues in an area of the Basque Country supports the second of the above two possibilities (Martínez Azumendi *et al.*, 1992). In the majority of first admissions, the family and the patient came to the mental health centre in search of help, with hospitalisation initiated by the latter. But in the case of re-admissions, we found that the family or the patient went directly to the hospital on their own initiative, without seeking guidance first from the centre, whether because they were more familiar with the hospital or because they had lost their previous fears or guilt.

It is of course the women within the families who shoulder the greatest burden for the care of those who are ill. Durán calculated that if those who can help themselves or get help beyond the family household are excluded, 59 per cent of the disabled are cared for by the 'housewife', with more than seven out of ten of them having experienced the care situation for more than six years. Durán's calculations are all the more dramatic when it is appreciated that most women caring for the disabled at home are over 64 years old. Indeed, so important is the care role economically that it has been estimated to account for between 11.4 and 20.2 per cent of the Spanish Gross Domestic Product (Caillavet, 1988).

It is quite possible that the present deployment of the family for support of the person with a chronic illness, without the offer of facilities to relieve the family's burden is acting as a time bomb for a not-too-distant future. Gómez Beneyto's 1986 study in Valencia which was referred to above is useful in highlighting this state of affairs. It contains a profile of the typical relative who is at present the most involved in the care of the ill person. This profile corresponds to that of a woman, usually the sister or mother of the person cared for, who is aged 62, and who has mortgaged her life in the service of a cause that is in many instances beyond her powers, and which of course imposes an onerous burden of suffering.

The picture of this typical carer poses the question of what will happen when she dies. How will the mentally ill member of the family whom she cared for be able to face the basic demands of life in this new situation? When the sorry moment arrives, will the family find itself unable to cope with a person of advanced age, and therefore with less capacity for adaptation, who is accustomed to having his or her needs satisfied because of the attitude, perhaps over-protective in many cases, of the relative who has up to this point shielded the person from 'ordinary' social responses to all his or her peculiarities and extravagances? In a brusque way, he or she will find himself or herself alone, disorientated and without the capacity to respond to the contingencies of daily life. It is then very possible that the social resources that must be placed at his or her disposal will be much greater than those that might initially have been needed to achieve a certain personal autonomy. And in fact it is just this distressed question that I and my colleagues hear in our daily practice from the parents of our patients: 'Doctor, what will happen when we are not there? There are his brothers, but they already have families and couldn't (or will not wish to) take charge . . .'.

All this argues in favour of the early development of (a) provision for domestic help, (b) home care assistance in the form of vocational, labour and leisure programmes for the person cared for, and (c) alternative sheltered lodgings for those families in this predicament and for whom the possibility of developing a relationship with the long-stay hospital is fast receding. It is clear that, for all its burdening of women, its ambivalence, its feelings of guilt, and its lack of popularity as a care arrangement with a fair minority of the mentally ill, if the family is to continue to play a role in providing forms of asylum, then these types of service are the very least that can be done.

Patients' views

So far, I have referred only to the opinions and attitudes of the family and community as providers of placements for care, but what forms of setting and protection do the sufferers themselves look to? This is the vital issue to which I will now turn.

At present there is an abundance of descriptive studies of different socio-demographic, clinical and diagnostic variables relating to the mentally ill, with consequent advances proffered for improving the structure of assistance. This process will be taken further as the concept of quality of life is applied in the evaluation of outcomes for the patients of services. However, these technical advances remain outwith the control in any way of the patient or the members of associations for the mentally ill. Studies of satisfaction with the service received have, it is true, represented one of the strategies employed, from the perspective of evaluation and quality control, as a way of actively involving the user. However, this type of study provides us with an evaluation of the process as perceived *a posteriori*: it does not give us an indication of the beliefs, attitudes, desires and expectations of the sufferer at the moment he or she first sought help.

Unfortunately, in this respect, there are few Spanish studies offering such information, and many aspects of the user demand remain that have not been well studied. One of these aspects would be the 'prior expectations' with which patients direct themselves to the health service. Little effort has been made to discover what the potential user and his or her family wants or, what is more important, what differences there are among different cultures or groups, depending on socio-demographic or diagnostic variables respectively (Martínez Azumendi *et al.*, 1995).

One of the bitterest criticisms of the process of deinstitution-alisation is that it is held to be responsible for increasing the number of homeless persons. The argument is that shelters for the homeless have begun to act as places of refuge for those with chronic illnesses, out of lack of psychiatric shelters for those who would otherwise have sought this facility.

Although there are no detailed Spanish studies which could confirm or disprove this belief, it is evident that a significant number of those who make their way to the shelters for the home-less do suffer from severe mental health problems (Rico *et al.*, 1994). On the one hand, as noted above, the non-existence of alternative resources could be the motive for most of those in this group. On the other, since mental illness can further incapacitate the individual in taking advantage of the available resources, it may be that opting out of care plays an important part in the decision to seek a shelter for the homeless.

What one can detect in the work that has been done is a clear difference of opinion between professionals and the homeless mentally ill about what their primary needs consist of, with the former arguing that psychiatric treatment is of the highest impor-tance, and the latter that meeting shelter and income needs should come first (Mansilla, 1993). It is thus probable that this lack of correspondence between views explains the fact that the mentally ill who have become homeless, like those who have come to be called 'difficult' for the health care system, have rather disengaged themselves from the available sources of support than have been denied the use of them.

Prospects for the future

As in most areas of social and health care, there can be little doubt about the scale of the movement in Spain towards a mental health model consistent with wider European values. Starting from what can be described as a somewhat retarded position in the post-war period, anchored in a very conservative and traditional way of thinking, the last three decades have seen great changes in Spanish society which have influenced mental health care. But progress has been slow in mental health not only because of the dominance of the institutional model but because of a certain lack of rehabilitative values.

The first few years of community mental health services development, thanks to the ideological energy underpinning it, laid down some alternatives to institutions, but, as was noted above, the initial impetus has since died down. Not only is there a predictable lack of resources for further development but there is a lack of campaigners from the voluntary sector or from popular associations who can exert pressure for change. The net result is that individual families, whatever their dissatisfactions with the situation, continue to take responsibility for the care of the mentally ill, and are likely to continue to do so.

The role of the community, on the other hand, given what has been said about the 'immaturity' of Spanish civil society does not appear to be a source in the near future of succour for the sufferers. The concept of community, of course, tends to be associated with an image of harmony in society, where everybody gets along with everybody else. This is the received wisdom about traditional folk communities, where face-to-face relations would be the norm and the individual would be integrated into a group having a social life in common and one sharing beliefs and attitudes. With urbanisation and social mixing such communities, in so far as they ever existed, have become extinct. The right to be oneself, and to have an individual identity is thus as important in Spain as it is in the rest of western, and increasingly of eastern, society.

The placing of the individual's need for identity above the need for him or her to conform to the identity of the community results in the individual searching for a private haven from the stresses of being in the community, a haven where he or she can be as he or she likes, and at the same time be loved and appreciated.

The private haven in question in the developed countries has normally been provided in the individual's home, in Spain this is overwhelmingly the family home, as has been indicated, to an extent greater than elsewhere in Europe.

The intimate and private space of the home is required for two main reasons. First, what one might call the 'individual centralism' of the situation in regard to the community is associated with an intense over-privatisation of life, and, to an extent, self-exclusion from local public life. One begins to look for a meeting with others outside the home not as an affirmation of common identity but as an opportunity to seek support for one's choice of particular privatised activities. Second, and as a corollary of the first reason, one pursues 'associationism', that is to say an identity with others only in relation to the specialised activity – be it in sport, culture, gastronomy or 'hobbies', rather than identity with the 'we-feeling' of communities which embrace many kinds of activity (Gurrutxaga, 1993).

Given these trends in the use of the home as a retreat from a local community that no longer provides the individual with a source of identity and purpose, the person suffering from mental illness, who is already excluded from many associations, will be all the more in need of a private place in which she or he can be loved and appreciated. As has been indicated so far in this chapter, the family often provides such a place at present, and what is required for the future are those minimal facilities of home support and family respite already mentioned to ensure that this particular strength and depth of Spanish asylum in the community is secured. But given the fact that some of the chronically mentally ill who live with their family would prefer an alternative, while the families in question may be expressing some intolerance towards them, then there is clearly a pressing need to provide structures of supported apartments outside it.

In the context of the EEC, and the rights of those with disabilities to 're-insertion', and to expect the 'social solidarity' of the able (Flynn and European Commission, 1993), supported havens can be considered a right of citizenship for those with serious mental illness.

In spite of the fact that the results of community care are criticised or questioned on many occasions, it seems evident that in general they are positive and that they hold out the prospect of asylum in the community in Spain being a viable proposition

(Martínez Azumendi, 1991). It is a movement in the country that deserves new energy, to offset the discredit that it is often threatened with, as well as to avoid the potential pressures of the re-institutionalising movement such as have been witnessed in other countries. The closure of large hospitals has, it is true, been one of the principal objectives, from the very outset, of community psychiatry, and it gives one satisfaction to see this being achieved. Nevertheless, one is assailed by doubt when, on visiting some of the hospitals programmed for closure one can see the staking out of the turf by the surveyors from the development companies that have bought the sites. While it is projected that the money thus obtained by government and churches will make it possible to develop services outside hospitals, their replacement by exclusive residential complexes, from which patients are obviously excluded, is not a good omen.

Is the present community movement motivated by scientific and ideological conviction or is it only a political strategy for reducing the costs of the large institutions, supported by other economic interests whose attention is directed towards the splendid hospital sites? In any case, what will happen when the easy money obtained from selling the sites has been spent after a few years?

These are some of the questions to be answered if one wishes to avoid the history of the alienation of madness repeating its cycle again, madness that is 'integrated' but not acknowledged and addressed in the community, largely out of sight and further away from the well population even than the present large hospitals, which are so big that it is impossible to ignore them. To provide a variety of kinds of shelter and support from the resources of the large hospitals, so that asylum in the community can be assured both within and without the family, is the challenge facing Spain in the twenty-first century.

REFERENCES

Aguado, A.M. *et al.* (1994) *Textos para la historia de las mujeres en España*, Madrid: Cátedra.

Alonso-Fernández, F. (1989) 'Algo más sobre el padre Jofré (La época de oro de la psiquiatría española)', *Psicopatología* 9, 3: 149–155.

Angosto, T. (1992) 'La asistencia psiquiátrica en España en la última década', in Espino, J.A. (ed.) *Libro del año de psiquiatría 1992*, Madrid: Saned, 141–157.

Aparicio, V. (1993) 'La reforma psiquiátrica de 1985', in Aparicio, V. (ed.) *Evaluación de servicios de salud mental*, Madrid: Asociación Española de Neuropsiquiatría, 127–182.

Ararteko (1992) *Los psiquiátricos, Situación de los enfermos mentales en los hospitales psiquiátricos*, Vitoria, Ararteko-O.M.I.E.

Baca, E. (1992) 'Atención primaria de salud y asistencia psiquiátrica comunitaria: origen, desarrollo y perspectivas', in Espino, J.A. (ed.) *Libro del año Psiquiatría*, Madrid: Saned, 119–140.

Bellot, J. (1980) 'Los Centros de Salud Mental institucionales en la práctica psicosocial', in González de Chávez, *La transformación de la Asistencia Psiquiátrica*, 151–168.

Blázquez, M.J. (1986) *La Inquisición en Castilla-La Mancha*, Madrid: Librería Anticuaria Jeréz y Servicio de Publicaciones Universidad de Córdoba, Monografías, no. 86.

Caillavet, F. (1988) 'El trabajo gratuito de las mujeres: de la economía familiar a la economía nacional', in Durán, M.A. et al., *De puertas adentro*, 379–452.

Central Statistical Office (1995) *Social Trends*, London: HMSO.

Defensor del Pueblo (1991) *Situación jurídica y asistencial del enfermo mental en España*, Madrid: Publicaciones Oficina Defensor del Pueblo.

Delgado, M. (1993) *Cambios recientes en el proceso de formación de la familia*, REIS (Revista Española de Investigaciones Sociológicas), 64: 123–153. A version of this paper has been published as 'Spain', in Blossfeld, H.P. (ed.) (1994) *Family Formation in Modern Societies and the New Role of Women*, Westview Press.

Durán, M.A. (1988a) 'El cuidado de la salud', in Durán, M.A. et al., *De puertas adentro*, 83–104.

Durán, M.A. (1988b) 'Los límites del hogar', in ibid., 31–50.

—— (1990) 'La initiativa privada en la acción social', in Montalvo, J. (ed.) *El futuro de la protección social en España*, Servicio de publicaciones de la Junta de Comunidades de Castilla-la-Mancha.

Durán, M.A., Heras, D., García, C., Caillavet, F. and Moyer, M. (1988) *De puertas adentro*, Madrid: Ministerio de Cultura, Instituto de la Mujer.

Espinosa, J. (1980) 'La evolución de la Asistencia Psiquiátrica en España', in González de Chávez, M. (ed.) *La transformación de la Asistencia Psiquiátrica*, Madrid: Asociación Española de Neuropsiquiatría: 109–115.

—— (ed.) (1986) *Cronicidad en psiquiatría*, Madrid: Asociación Española de Neuropsiquiatría.

Fernández Zapico, E. (1993) 'Experiencia del voluntariado social en salud mental', *Informaciones psiquiátricas*, 131: 57–60.

Flynn, P. and European Commission (1993) *European Social Policy: Options for the Union*, Brussels: Office for Official Publications of the European Communities.

Gamo, E. (1992) 'Información sobre salud mental en la prensa: Su repercusión en la educación sanitaria', *Revista Asociación Española de Neuropsiquiatría*, 12, 40: 43–57.

García de Cortázar, F. and González Vesga, J.M. (1994) *Breve historia de España*, Madrid: Alianza Editorial

García Granados, J., Girón, F. and Salvatierra, V. (1989) *El Maristán de Granada: Un hospital islámico*, Asociación Española de Neuropsiquiatría, Granada: Asociación Mundial de Psiquiatría.

Gil, R.M. and Boadas, J. (1987) *El psiquiàtric de Salt Cent anys d'història*, Col·lecció Joaquim Botet i Sisó, 4. Institut d'Assistència Sanitária, Diputació de Girona.

Gobierno Vasco (1984) *Legislación psiquiátrica: Crítica y alternativas*, Vitoria: Departamento de Sanidad y Seguridad Social.

Gómez Beneyto, M. *et al.* (1986) 'Desinstitucionalización de enfermos mentales crónicos sin recursos comunitarios', in Espinosa, J. (ed.) *Cronicidad en psiquiatría*, Madrid: Asociación Española de Neuropsiquiatría, 237–263.

González de Chávez, M. (1980) 'Necesidades y objetivos de la transformación psiquiátrica', in González de Chávez, M., *La transformación de la Asistencia Psiquiátrica*, 171–202, Madrid: Asociación Española de Neuropsiquiatría.

Gonzáles Duro, E. (1987) *Treinta años de psiquiatría en España, 1956–1986*, Madrid: Ediciones Libertarias.

—— (1994) *Historia de la locura en España, Tomo I: Siglos XIII al XVII*, Madrid: Ed. Temas de Hoy.

Guimón, J. (1990) *Psyquiatras: De brujos a burócratas*, Barcelona: Salvat.

Guimón, J. and Sota, E. (1993) 'Evaluación de la deinstitucionalización del paciente psiquiátrico crónico', in González, de Rivera, *et al.*, (eds) *El método epidemiológico en Salud Mental*, Barcelona: Masson-Salvat.

Gurrutxaga, A. (1993) 'El sentido moderno de la comunidad', *REIS, Revista Española de Investigaciones Sociológicas*, 64: 201–219.

Health and Health Care Research Unit, Queens University (1991) *Leaving Hospital in Northern Ireland*, Belfast: Queens University.

Hernanz, M.M. (1982) 'Actitud de la familia ante el enfermo psíquico crónico hospitalizado', *Documentación Social, Revista de estudios sociales y de sociología aplicada*, 47: 65–74.

IASAM (1987) *Salud Mental y prensa*, Andalucía: Consejería de Salud, Junta de Andalucía.

——, Gabinete técnico (1989) *Actitudes de la población andaluza ante los enfermos mentales*, Sevilla: Instituto Andaluz de Salud Mental.

Igartua, J. *et al.* (1994) *Enfermedad mental: Grupos de autoayuda e integración social*, Vitoria: Gobierno Vasco, Vicepresidencia Asuntos Sociales.

Instituto Nacional de Estadística (1993) *Encuesta sociodemográfica 1991, Tomo II: Resultados nacionales, Volumen I*, Madrid: Hogar y Familia.

Jordá, E. *et al.* (1993) 'Evaluación del resultado de la desinstitucionalización de pacientes mentales crónicos: un estudio de cohorte', *Revista Asociación Española Neuropsiquiatría*, 13, 45: 113–123.

Ley General de Sanidad, Boletín Oficial del Estado, 29 April 1986.

López Linage, J. (ed.) (1977) *Grupos marginados y peligrosidad social*, Madrid: Campo Abierto Ediciones.

Mangen, S. (1986) *Mental Health Care in the European Community*, Beckenham: Croom Helm.

Mansilla, F. (1993) 'Red social y apoyo social en enfermos mentales sin hogar', *Revista Asociación Española de Neuropsiquiatría*, 13, 45: 124–129.

Martínez Azumendi, O. (1991) 'Revisión en torno al concepto psiquiatría comunitaria, *Documentos de Psiquiatría Comunitaria*, 1: 30–36.

Martínez Azumendi, O., Araluze, K., Grijalvo, J., Beitia, M. and Mendezona, J.I. (1995) 'Expectivas de la demanda sobre un centro de salud mental comunitario: evaluación de un nuevo cuestionario', *Revista Asociación Española Neuropsiquiatría*, 15, 52: 25–43. Erratum published in Revista Asociación Española Neuropsiquiatría, 15, 53: 198.

Martínez Azumendi, O., Beitia, M. and Ballesteros, J. (1992) 'Ingreso psiquiátrico. Análisis del tiempo de hospitalización y flujos entre C.S.M. y hospital', *Psiquis*, 13, 2: 57–62.

Mediavilla, J.L. (1992) 'Antipsiquiatría y psiquiatría: Veinte años después', in Antón, P. (ed.) *Medio siglo de psiquiatría en España: Homenaje al Profesor Ramón Sarró*, Madrid: Libro del Año (ELA).

Ministerio de Sanidad y Consumo (1985) *Informe de la Comisión Ministerial para la reforma psiquiátrica*, Madrid: Ministerio de Sanidad y Consumo.

Montalvo, J. (ed.) (1990) *El futuro de la protección social en España*, Servicio de Publicaciones de la Junta de Comunidades de Castilla-la-Mancha.

Moya, V. and González Navarro, F. (1993) *La Sanidad Española en la Europa de Maastricht*, Madrid: I.M. & C Lab. Beecham.

O.M. (1942) 'Memoria histórica: Bodas de diamante de la restauración de la orden hospitalaria de San Juan de Dios en España, Portugal y América', *La Caridad*, 2: 24.

Ozámiz, A. (1985) *Actitudes hacia las enfermedades mentales en el País Vasco*, Oñate: Instituto Vasco de Adminstración Pública.

Palacios de Borao, G. (1954) Introduction and notes, in Vander Veldt, J.H. and Odenwald, R.P. (1954) *Psiquiatría y Catalocismo*, Barcelona: Luis de Caralt.

Rico, P., Vega, L. S. and Arangureu, L. (1994) 'Transtornos psiquiátricos en transeuntes: un estudio epidemiológico en Aranjuez', *Revista Asociación Española Neuropsiquiatría*, 14, 51: 633–649.

Rodríguez, A. *et al.* (1982) 'Actitudes hacia la enfermedad mental la psiquiatría en Galicia', *Documentación Social, Revista de estudios sociales y de sociología aplicada*, 47: 139–154.

Rubí, M.L. (1988) 'Salud Mental: Repetición de un conflicto, superación de un conflicto', in Sáez Buenaventura, C., del Río García, L. and Sánchez Carrero, P., *Mujer y salud mental*, Madrid: Ministerio de Cultura, Instituto de la Mujer.

Secretaría Federal de Acción Social P.S.O.E. (1982) *Bases para una política sanitaria en salud mental*, Madrid: Secretaría Federal de Acción Social P.S.O.E.

Tomlinson, D.R. (1991) *Utopia, Community Care and the Retreat from the Asylums*, Buckingham: Open University Press.

Vander Veldt, J.H. and Odenwald, R.P. (1954) *Psiquiatría y Catolicismo*, Barcelona: Luis de Caralt.

Xunta de Galicia (1991) *Salud Mental y prensa en Galicia: Análisis de contenido*, Santiago de Compostela: Servicio Galego de Saúde, Servicio de Saúde Mental e Drogopendencias, Colección Saúde Mental, Serie Reforma Psiquiátrica, no. 7.

—— (1993) *Aspectos xurídico-asistenciais do enfermo mental*, Santiago de Compostela: Servicio Galego de Saúde, Servicio de Saúde Mental, Colección Saúde Mental, Serie Reforma Psiquiátrica, Documentación básica, no. 9.

Ylla, L., Ozámiz, A. and Guimón, J. (1982) 'Sociedad, cultura y actitudes hacia la enfermedad mental', *Psiquis*, 3, 3: 82–93.

Chapter 4

The appeal to madness in Ireland

Lindsay Prior

The concept of witchcraft provides [the Azande] with a natural philosophy by which relations between men and unfortunate events are explained and a ready and stereotyped means of reacting to such events.

E.E. Evans-Pritchard 1937: 63

THE INSTITUTIONALISATION OF THE INSANE

In 1915, the Sixty-Eighth (and final) Annual Report of the Lunacy Commissioners for England and Wales was published. It provided an ideal occasion for the Commissioners to review the result of the efforts which they had expended during the period from 1847 (the very first year of their existence) until 1914 (the final year). As part of their review exercise they included a graph which illustrated how, throughout the critical period, the number of asylums had increased from twenty-one to ninety-seven; how the mean number of inmates per asylum had increased from 261 to 1,088; and how the absolute number of lunatics contained in such asylums had increased from around 5,000 to something approaching 105,000. By any standards they were phenomenal increases and the pattern of augmentation was, as we now know, paralleled in many other parts of the western world – from France and the USA to Germany and Ireland. And as far as Ireland is concerned, this pattern of growth and development has been more than adequately dealt with in Finnane's (1981) work. I have no intention of summarising that work here, though a graphical representation of patterns of admission and residence relating to the twenty-two Irish asylums which were extant in 1914 is provided in Figure 4.1.

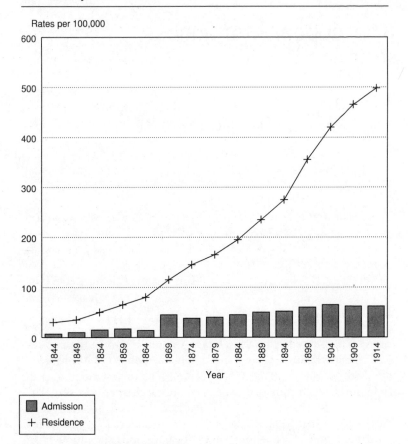

Rates per 100,000

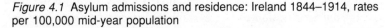

Year

- ▨ Admission
- + Residence

Figure 4.1 Asylum admissions and residence: Ireland 1844–1914, rates per 100,000 mid-year population

In what follows my intention will be to say something about the role of asylums in late Victorian Irish society, and I shall execute that task by concentrating upon the activities of just one asylum – that of Omagh, which served the area of County Fermanagh and part of Co. Tyrone. Before focusing on the Omagh asylum, however, I would like to place the entire discussion in a much broader context by referring to the overall aims of this book, which are concerned with the purposes and ends to which the notion of asylum might be directed.

The origins of the nineteenth-century asylum system are far from clear when we consider 'origin' in its rounded Aristotelian sense. And this state of confusion is in large part reflected in the literature relating to the growth of the asylum system in Europe and America. For example, some of those who have sought to analyse the growth of the asylum system have pointed to the fact that its augmentation correlates closely with urbanisation and industrialisation – that the growth of large-scale factory production, the growth of metropolitan areas and the appearance of the asylum system are in some way linked. In a few cases the association is introduced in a rather vague and general way (Mechanic, 1969), and in other cases it is introduced a little more specifically – as a term in a causal model (Sutton, 1991). When applied to the sparsely populated lake lands of Fermanagh or to the thinly inhabited townlands of Tyrone, such broad brush hypotheses can, of course, seem a little unconvincing, but at this stage I merely wish to note the general tenor of such claims without in any way criticising them.

Should it be considered that urbanisation, industrialisation and 'modernisation' appear to offer little in the way of explanatory power, then the analyst can call instead upon some variant of a 'social control' thesis. That is to say, some variant of a thesis which claims that asylums were built for the purpose of organising and controlling vast numbers of otherwise ungovernable people – ungovernable because they were unruly *per se*, surplus to the requirements of industrial capitalism (because they were insufficiently skilled or educated), or because they were uprooted, homeless, dispossessed and desolate, or perhaps because the very nature of social relations in a capitalist society meant that the old social ties of care and control (previously based in the family and in local rural communities) were routinely burst asunder. The names of Digby (1985), Rothman (1971, 1985) and Scull (1979, 1989) obviously come to mind when we consider such possibilities, though perhaps Foucault (1967, 1977) too, in his own way, may be said to have related the origin of the 'great confinement' to the need for what is commonly called social control.

These views are not, of course, beyond criticism and authors such as Arieno (1989) have not only sought to contradict specific hypotheses which are implied by the social control thesis, but also to substitute their own hypotheses. Arieno argues that asylum growth represents a particular expression of a more general nineteenth-century trend for governments to bureaucratise social life and its attendant problems.

All of this, of course, is to overlook what is perhaps the most obvious of hypotheses; that the growth of the system represented a suitable response to real and genuine needs of the asylum inmates. That is to say, that the growth of asylum building represented in its day a humane and rational way of dealing with a very real set of personal medical or medico-social problems. Kathleen Jones (1972) and Gerald Grob (1973) have both been prone to what one might call this Whig interpretation of history. It is an interpretation which has charm. For modern treatment programmes are clearly underpinned by the belief in rational and systematic scientific solutions to personal human problems. In that sense it is easy to see how asylums may well have been built on the promise of their curative powers. That the 'cures' sometimes turned out to be worse than the original complaints is beside the point.

And linked to this notion of cure it is necessary to consider the possibility that there was indeed a real increase in rates of insanity during the nineteenth century. That is to say that the spread of a virus or some other biological agent may well have generated an explosion of mental pathology. Asylums in this sense could be seen to have represented an appropriate medical response to a growing medical problem. I suspect that Gottesman and Bertelsen (1991), Hunter and Macalpine (1974), and Turner (1989) would choose to pitch their tents in this particular camp, together with Hare (1983) who has linked the rise in English County Asylum populations to a real increase in rates of schizophrenia.

At the considerable cost of leaving aside the fine print which substantiates these various claims and hypotheses, I would simply like to highlight one or two difficulties which arise out of these diverse accounts of asylum growth. The first concerns the fact that they each tend to consider the development of the asylum system as something which was primarily instigated by members of an elite – here a political, there a medical or juridical elite – rather than something which was initiated in response to the needs expressed by the 'lower' orders by society. In other words, asylums were built in increasing numbers because well-intentioned (or even not so well-intentioned) reformers realised their potential benefits vis-à-vis the ills of the masses (Jones, 1972; Rothman 1971; Grob 1973). Indeed Rothman (1985: 115) at one point argues that to understand the growth of the system we must begin with 'the rhetoric of the reformers'. Though should one choose to shun the intentions of the reformers, then we can instead turn to consider 'moral entrepreneurs' (Scull, 1979), or the machinations of the medical profession (Scull, 1979), or simply 'the dominant classes' (Szasz, 1994: 105).

Second, there seem to me to be difficulties in the ways in which these accounts link (or fail to link) the growth of asylums to an increased prevalence in insanity. Thus some commentators, for example, seem to be intent on denying that the inmates of asylums were truly insane in any sense at all – 'deviant' they may have been, but only occasionally 'insane' (Scull, 1989; Szasz, 1994). This mistrust in the accuracy of nineteenth-century diagnostic prowess stems mainly from the assumption that real insanity would have to have been, at base, a biological problem – and there is no evidence to suggest that the majority of inmates in nineteenth-century asylums exhibited, say, any brain pathology. Of the commentators who do link the growth of asylums with an increase in mental pathology, the link is of course made exactly and precisely on biological grounds. Thus Renvoize and Beveridge (1989) seem to suggest that asylums truly did confront various forms of bodily, pathological (mental) disorder, whilst Gottesman and Bertelsen (1991), as I have already stated, argue that the increase in asylum inmate numbers can be associated with the transmission of some form of biological agent. In both cases, however, we are left to grapple with a very narrow interpretation of what insanity might have been. And in neither case is it recognised that true insanity might be defined in terms of human culture rather than in terms of human biology.

Now, it is not my purpose to dismiss these various claims on the basis of one or two hastily conceived misgivings, but I would like to suggest a different tack to our problem by asking what these accounts might look like if they were applied to something akin to the Azande belief in, and use of, witchcraft. Might they hint, for example, at some kind of colonial conspiracy? Or the existence of some underhand means of social control? Or yet again at a devious system of indigenous ruling-class manipulation? Or maybe the presence of some undiagnosed biological illness? Or might it be argued that Azande witchcraft was not real witchcraft after all? What Evans-Pritchard (1937) demonstrated, of course, was that witchcraft was not something imposed on unfortunates by a dominant other, but a phenomenon which was integrated into the very fabric of social life. That it was a self-contained belief system

– a cosmology – which enabled its adherents to cope with and explain the misfortunes which confronted them, and that it persisted because people found it useful and practical. In this respect I would like to suggest that rather like witchcraft, there is a sense in which beliefs in insanity and madness are also embedded in the quotidian nature of human existence. That is to say, references to lunacy, madness or whatever, cannot just be imposed on a population or introduced from afar, but have to form part of a system of explanations which people regularly call upon to account for the turmoil in their social relations or their personal misfortunes. And in the Irish case, this is a state of affairs well illustrated in Synge's *Playboy of the Western World* (1907) (a play sited in the wild west of Ireland during the opening decade of this century). A central theme of the play concerns father–son relationships, and it is of some interest to note that it was the doctrine of madness that was called upon to account for the disruption which existed between Mahon and his son. And when the father tried to return his son to home, it was the selfsame doctrine which was applied to him. Indeed, as the widow Quinn said to the boy's father, 'It's mad yourself is with the blow upon your head. That lad is the wonder of the western world.'

In this vein, therefore, what I would like to investigate here is something about the manner in which ordinary people (the afflicted and their relatives, together with minor and medical functionaries of the asylum) might have used the facilities of the asylum both to make sense of the various difficulties with which they were confronted, and to organise their lives in general. In order to achieve these aims I shall divide my discussion into three parts – a discussion of inmates' characteristics and 'careers'; a discussion of symptoms and therapeutics; and a discussion concerning the etiology of madness.

THE OMAGH ASYLUM

Before his eyes appeared, sad, noisome, dark
A lazar-house it seemed, wherein were laid
Numbers of all diseased, all maladies
Of ghastly spasm, or racking torture, qualms
Of heart-sick agony, all feverous kinds,
Convulsions, epilepsies, fierce catarrhs.
Intestine stone and ulcer, colic pangs,

Demoniac frenzy, moping melancholy,
And moon-struck madness . . .

(Milton, *Paradise Lost* XI, 478–486)

Inmates and their 'Careers'

The Omagh Asylum was opened in 1853 with 300 beds, by the turn of the century the number of beds had more than doubled and on census night 1901 the asylum contained some 660 individuals. But who were these people and why were they incarcerated there?

In many ways the answer to the last question leads us directly back to our opening problem. So, for example, if one was to discover that the 660 individuals were mainly drawn from the poor, dispossessed and frail we might argue that it was their poverty and frailty which formed the occasion for their incarceration. Unfortunately for us perhaps, at least one thing is clear and it is that the inmates of Omagh Asylum were far from being a homogeneous group and almost any generalisation which we may be tempted to make about their common condition would soon be overturned by contrary evidence. Indeed, in what follows I am going to argue that the Omagh Asylum contained at least two very different populations – a long-term and a short-term population – each of which had very different demands and needs to be met. And, what is more, the two populations were drawn from very different sections of the rural community. The data on which I have chosen to base my argument are drawn from two sources. The first is a 10 per cent sample of cases entered into the Acute Case Books of the Asylum between 1895 and 1905. The second is a 25 per cent sample of census records relating to the 1901 Census for Co. Tyrone.

In the analysis of asylum inmates, two sets of questions ordinarily arise. The first concern the social characteristics of the inmates and the second concern their movement in and out of the institution. For the purpose of discussing movement I have borrowed Goffman's (1961) concept of career. By social characteristics I mean to report merely on simple measures of age, sex, marital status and occupation, and in this section I intend to draw a few comparisons between the two inmate groups (as defined above), and the population of Irish asylums on census night 1901.

Table 4.1 Selected characteristics of inmates

Selected characteristics	(a) %	(b) %	(c) %
Male	56	53	53
Age:			
0–19	5	1	5
20–49	72	61	70
Married	31	19	17
Catholic	68	67	82
Farmers or labourers			
(or wives and daughters of)	52	44	32
Melancholic	32	31	15
Manic	54	54	45
Hereditary causation	26	20	19
Numbers	188	164	25050

Note: Inmate profiles for (a) a 10 per cent sample of acute cases of the Omagh Lunatic Asylum 1895–1905; (b) a 25 per cent sample of cases listed in the 1901 Omagh Lunatic Asylum Census Returns; and (c) all inmates of Irish Lunatic asylums reported in the 1901 Census of Ireland

The best starting point for our analysis of careers is Table 4.1 in which selected inmate characteristics are listed for the case book sample and the census sample. From this table one may note that as far as Omagh was concerned, the inmates were predominantly small Catholic farmers, and unskilled labourers. They were predominantly unmarried and predominantly male (in contrast to England it seems where, according to Showalter (1981), women predominated). Furthermore, most Omagh inmates were to be found in the 20–50 age group with just a small percentage in the younger age range and the remainder in the higher ranges. The major disease categories were mania and melancholia (which together accounted for over 80 per cent of the inmate population). This, of course, presents only a static picture of the inmate population. In order to gain knowledge of the various routes which different inmates took through the asylum it is necessary to make an examination of the case book sample in greater detail. Before I do this, however, it may be useful to glance at a few of the physical characteristics of the inmates.

As will be demonstrated below, the case book material contains an inordinate amount of detail on the physical characteristics of inmates, and among such detail are data on the heights and weights of inmates. Measures of height and weight are often used

Table 4.2 Mean height (ins) and weight (lbs) for Omagh Asylum acute case book sample 1895–1905

	Females			Males		
	Mean	*Standard error*	*n*	*Mean*	*Standard error*	*n*
Height (ins)	62.83	0.30	70	67.04	0.257	95
Weight (lbs)	126.2	2.65	70	144.189	1.755	95

these days as indices of health and nutritional history, (see, for example, Floud *et al.*, 1990). And in that respect the Omagh measures can be used to form some judgement concerning the extent to which any given population displays characteristics of social deprivation. Naturally, the information contained in Table 4.2 needs to be compared to that obtainable from other populations in order to be meaningful (and had the sample been larger, it would have proved useful to break it down into age cohorts as well). Nevertheless, on the basis of information provided by such researchers as Floud *et al.*, (1990) on the average height of nineteenth-century European males, and O'Grada (1991) on Irish prisoners at Clonmel, these data suggest a relatively well fed and very healthy population. Indeed, the detail gives the lie to the notion that asylum inmates were 'physically decrepit' (Scull, 1979), or that asylum inmates were in any way drawn disproportionately from the feeble, infirm and severely deprived strata of Irish society.

As for movement through the asylum, the case books demonstrate that almost half of the patients were discharged as recovered within the first four years, that 26 per cent died during the same period and that the remaining 27 per cent became 'chronic' patients (cf. Renvoize and Beveridge, 1989). Admission into the chronic book, of course, usually signified the beginning of a very lengthy internment. (One half of those in the 1901 sample had been asylum residents for more than six years, whilst the average stay was 10.5 years.) But nevertheless it would be wrong to think of the asylum system as providing a unidirectional mechanism – for people left it as regularly as they entered it. Indeed, some 25 per cent of the case book sample were readmissions, and in some cases inmates manifested what is known today as 'the revolving door syndrome'. Thus the manic 7052 first admitted April to July

1888, was subsequently readmitted July to October 1896, August to November 1898, May to September 1901, September 1901 to November 1903, before her sixth admission on 3 December 1901. The last reference to her concerns her transfer to 'Chronic Females' during March 1909. In a similar way, 6972 was admitted during 1885, 1894 (twice), 1899, 1900 and 1901 (April to July) before being discharged once again as 'recovered'.

What this detail does not reveal, however, is how the recovery rate was associated with specific social factors. Given the difficulties posed by research on historical data of these kind, it is not of course possible to reconstruct a plausible causal model of inmate 'careers'. The information in Tables 4.3 and 4.4, however, provide some clues that the acute patients did differ from the chronic patients. The tables provide some results from a statistical investigation using discriminant analysis. In this context the analysis has been used more as an exploratory technique than as an aid to the production of a fully polished model. The central question which was posed was 'does the acute population differ from the chronic population in any recognisable way?' And broadly speaking, discriminant analysis responds to such questions by trying to predict who would and would not be included in different groups (such as acute and chronic) on the basis of information about patient's social background. Since the case files contained information on such things as patient age, sex, marital status, previous occupations, religion, the nature of patient diseases, the cause of their admission, their height, weight and length of stay, it was possible to introduce various combinations of factors as suitable predictors into the statistical model. For the case book sample the acute group was defined so as to include those who entered and left the asylum within twenty-four months; for the census group it was defined so as to include those who entered and left in the first forty-eight months. (The census sample had a much bigger spread of lengths of stay and the data set proved too awkward to handle with a twenty-four month cut-off date).

In general, the only models which seemed to have any real predictive force for the case book sample were those which included the variables of marital status, age, weight and reason for admission. The only predictive factors which emerged from the analysis of the census sample were age (naturally enough), marital status and age at admission. Of these, the most powerful

Table 4.3 Factors associated with length of stay in the case book sample

Canonical Discriminant Functions

Eigenvalue	Correlation	Wilks'Lambda	Chi-square	DF	Significance
0.1459	0.3569	0.8727	16.18	4	0.002

Correlations between discriminating variables and length of stay:
Marital status   0.765
Body weight (lbs)   0.546
Reason for admission   0.369
Age (in years)   −0.131

Classification results:
Group 1: length of stay 0–24 months *N = 74   Misclassified = 41%
Group 2: length of stay 25+ months *N = 49   Misclassified = 25%

* Excludes those who died

Table 4.4 Factors associated with length of stay in the 1901 Census sample

Canonical Discriminant Functions

Eigenvalue	Correlation	Wilks'Lambda	Chi-square	DF	Significance
0.7050	0.6430	0.5865	85.63	3	0.000

Correlations between discriminating variables and length of stay:
Age in years   −0.3248
Age at entry in years   0.1972
Marital status   0.1568

Classification results:
Group 1: length of stay 0–48 months N = 59   Misclassified = 0%
Group 2: length of stay 49+ months N = 105   Misclassified = 31%

predictors were marital status in the case book sample and age in the census sample. In both cases being married made a difference in the sense that it was related to shorter stays. Since the married were on average somewhat older than the single, age at entry also played a part in the predictive process. As for reason for admission, it was clear that those admitted on the basis that they might harm themselves (had made suicidal threats or attempted suicide) were more likely to return home after a short period than those who had threatened harm to others.

The connection between weight and length of stay (in the case book sample) remains something of a puzzle – except to say that the well fed left sooner than the remainder of the group. Looking at Tables 4.3 and 4.4, we can interpret Wilks' Lambda (translated into a chi-squared measure) as telling us that there is a real difference between the two groups of inmates (acute and chronic) in terms of the discriminant factor. The canonical correlations provide a measure of the association between the discriminant scores and the groups. The pooled within groups correlations are correlations between the variables stated and the discriminant function. (Crudely put, they give us some indication of the relative contributions of each variable.) A good model would have had larger eigenvalues and canonical correlations than are evident in Table 4.3. But nevertheless the two models had a certain amount of predictive power. In the case book sample the model misclassified only 34 per cent of cases, and in the census sample it misclassified 20 per cent. In both cases the results are far better than could have been achieved by making predictions with a toss of the coin or by throwing dice. By implication, of course, such factors as nature of 'disease', occupation, religion and gender seemed to have made little if any discernible difference to length of stay *per se*.

There is a sense, therefore, in which the Omagh Asylum may be said to have contained a 'fast stream' of older, married individuals who often displayed bizarre beliefs and behaviours and sometimes exhibited tendencies to self-harm; and a 'slow stream' of younger, single individuals who in some way or other had been perceived at entry as being disruptive to the family or community order. For the one group the asylum acted as a temporary haven; for the other, as a long-term form of containment.

It seems likely then that patterns of marriage and family life did have an impact on the admission and residence patterns of Omagh inmates. In the twentieth century, of course, the recognition of family and community factors in the genesis of psychiatric disorder emerged slowly but surely in both the literature and the practice of psychiatry. In the nineteenth century, however, madness was solely regarded as being 'in' the body or brain of the afflicted person, and the conceptualisation of disturbed interpersonal relationships had not yet begun. It was, therefore, individual abnormalities rather than family abnormalities which had to be treated (or restrained); and that treatment necessitated a detachment of the sick person from his or her usual network of social relations.

Symptoms and therapeutics

The patient presents nearly all of the characters of a cretin of that class of sporadic cretinism in which the (thyroid?) is absent or at any rate greatly atrophied. The body is squat and stout, head broad but not unusually large. Weight 4 st(ones) 6. Height 3 (foot) 3. Skin is sallow, coarse, rough, wrinkled and covered with an eruption resembling scabies. Eyes, blue, hollow, oblique. Hair on head; absent on eyebrows and pubis. Nose flattened, nostrils large perpendicular. Mouth large and repulsive, always open, lips thick. Ears misshapen, chest narrow, back curved ... limbs misshapen. Is unable to stand or sit up unaided – abdomen like a bag. Shy of strangers. Those who know her well say she is capable of some understanding, is said even to laugh ...
(Omagh Asylum Acute Female Case Book 1895 + : Case 7914)

Perhaps the most striking feature of the Omagh case books is the fact that they express an inordinate amount of interest in the physical health of the body and generally fail to tell us anything substantial about the ideas, beliefs and actions of the insane. Indeed, for each inmate very detailed information is recorded at entry on almost every aspect of the physical body. Each case record, for example, contains detailed information on all of the following: height (to the quarter inch), weight (to the half pound), eye and hair colour, specific gravity of the urine, the presence of sugar in the urine, the pulse rate, the body temperature, the forms of the head and the shape of the nose and the eyes and the chin, the expression of the countenance, and the possibility of hereditary disposition. This in addition to data on the digestive, dermic, circulatory, respiratory and glandular systems. Inmate 6051, for example, has a 'red face, short and turned up nose, large ears, prominent teeth. Sullen expression, and mutters.' Inmate 6179 has a short nose, well-shaped forehead and small ears. The head of 8639 is fuller on the left than the right side, her expression is dull and melancholy. Inmate 6973 has a head which is, 'Very broad across the front. A high forehead.' Her countenance is 'dazed and vacant'. Inmate 5891 is 10.5 stone and 5 foot 3.5 inches, his countenance is 'quiet and cheerful'. Inmate 6778 has urine with a specific gravity of 1,020 and an alkaline reaction. No albumen or sugar is present. (On the significance of urine to mental pathology see Tuke, 1976.) And this focus on the body is well represented in the case book entry for Margaret Hampton which opened this sub-section.

Data on the non-physical characteristics of inmates are, however, much harder to come by. The reader is informed, for example, that inmate 6191 'speaks in a loud excited manner', that inmate 6265 is 'incoherent, irrelevant and evasive', and that 6081 is 'noisy and violent. Dirty in his habits', but in none of these cases is anything noted about the substance of their talk or behaviour. True, symptoms are sometimes described on admission. Thus, 6171 claims that 'The divil (sic) has castrated him', while 7510 says that he is the son of God. Inmate 9469 believes that the Coroner and 'The Clinicman' are out to destroy him. Inmate 6553 wanders aimlessly, muttering repeatedly, 'I am lost, dreadful, horrible, awful' and 6749 'Imagines her soul is lost and that she is going to be killed.' Inmate 6777 says, 'How her neighbours got the heavenly men to destroy her, also the men under the earth turned her inside round and pushed her heart over to the wrong side.' Inmate 6116 says that she has seven children and that they each have sacks of gold. She denies having attempted suicide on the grounds that she is 'already dead'. Inmate 6873 (who died from General Paralysis of the Insane), imagines that he has had 'connexion' with six of the Sultan's wives. And data on the social backgrounds of patients is included almost only as an afterthought to the admission process. Thus we know, for example, that Margaret Hampton was brought to the asylum 'crying and fretting' a few days after the death of her mother, but that is about all that we know except that she died of 'cretinism' within the month.

In contrast to the relative dearth of information on the subjective or social dimensions of madness there is, as I have already stated, a surfeit of data on the bodily condition of inmates and one assumes that this is precisely because the asylum doctors either regarded only bodily conditions as real, or saw bodily health and illness as the substratum on which 'the mind' was built. Indeed, Clarke (1981) describes how the 'doctrine of concomitance' (or psycho-physical parallelism) dominated late nineteenth-century psychiatric thought. And it is clear from the English language texts of the like of Maudsley (1895), Tuke (1976), and Kraepelin (1902, 1904), that for psychiatry it was the body (and specifically the brain) rather than the mind or social relations which constituted the true object of attention.

Given such a point of focus, then, it can come as no surprise to realise that the therapeutic effort of the asylum staff was directed mainly towards the insane body. On the basis of case records there can, in fact, be little doubt that in the Omagh Asylum therapy was first and foremost about the control of the body, for the category of 'mind' appears only dimly in the case book accounts, and that of social relations not at all. Indeed, the details of medication which appear in the records seem, for the most part, to be directed towards the manufacture of docile bodies. Inmate 5941, for example, is dosed with 'potass. bromide' – the most popular of the means of chemical control while 6065 is dosed with potassii bromide and foul-tasting paraldehyde. Inmate 6864 is dosed with what seems the excessive amount of 320 grains of bromide and 6227 is unfortunate in that his acute melancholia and suicidal impulses are treated with both bromide and chloral hydrate (ether also figures in his therapy). For an episode of acute mania 6658 is dosed with potassii bromide (30 grs) and spirits of ammonia. The suicidal 5970 (who had slit his throat to such an extent that when he drank water it gushed out through the oesophagus) was dosed with morphine. Inmate 7375 is dosed with sulphonal (25 grs) and paraldehyde (3 drachms). The luckier 7648 seems unaffected by any of the substantial doses of paraldehyde or bromide which are administered to him and is therefore treated with cannabis. After three years, 7139 displays cyanosis of the extremities and poor circulation as a result of bromide treatment and is therefore dosed with a quinine and strychnine mixture – to no visible effects, as his epileptic convulsions continue at a rate of seven to ten per month.

In addition to sedatives and hypnotics for the quelling of loud behaviour, great attention was also paid to bowel movements and endless doses of calomel, potassii sodium and dilute hydrochloric acid were dispensed to the intestines. Enemas were also frequently used. The comatose and dying 6371, for example, was nevertheless given an enema of oil of ricin and turpentine, whilst 6387 was fed beef tea and whisky through a nasal tube in the mornings and given an enema each evening. (For a wider discussion of asylum posology see Cullum, 1905.) When chemical control failed, mechanical restraint was used in its stead. Inmate 6658 was placed 'in seclusion' (that is, in the cells), for a number of hours. The use of seclusion, however, is little recorded and more frequent are references to the 'Refractory division'. Thus, the hyperactive 5914 was dosed with potassii bromide and spirits of ammonia for three months during 1895 to no effect. Subsequently, her medication was changed to bromide and tincture of cannabis. Two weeks later the medication was again changed – to chloral hydrate and bromide. When that failed she was taken off all medication and subjected to the mechanical restraint of the refractory division alone.

It is clear, then, that the therapeutics of the asylum were primarily directed towards restraint and confinement. (See also Renvoize and Beveridge (1989).) There is no hint here that anyone confronted the delusions and imaginings of the insane on anything other than a physical basis. In fact, it was the body which was observed and treated and dosed with bromides. The 'mind', family and interpersonal relations were ignored. Such a focus on the restraint of the body had, as I will discuss below, a resonance in some of the wider aspects of nineteenth-century Irish (even European) culture. For now one need only note that asylums were, in the main, repositories for insane bodies – and as such they were eminently suited to their purpose. Indeed, it was only when the problem of insanity (a legal category) was theorised anew as mental illness – during the twentieth century – that the isolated asylum appeared to be mismatched with aims of psychiatric practice.

The etiology of madness

Each form of professional practice conceives and creates its own objects of focus and it is, I think, already clear that the object of asylum medicine was the physical frame. Omagh was not, of course, alone in underlining the body as the point on which asylum practice should concentrate, and Clarke (1981) in his study of nineteenth-century English psychiatry makes plain that all the dominant texts of the day were steeped in a form of psychiatric physicalism in which the brain (together with the body which it directed) played the central role. The discourse on symptoms and therapeutics is not, however, the only aspect of asylum practice which would lead us to this conclusion. The discourse on causation brings us to the same point.

To a modern researcher many of the details of causation contained in the asylum case books seem bizarre. Take for example the case of AB aged 45 years, who was afflicted with mania, its cause was listed as 'congenital', and yet her affliction was supposedly only of five years length. Or take case 6904 whose acute mania was supposedly caused by 'irritation of law courts', or 6245's mania which was caused by 'foreign service in the army', or 7357 whose mania was a product of masturbation. Even more puzzling is how, in 1903, 7318's General Paralysis of the Insane (GPI) could be attributed to syphilis, whilst a year later 7555 had his GPI attributed to 'pecuniary losses'. In the presence of such statements as these, it is probably safer to suspect that the registered 'causes' of disease tell us little about what were regarded as the sufficient and necessary conditions of insanity, and rather more about the broader vocabulary of causation which was manifest in asylum psychiatry at the turn of the century. Thus, from a study of the case books it is clear that mental disorders were believed to have a primary cause (in the same way as did physical diseases), that the range of primary causes was relatively limited, and that causation was perceived in terms of simple associations – one disease per person, one cause per disease.

According to the 1901 Irish Census, the causes of insanity could be divided into four categories: Moral or Mental Causes, Physical Causes, Hereditary Causes and Unspecified. Of the 3,861 Melancholiacs in Irish Asylums on the night of 30 April 1901, for example, 54 per cent had cause unknown allocated to them, 24 per cent had heredity assigned as a cause, 12 per cent moral causes and 10 per cent physical causes. For the 11,190 maniacs the percentages were: 56 per cent unknown, 20 per cent heredity, 14 per cent physical causes and 10 per cent moral causes. And this more or less reflects the picture presented to the enumerators for the Omagh Asylum.

When one compares the case book causes with asylum returns, however, one begins to discover interesting variations. For example, in the case book accounts hereditary associations appear with greater frequency than in census returns. In fact, such associations were noted (though not necessarily under the specific heading of 'causation') in 37 per cent of case book records as compared to only 20 per cent of census records. More interestingly, the causes allocated to the same case alter according to the document on which it is recorded. Thus the nature of 6955's acute mania is noted as being caused by hereditary factors in the case book, and as 'unknown' in the census returns.

Overall, then, there seems to have been a considerable degree of ambiguity about causation and about the role of hereditary factors in the etiological framework. It is, for example, quite clear that asylum doctors were more than ready to claim ignorance as to why particular individuals succumbed to insanity and that their understanding of causation was piecemeal and flawed. To that extent the evidence presented here is compatible with the image of late nineteenth-century (American) psychiatry presented by Blustein (1981). It conflicts, however, with that painted by Ray (1981) whose figures for hereditary causation at the Brookwood Asylum are much higher (namely 40 per cent), and who attributes to asylum doctors a coherent 'model of madness' in which hereditary degeneration played a major role. Indeed, Stewart (1976), and Decker (1971) also claim that the theories of racial and specifically family 'degénéréscence' held a central position in continental European psychiatry of the 1890s and early 1900s. Perhaps, then, there was a disjunction between the theory of causation as it was presented in the text books of psychiatry and the vocabulary of causation as it was used in asylum practice. This, I suspect, would fit in more squarely with a view of causation which looks upon causal explanations rather as others have viewed the attribution of motives (see, for example, Gerth and Mills, 1954). In other words a relevant 'cause' of an event is not so much the objectively necessary and sufficient condition for its occurrence, but merely one of a range of culturally acceptable factors chosen from a familiar array of solutions. And it is in terms of such a system that the everyday, the mundane, and the banal misfortunes and awkwardnesses which disrupted routines could be reinterpreted as being symptomatic of a personal pathology – that is, of insanity.

So what were these unfortunate and awkward events which disrupted the routines of social life? To answer that question one must turn not to the vocabulary of causes but to the vocabulary of 'reasons' by dint of which the Omagh inmates were legally committed to the asylum. And on doing so it can be discovered that the two great categories of reasons which underpinned committal to the asylum related either to self-harm (attempted or threatened suicide), or harm and violence to others. Inmate 5891, for example, had threatened to kill his brother; 5970 tried to choke his sister; 6002 assaulted his wife; 6265 threatened his wife, his father and his children; 7049 attacked a man with a pitchfork; 5990 attacked her father; and 6047 attacked her husband and burnt his clothes, and so on. Indeed, just over 55 per cent of the case book sample were admitted by reason of violence or threatened violence to a relative or neighbour; and 25 per cent by reason of self-harm or threatened self-harm. Only the remaining 20 per cent were, like Margaret Hampton, committed by reason of their symptoms.

So despite the fact that there is no inkling in the Omagh Asylum of a much later and specifically twentieth-century concern with relationships in the community or the family (except in the guise of a rather primitive and untheorised form of population genetics), there are grounds for arguing that it was damaged interpersonal relations which formed the basis for many of the admissions. Yet in the culture of the day it would seem that it was only the isolated individual (the morally weak subject) who was the object of shock, grief, fear, religious excitement, or whatever, that could contain the seeds and causes of madness. In that sense madness was seen as a product of personal weakness and as something individuals possessed. It was the solitary individual who cried out for treatment – a 'treatment' which was predicated on the geographical and social detachment of the subject from his or her usual habitat. Only some years later, when Adolf Meyer came to speak of mental disorder in terms of 'reactions' to 'life problems' (see Meyer, 1906; Winters, 1952), and Southard came to speak of his fledgling social psychiatry (Southard, 1917; Southard and Jarrett, 1922) did psychiatry in general begin to recognise the significance of the wider social environment to the etiology of madness. But that way of thinking did not, in all probability, reach the Omagh asylum until late into the twentieth century.

CONCLUSION

It is clear that the Omagh case books reveal a picture of admission and readmission which would not be unfamiliar in the late twentieth century. People could and did leave the asylum in quite large numbers – as long as they had families to return to, or families that would take them. This is not to deny (as if one could) that the asylum slowly but surely accumulated a long-term population during the 1853–1901 period. The long-term residents of

the asylum, as we have seen, tended to be drawn from a particular sub-set of the wider population. Indeed, it seems as if the
latter had entered as young unmarried individuals, and it also
seems as if their admissions were associated with disturbances in
the web of their personal or social connections. There is little
evidence, however, that they were either physically decrepit or
economically useless (in the sense of being predominantly drawn
from the unemployed or unemployable). And in any case there
existed a parallel but quite different institutional system for the
care of the economically disordered – namely, the workhouse
system.

However that may be, it is at least clear that the admission
patterns at Omagh fitted in very snugly with some of the fundamental cultural changes which swept across rural Ireland in the
post-famine period. And the most important of these changes
were those which affected marriage patterns. For as Fitzpatrick
(1985) has demonstrated, Ireland became a notably 'celibate'
nation towards the end of the nineteenth century. That is, it
became a country with a rather high average age of marriage and
a particularly low rate of marriage. Hence, as Walsh (1985) points
out, of those born at the turn of the century, one half of males
and almost three-quarters of females were still unmarried at the
age of 30. And these figures merely express a trend which had
commenced in the 1850s. In addition, we find in post-famine
Catholic Ireland the impact of what Larkin (1972) has called 'the
devotional revolution'. That is the impact of new religious ortho-
doxy which attempted to discipline the conduct of both
interpersonal relations and the deportment of the human body
(in terms of dress, manners, etiquette and so on). Indeed, the
devotional revolution can be viewed as having fostered a kind of
social Puritanism; an intensified regulation of sexual behaviour,
and a much sterner response to forms of daily life including forms
of peasant dance and music (see Inglis, 1987). Above all, perhaps
these structural and cultural alterations in the social fabric resulted
in lower levels of tolerance of disorder and deviations in everyday
family life.

Given that tensions (whatever their source) did exist, it seems
likely that everyday notions of insanity and lunacy provided
a plausible ideological (theoretical) canopy in terms of which
ordinary people (such as Mahon, in Synge's *Playboy*) could understand and explain the vagaries of personal misbehaviour. That

people called upon that system of explanation to address their problems – including their family problems – with increasing frequency is evidenced by the growing numbers of asylum inmates who populated both the old and the new worlds.

I will conclude, then, by suggesting that the ideology of insanity and madness is something which belongs to a culture. In that respect it is something which permeates the entirety of social life in the sense that nearly everyone in a given society will either actively support or pay lip service to the central beliefs. By implication, and as is the case with Azande witchcraft, such an ideology cannot be seen as some ploy devised by elites, moral entrepreneurs, and other interest groups to ensnare or to control and placate the masses; but, instead, has to be understood as something which arises out of everyday experience and which answers to certain difficulties that are related to such experience. It is undoubtedly the case that the multiple changes associated with the 'civilising process' in late nineteenth-century Ireland generated many such difficulties. In this vein one is reminded of the claims of Michael Oakeshott (1962) who argued that ideology had to be understood not so much in terms of abstract rules and distant intellectual themes, but rather in terms of the intricateness of humdrum daily life. In its way the asylum system (together with the ideology which its presence represented) provided an appropriate and tangible response to the numerous and intractable problems of interpersonal life. Consequently, the inevitable conflicts which arose between parents and their adult children could always be readily reinterpreted as expressions of madness – and in a social and economic structure where the capacity of children to establish a home of their own was extremely limited, the appeal to such explanations must have been frequent indeed. In any event, given that most of the people who entered the Omagh Asylum were committed there on the say-so of their relatives, it seems fair to suggest that the appeal to madness as an underlying explanation for family conflicts and tensions was far from being rare or unusual.

REFERENCES

Arieno, M.A. (1989) *Victorian Lunatics: A Social Epidemiology of Mental Illness in Nineteenth-Century England*, New Jersey: Susquehanna University Press.

Blustein, B.E. (1981) "'A Hollow Square of Psychological Science": American neurologists and psychiatrists in conflict', in Scull. A.T. (ed.) *Madhouses, Mad-Doctors and Madmen: The Social History of Psychiatry in the Victorian Era*, London: Athlone Press.

Clarke, M.J. (1981) 'The rejection of psychological approaches to mental disorder in late nineteenth-century British psychiatry' in Scull. A.T. (ed.) *Madhouses, Mad-Doctors and Madmen: The Social History of Psychiatry in the Victorian Era*, London: Athlone Press.

Cullum, S. (1905) 'Sedatives and narcotics in the treatment of the insane', *The Dublin Journal of Medical Science*, 120: 161–181.

Decker, H.S. (1971) 'The medical reception of psychoanalysis in Germany, 1894–1907: three brief studies', *Bulletin of the History of Medicine*, 45: 475–479.

Digby, A. (1985) *Madness, Morality and Medicine*, Cambridge: Cambridge University Press.

Evans-Pritchard, E.E. (1937) *Witchcraft, Oracles, and Magic among the Azande*, Oxford: Clarendon Press.

Finnane, M. (1981) *Insanity and the Insane in Post-Famine Ireland*, London: Croom Helm.

Fitzpatrick, D. (1985) 'Marriage in post-famine Ireland', in Cosgrove, A. (ed.) *Marriage in Ireland*, Dublin: College Press.

Floud, R., Wachter, K. and Gregory, A. (1990) *Height, Health and History: Nutritional Status in the UK 1750–1980*, Cambridge: Cambridge University Press.

Foucault, M. (1967) *Madness and Civilization*, trans. R. Howard, London: Tavistock.

—— (1977) *Discipline and Punish*, trans. Sheridan, A. London: Allen Lane.

Gerth, H. and Mills, C.W. (1954) *Character and Social Structure: The Psychology of Social Institutions*, London: Routledge and Kegan Paul.

Goffman, E. (1961) *Asylums: Essays on the Social Situation of Mental Patients and Other Inmates*, New York: Anchor Books.

Gottesman, I. and Bertelsen, A. (1991) 'Schizophrenia: classical approaches with new twists and provocative results', in McGuffin, P. and Murray, P. (eds) *The New Genetics of Mental Illness*, London: Butterworth-Heinemann.

Grob, G. (1973) *Mental Institutions in America: Social Policy to 1875*, New York: Free Press.

Hare, E. (1983) 'Was insanity on the increase?', *British Journal of Psychiatry*, 142: 439–455.

Hunter, R. and Macalpine, I. (1974) *Psychiatry for the Poor: 1851 Colney Hatch Asylum: Friern Hospital 1973*, Folkestone: Dawsons.

Inglis, T. (1987) *Moral Monopoly: The Catholic Church in Modern Irish Society*, Dublin: Gill and Macmillan.

Jones, K. (1972) *A History of the Mental Health Services*, London: Routledge and Kegan Paul.

Kraepelin, E. (1902) *Clinical Psychiatry: A Text-Book for Students and Physicians*, A.R. Defendorf (ed.), London: Macmillan.

—— (1904) *Lectures on Clinical Psychiatry*, London: Ballière, Tindall and Cox.

Larkin, E. (1972) 'The devotional revolution in Ireland 1850–1975', *American Historical Review*, 77: 625–652.

Maudsley, H. (1895) *The Pathology of Mind: A Study of Its Distempers, Deformities and Disorders*, London: Macmillan.

Mechanic, D. (1969) *Mental Health and Social Policy*, Englewood Cliffs: Prentice Hall.

Meyer, A. (1906) 'A fundamental conception of dementia praecox', *British Medical Journal*, 2: 757.

Oakeshott, M. (1962) *Rationalism in Politics and Other Essays*, London: Methuen.

O'Grada, C. (1991) 'The heights of Clonmel prisoners 1845–9: some dietary implications', *Irish Economic and Social History*, 18: 24–33.

Ray, L.J. (1981) 'Models of madness in Victorian asylum practice', *European Journal of Sociology*, 222: 229–264.

Renvoize, E.B. and Beveridge, A.W. (1989) 'Mental illness and the late Victorians: a study of patients admitted to three asylums in York, 1880–1884', *Psychological Medicine*, 19: 19–28.

Rothman, D. (1971) *The Discovery of the Asylum*, Boston: Little, Brown.

—— (1985) 'Social control: the uses and abuses of the concept in the history of incarceration', in Cohen, S. and Scull, A.T. (eds) *Social Control and The State*, Oxford: Blackwell.

Scull, A. T. (1979) *Museums of Madness: The Social Organization of Insanity in Nineteenth-Century England*, London: Allen Lane.

—— (1989) *Social Order/Mental Disorder: Anglo-American Psychiatry in Historical Perspective*, London: Routledge.

—— (1993) *The Most Solitary of Afflictions: Madness and Society in Britain, 1700–1900*, London: Yale University Press.

Showalter, E. (1981) 'Victorian women and insanity', in Scull, A.T. (ed.) *Madhouses, Mad-Doctors and Madmen: The Social History of Psychiatry in the Victorian Era*, London: Athlone Press.

Southard, E.E. (1917) 'Alienists and psychiatrists', *Mental Hygiene*, 1: 567–571.

Southard, E.E. and Jarrett, M.C. (1922) *The Kingdom of Evils*, London: George Allen and Unwin.

Stewart, L. (1976) 'Freud before Oedipus: race and heredity in the origins of psychoanalysis', *Journal of the History of Biology*, 9, 2: 215–228.

Sutton, J.R. (1991) 'The political economy of madness: the expansion of the asylums in progressive America', *American Sociological Review*, 56: 665–678.

Synge, J.M. (1907) *The Playboy of the Western World*, in Hein, T.R. (ed.) (1981) *J.M. Synge: The Complete Plays*, London: Methuen.

Szasz, T. S. (1971) *The Manufacture of Madness*, London: Routledge and Kegan Paul.

—— (1994) *Cruel Compassion: Psychiatric Control of Society's Unwanted*, New York: John Wiley.

Tuke, D.H. (1976) *A Dictionary Of Psychological Medicine*, New York: Arno Press.

Turner, T. (1989) 'Rich and mad in Victorian England', *Psychological Medicine*, 19: 29–44.

Walsh, B.M. (1985) 'Marriage in Ireland in the twentieth century', in Cosgrove, A. (ed.) *Marriage in Ireland*, Dublin: College Press.
Winters, E.E. (ed.) (1952) *The Collected Papers of Adolf Meyer* Vol. IV, Baltimore: Johns Hopkins Press.

Other written sources

Sixty-Eighth Annual Report of The Lunacy Commissioners (1915), London.
The Census of Ireland 1901: General Report, Dublin: HMSO.
File *Hos* 29. Public Records Office of Northern Ireland: Belfast.
1901 Census Returns. Co. Tyrone. MFGS 28/34. National Archives: Dublin.

Chapter 5

Law and the social uses of the asylum in nineteenth-century Ireland[1]

Mark Finnane

INTRODUCTION

The high rate of use of lunatic asylums in nineteenth-century Ireland was accomplished through extensive use of the procedure of legal certification under a statute known as the Dangerous Lunatics Act. In this chapter I explore the social context of the use of this Act in order to understand better the role of the asylum as an institution in Irish society. The evidence suggests that historically the psychiatric hospital was an institution which performed a variety of social functions. Irrefutably, these included simple social control objectives for some proportion of its inmates. Other inmates were there because their personal and social behaviour was increasingly seen as explicable through the taxonomies of alienism, soon to become psychiatry.

Yet the patterns of movement in and out of the asylum as Prior indicates in Chapter 4 suggest that this nineteenth-century institution had a social function which made it something other than simply an elite's instrument of social control or the plaything of over-ambitious medicine. For very many it appears that the lunatic asylum functioned just as that – an asylum, or refuge, from an intolerable condition. For some, consistently about one in three of admissions, asylum was temporary, lasting less than a year. For others asylum was more permanent, their long-term residence contributing to the phenomenon of the over-crowded mass psychiatric hospital, persisting longer in Ireland than in many other western societies. In understanding the development of this situation I focus in this chapter on the uses of the law in seeking asylum, showing how social uses of its remedies expanded the use of the asylum in a changing society.

The widespread use of the asylum was the product, I argue, of a complicity between a number of social actors, including police, magistrates, doctors, relatives and friends of the inmate – and even of the inmate himself or herself, in a gesture sometimes quite conscious, seeking separation from the social world or the prospect of recovery from debilitating depression or alcoholism or other concerns. The meanings of asylum in Ireland were structured less, I suggest, by the forms of public political and social conflict (dominated as they were by such issues as the national question and land reform) than by the more mundane adjustments and pressures of a society faced by rural transformation and massive emigration. In this society asylum was a dumping-ground, certainly, but its functions and meanings were ultimately more complex than such a characterisation would allow.

The public provision of lunatic asylums was one of the most substantial achievements of the nineteenth-century state in Ireland. The imposing physical presence of the twenty-four district asylums by 1900 was testimony to the capacity of government to prescribe and administer an institutional tonic which it was hoped would relieve those who had fallen prey to mental illness. In a judgmental century the asylums were rather remarkable institutions. While the birth of eugenics at the end of the century was something of a setback for the more benign vision of the asylum as a curative institution, the striking thing about reading the asylum case books is the degree of acceptance of human failing and weakness, not to mention sympathy for the tragic condition and lives of some of those who passed through the doors of the asylum. In Ireland, a country troubled by sectarian conflict over some other social policies, especially in education, the public asylum appeared mostly free of such difficulties, an institution informed largely by secular notions of care and treatment.

The doctors and staff had their own limited standards, as we do, but their role testified to the prevalence of a nineteenth-century view that mental illness was essentially a providential matter. The ambition of medical science was to give an account of its course and incidence in individuals and, as became increasingly common in late nineteenth-century British psychiatry, in whole populations. Yet this ambition was mediated by a consciousness of the apparent randomness of illness in so many cases. Unlike poverty or crime, madness could not, in many instances, be attributed to the voluntaristic actions of its victims: hence the view of Dr Oscar Woods of the Cork Lunatic Asylum who wished as late as 1881 to 'separate visitations of Providence [i.e. insanity] from vicious acts [i.e. crime], (Medical Press and Circular, 6.4.1881). Characteristically of those who spoke the language of social evolution, the eminent alienist James Crichton Browne observed, as President of the Medico-Psychological Association, in 1878 that in their work in asylums, medical men 'have to oppose evolution, promoting the survival of the unfittest, of weakly and crippled beings' (*Journal of Mental Science*, 24, 1878: 345–373). Like the families of those admitted or confined to the asylum, doctors commonly professed their helplessness in the face of the intractable language and behaviour of those in their care.

To read the case books, however, is to become aware also of the fluid relation of the asylum to its social milieu. The asylum performed a myriad of functions. This was an institution shaped for a specific purpose but capable in fact of performing a role for other purposes. To understand its variety of purposes we need to take account of the different types of social actors in the various contexts in which the asylum functioned. One needs also to understand the institutional conditions which structured the possibilities of action.

Taking this perspective I will examine the effect and operation of the Dangerous Lunatics Act in Ireland before the First World War. Elsewhere I have shown that this Act was the dominant means of admission to the public asylums in Ireland (Finnane, 1981). The research question in that study was concerned primarily with the notion that admission to asylums in the nineteenth century was above all a process of incarceration. Yet, even so, that study suggested that the quickly established legitimacy of the asylum in Ireland (the point could be made as easily elsewhere) derived from the 'complicity of Irish society in readily resorting to the use of the state's institutions'. However tempting it might have been to suggest that the asylum was a nefarious construct for the misgovernment of Ireland (in fact, a suggestion not mooted to my knowledge in the nineteenth century), the fact was that 'to the relatives, friends or neighbours of the committed the asylum offered the possibility of relief from the burden of care, or else from the fear of violence' (Finnane, 1981: 13).

Of most relevance to the concerns of this chapter, however, is another conclusion from that earlier study which focuses on what the asylum may have offered to those inside. To at least some of these, I concluded, 'the asylum offered refuge from the treacherous and harsh world outside' (ibid.). The characteristics of that world were distinctive. They include a number of facts which marked the changing conditions of life in Ireland after the famine. Most notably these facts included a large-scale post-famine emigration and accompanying rural depopulation. This may well have reduced the capacity of families and communities left behind to support those prone to mental illness. In other respects Ireland continued to be a poor society. This is not to say that it did not have its share of prosperity. Land reform benefited many of the farming class who avoided emigration. But outside the industrial north-east, Ireland's urban centres were home to pervasive unemployment and insecurity for those who did have a job. Recounting these social ills, however, cannot explain conclusively the tendency in Ireland to a very intense use of the asylum. Different kinds of conditions (urban prosperity and affluence, the pace of modern life, for example) were commonly cited by doctors and others as reasons for the 'growth in insanity' in more urbanised and industrialised societies in the nineteenth century. Regardless of the larger structural reasons for the incidence of use of the asylum, the prospective inmates of the asylum were likely to see their worries as more immediate and personal.

This at least seemed the irrefutable message of such admissions as that to Omagh Asylum in the 1880s of John, a Tyrone labourer, who 'threatened ... that he would do injury if he was not taken to the Asylum where he said that he would get better' (ibid.: 168). The possibility that some of those in the asylum were there of their own volition is a feature of the use of the asylum that I want to explore later in this chapter. At the time, however, this function of the asylum seemed less significant than the uses of the asylum by the associates of the insane for the purpose of removing the ill or the merely troublesome. The revival of interest in the refuge functions of asylumdom offers, therefore, a new opportunity to view the Irish evidence about the uses of the asylum through a different perspective (Wing, 1990: 822–827).

The argument runs like this. The Irish district asylum system, a comprehensive public institutional apparatus by the 1850s, became a central social institution in later nineteenth-century Ireland. It did so through the process of admission established by the Dangerous Lunatics Act. This Act made it possible for large numbers of individuals to be admitted to the asylums at minimal direct cost to themselves or their families. The use of the law in this way may have been at odds with its original intention. But laws are only what people make of them.

Large numbers of individuals, therefore, were incarcerated by legal certification, involving the use of police and magistrates as well as medical opinion, and acting at the instance of family or other associates of the person being incarcerated. But did this mean that other possible, more benign, uses of the asylum were avoided or precluded or restricted? Case evidence suggests not. Instead, admission to and residence in the asylum were the product of sometimes quite detailed negotiation. In this process, as the above case of John from Tyrone shows, the inmates themselves occasionally played a part. By the nature of the illness of many inmates, however, this possibility was necessarily a limited one. And the problems of evidence restrict our opportunity to assess quantitatively the incidence of such active participation in the process of asylum admission by the prospective inmates. Nevertheless its significance bears consideration.

Examining the uses of the asylum involves a number of approaches. I commence with the formalities of admission, in part legal, in part administrative. Then I review some of the quantitative evidence about admission, residence and discharge. In the last section I discuss some of the qualitative evidence which suggests the degree to which the asylum as a refuge, for temporary retreat or long-term care, was a reality in pre-partition Ireland.

FORMS OF ADMISSION

The primary mode of admission of inmates from the 1850s to the First World War was under the Dangerous Lunatics Act. From 1838 to 1867 the Act provided for confinement in gaol before transfer to asylum of those deemed to be of unsound mind. Medical opinion could be called but was not essential to the process of committal by the justices. A major change to the law in 1867 ended committal to prison, substituting the district asylum instead. The new Act also required medical certification, by the medical officer of the local Poor Law dispensary district.

Non-judicial admission to the district asylums was governed by local as well as Privy Council rules. Application to the board of governors of the district asylum was one means. More important after 1843 was emergency admission by the visiting physician, or later the medical superintendent.

Given a variety of possible means of admission to the asylum in Ireland, what were the conditions which governed the use of one or the other modes of admission? And why did judicial committal become so important in Ireland in contrast with the experience in England (where certification was less important than admission by authority of relieving officer of the Poor Law unions) (Finnane, 1981: 104)?

It is not surprising to find that a key issue was the financial one. Every actor in the world surrounding the insane was involved in some calculation bearing on the financial burden of a dependent person. Policy-makers determined in the 1860s that not just any doctor could certify a dangerous lunatic: it had to be the district dispensary doctor. This was a means of limiting the costs of certification to the state. Asylum governors, on the other hand, were concerned probably above all with the impact of the institutions on the rates. In the 1880s when it was proposed to remove non-attending governors from the boards, there were objections from some of the latter that the 'interests of ratepayers' might be affected (CSORP, 1887/10943). With local government reform after 1898, the asylums remained vulnerable to the ruling interest of the 'ratepayers', a situation which continued after partition in Northern Ireland when Belfast Corporation repeatedly sought to relieve the financial burden of these large institutions (Prior, 1993: 34).

In the front line of reception into the asylums was the medical superintendent. He had, as noted above, some autonomy in relation to admission of emergency cases, and correspondence indicates that this was taken seriously. Overcrowding was a constant threat, and the medical superintendent had to combat the parsimony of the boards of governors (later, after 1898 local government reforms, the committees of management) (Finnane, 1981: 73–82).

The list of interested parties participating in the negotiation of fiscal responsibility for the lunatic could lengthen to include justices, and police. But the most important of all, in many cases, was the family of the person whose admission was sought. In this respect it is not likely that the Irish asylums were unique. As the Scottish Lunacy Commissioner, John Sibbald, had commented in 1877, 'the decision of the question whether a particular individual is or is not to be counted as a lunatic from the social point of view, depends more on the mental condition of his friends than on his own' (*Journal of Mental Science*, 23, 1877: 549).

Yet the institutional and financial arrangements governing the provision of asylum care in Ireland appear to have created a powerful culture of family initiative in the committal to an asylum in Ireland. It has been observed recently by Pauline Prior that the longevity of this tradition survived partition so that in Northern Ireland families rather than relieving or later welfare officers have continued to play the dominant role in applications for admission, in contrast to England (Prior, 1993: 42). Official statistics on the contexts of admission are limited in their information. But on the basis of a survey of Omagh admissions at decade intervals from 1861–1901 it appears consistently that about 80 per cent of admissions had a direct family relation (spouse, parent, sibling or child) living in the same locality (Finnane, 1981: 132, 170; ODHAR, HOS 29/1/5/601–7000). Case evidence confirms the impression that those admitted to the asylum were usually people with living relatives, more than likely in close association with them at the time of admission.

For these people the evaluation of financial burden was endless, and even subtle. What did one do with a relative who was incapable of providing income or contributing to subsistence in kind? That was one kind of calculation. But paying an institution (whether public or private, see Malcolm, 1989: 145–147) for their care was undoubtedly expensive. That was another. There were still other levels of reckoning. Women particularly may have been glad to be relieved of the presence of a maniacal, or drunken, or simply depressed husband. But if he was at all capable of work then his early discharge might be actively sought before too long.

All these calculations enter into the explanation of the use of the judicial committal. Basically they reduce to this. The judicial committal through the Dangerous Lunatics Act was a means of responding quickly to an immediate threat or to a longer-standing conflict with family members. While an asylum board might subsequently attempt to negotiate a degree of family maintenance payment for the confinee, there was little they could do to enforce such payments. Whatever the reason for committal there was little incentive on the part of relatives to seek a committal through the asylum board. Put another way, there was in fact every incentive to avoid doing so, especially since magistrates seemed so compliant. Hence the pessimistic advice of the Dublin Castle Law Adviser in 1876, after eight years experience of the new Act.

> I doubt that any system not liable to abuse could be devised . . . Under the present system I think the only step remaining to be taken would be to call attention of individual magistrates to any particularly bad cases and to discharge a few for the sake of example.
>
> (CSORP, 1876/19445 (Law Adviser, 21 Nov 1876, 17221/76))

Indeed, such was the evidence of abuse of the procedure that the inspectors had been advised in the same year to undertake an action for habeas corpus in a number of cases in Ballinasloe (CSORP, 15913/76).

Why then was the matter never seriously addressed in law reform? The answer is somewhat difficult to fathom since there appears little evidence of serious attention having been paid to the possible reform, at Dublin Castle. Nevertheless, the most mundane is probably the best explanation in this case. The fundamental difference between the organisation of Irish and English public lunacy institutions was the tax base. In England, the asylums were essentially Poor Law institutions, supported on the local rates (though the form of governance removed them from direct control by the Poor Law guardians (Walton, 1985)). In Ireland they were district institutions supported (for the local contributions) by the county cess. This was raised on landowners only, though undoubtedly its effects were felt indirectly by tenants. In a country which was in any case a hotbed of discontent over the rights and burdens of the tenantry, any serious political move towards changing the tax base of the asylum (and possibly creating a more demanding government board, even less sympathetic to the impositions of the Dangerous Lunatic Act) was scarcely to be contemplated. I suggest that the tax base of the asylum, combined with the lax administration of the law by magistrates, explains the high rate of use of the Dangerous Lunatic Act, including its use by family and associates of the insane, during the nineteenth century. The mundane reasons of pecuniary advantage seemed to apply equally to doctors, key players in the post-1867 world of lunacy certification. They were the object of criticism in 1905 by Dr Drapes of the Enniscorthy Asylum, for their role in popularising the dangerous lunatic warrant. The warrant form of admission was popular with dispensary doctors, he noted, because

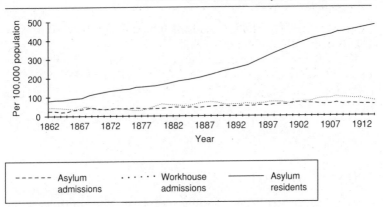

Figure 5.1 Asylum and workhouses, Ireland, 1862–1914

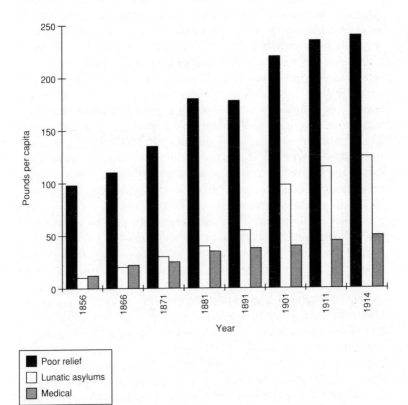

Figure 5.2 Social expenditure, Ireland, 1856–1914

a fee was payable, which it was not for other forms of admission (*Medical Press and Circular*, 20.12.1905).

These factors, however, explain only the legal and administrative context. What do we know about social uses of the law which patterned admission into the asylum? My comments below are directed towards highlighting some evidence on the specific issue of asylum seeking. It will be useful, first, to establish just how dominant was this mode of committal in Ireland.

USING THE ACT

The pattern of admissions to public lunatic asylums in Ireland can be summarised briefly. By 1870, just a couple of years after the enactment of the revised Dangerous Lunatics Act, the recent addition of asylums in Down and Monaghan meant there were now twenty-two public asylums in Ireland. At the end of the century two more were added, at Portrane, north of Dublin, and in Antrim.

Between 1845 and 1914 these twenty-four asylums received about 130,000 first admissions. Asylum admission rates of about 8 per 100,000 population on the eve of the famine increased by a factor of 8 in the following seventy years. In some years the admission rates to lunatic asylums in Ireland exceeded those to the 130 workhouses. Asylum residence rates increased at an even more rapid rate, by a factor of 16 times between the mid-1840s and 1914. The asylums consistently rivalled the 130 workhouses as a major destination of institutional admission of dependent people throughout this period (see Figure 5.1).

By the end of the period the total expenditure on public asylums was half the total spent on poor relief in Ireland and double the amount spent on the public health (medical dispensary) system (Figure 5.2).

When one compares residence rates in public asylums, there can be no doubting the very substantial use of the public asylum system in Ireland: in 1914 the rate was 490 per 100,000 population in Ireland as compared to England (298) and Scotland (283) (Finnane, 1981: 224).

The dominant mode of committal throughout this period remained that under the Dangerous Lunatics Act. Figure 5.3 indicates that the proportion of dangerous lunatic admissions made by magistrate's order under this statute increased steadily until the 1890s when it stabilised. There were gender differences in

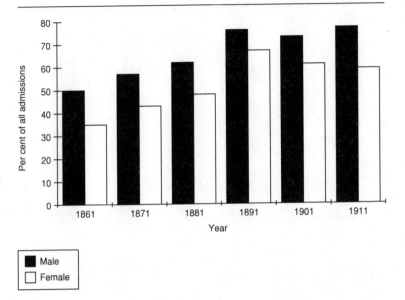

Male
Female

Figure 5.3 Dangerous lunatic admissions, Ireland, 1861–1911

these rates, with males rather more likely than females to be judicially committed on admission to the asylum. This sex difference in committal patterns was characteristic of almost all asylum districts in Ireland throughout this period.

The route to the asylum was not a one-way street. Rates of discharge after less than a year's stay, as shown in Figure 5.4, were consistently more than 30 per cent of admissions. Conversely most of those discharged had been less than one year in the asylum (Figures 5.5 and 5.6). There was little variation in these rates across the later nineteenth century, as is consistent with results of research elsewhere (e.g. Mackenzie, 1985: 149–151).

From one perspective these discharge figures are less than impressive: their obverse is the high retention rates which led to the accumulation of patient numbers by the end of the century. That has been the perspective informed by a desire to assess and judge the extravagance of early psychiatric claims about the possibilities of asylum care. However, a larger assessment has to examine such rates against the social and medical expectations and norms which moulded the uses of the asylum.

The statistical patterns of use make little sense on their own. In order to assess what sorts of decisions were being made at a

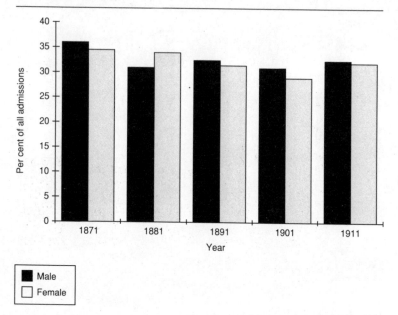

Figure 5.4 Discharge rates (resident less than one year), Ireland, 1871–1911

micro-level which produced these larger patterns we need to inspect the case registers and admission warrants. Some gleams of evidence appear in what are frequently highly bureaucratised record-keeping procedures by the end of the nineteenth century.

The process by which the Dangerous Lunatics Act could be turned to advantage of all concerned is thus well illustrated by a detailed case account by Conolly Norman in 1905. As the Resident Medical Superintendent of the country's largest asylum, the Richmond at Grangegorman in Dublin, Norman was the senior psychiatric figure in Ireland during this period, explaining his passing acknowledgement in Joyce's *Ulysses*, when Buck Mulligan refers to a drinking mate being 'up in Dottyville with Conolly Norman' (with general paralysis of the insane, of course) (Joyce, 1968: 12). Committed to the ideal of individual treatment, Norman found by the 1890s that the asylum was an institution which threatened not only the patients but also doctors and attendants with a 'wearing, depressing and monotonous existence'. Countering this effect was one of his objectives, achieved in part through an approach which attempted to facilitate the return of inmates to

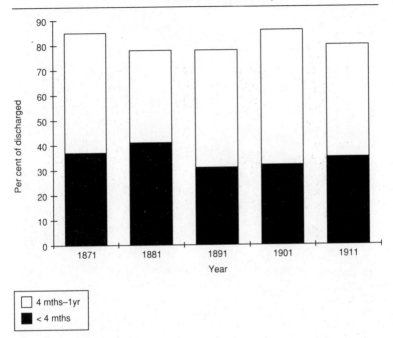

Figure 5.5 Males discharged, length of stay

the community, after a period of recovery in the asylum (Finnane, 1981: 185).

Norman's case notes indicate a considerable sensitivity to the social context of his charges. His address to the 1893 meeting of the Medico-Psychological Association (later the Royal College of Psychiatry) noted the informal consulting day clinic which had apparently developed at Grangegorman (*Journal of Mental Science*, 39, 1893; 308–311). It is not surprising then to see him record the following circumstances of one dangerous lunatic admission in 1905. Edmond, a 38-year-old single shop assistant from Dublin city, came to the asylum with his brother and sister at 12 noon on 10 October 1905 and begged to be admitted to the asylum. He said he had been drinking all his life, had been in jail recently for an act of violence while drunk, then celebrated his discharge from jail with a particularly heavy drinking bout. 'He insisted [records the case note] that he was ill and that he was insane. He entreated to be at once admitted to the asylum as he would commit suicide if he were not.' He spoke first and got his

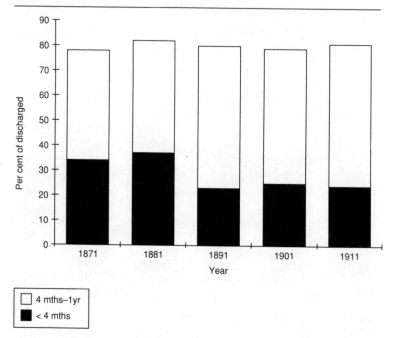

Figure 5.6 Females discharged, length of stay

brother and sister to confirm the story. Norman then explained that he could only admit him under warrant and outlined the procedure involved. The next day Edmond was admitted to the hospital as a dangerous lunatic. The medical evidence cited on the warrant was an 'attempt to commit suicide'. He was there for about seven months, by which time it was noted that he could be discharged as 'recovered', as the voices in his head had been absent for some time (RMCB, 1905–1906: 9).

It is evident from this account that what we have is a straightforward example of the law being deployed in creative fashion by the potential inmates of the institution. Moreover, what is most interesting is Norman's advice that the law should be used in this way. On the basis of the notes we can confidently say that the occasion for committal was not an 'attempt to commit suicide', the sort of threatening event which the Act was intended to cover, but rather a state of behaviour including threats to commit suicide if admission to the asylum was not obtained. What is not clear from the case book is why Norman felt that in this instance he could only admit on the basis of a dangerous lunatic warrant. Nevertheless, the more relevant detail is the probability of obtaining admission to the asylum, by seeking a magistrate's warrant. It is that high probability which explains the existence of cases such as Edmond's, of people seeking refuge in the asylum, for a quite specific need, and perhaps for a limited period of time.

Such a strategic use of the asylum by those seeking help was an undeniable if incalculable feature of its function. So we have the perhaps confounding phenomenon of a person trying to break into the asylum for assistance. 'Last evening,' records a Cork case note in the 1890s, 'he appeared at the Asylum and asked to be taken in he was handed over to the police and brought in on a Magistrates warrant.' The same man, discharged after seven months, was back in a month later:

> it is said he threatened to commit suicide. It appears he did not go home with his sister but remained in Cork and evidently took to drink last night he broke into asylum & sought to be taken in he was handed over to the police.
>
> (CMCB, 1892–1894, fol. 181,91/22/67/1)

Qualitative evidence of this kind suggests an active sense on the part of some prospective inmates of the idea of the asylum as a refuge. On the other hand, a quite different sense of the asylum as a refuge is suggested by the ever-widening gap between first admission and residence rates. While discharge rates were of the order of 30–40 per cent within the first year of admission (see Figure 5.4), this left a substantial number of people whose remaining life would be closely if not entirely associated with the asylum. Case study evidence again indicates some of the processes and self-perceptions which underlie this statistical reality.

Discharge, for example, was dependent on having a friend or institution to go to. One was not turned out on the street, as at the end of a prison sentence. For some of the discharged, we have evidence of application for their release from the relatives, usually a spouse, but occasionally others.

But what happened when a dischargeable inmate had nowhere to go? In Cork in 1894 a 44-year-old labourer's wife was admitted with melancholia. Case notes indicate that she was much recovered within a few weeks of admission, although her formal discharge as 'recovered' did not come till seven months after admission. A month after the discharge decision, however, the case book records that her husband had not come for her. Twice in the next fifteen months she was again discharged but her husband did not come for her. Other friends were contacted, together with the master at the Mallow workhouse. She was removed to the care of the latter at the end of 1896, two and a half years after admission and nearly two years after formal notice of recovery (CFCB, 1894, fol. 29,91/22/66/3).

Active interest on behalf of friends was in itself no guarantee of early, if any, removal. But there is case evidence from throughout the period I am concerned with here of requests from relatives for removal. Hence, around 1850 the Cork asylum has the wife of an inmate requesting his discharge and undertaking to protect him and others from harm (CDLA, 91/22/65/3). In Dublin in 1905, the wife of an alcoholic bottle-maker, who is periodically in a state of delirium tremens, regularly visits him and asks for his discharge. The reason, she says, is that 'myself and my child is solely dependent on him': 'between sprees he is a model husband, quiet, intelligent and attentive at home' (RMCB, 1905–1906, 49). Such instrumental use of the asylum as a resort for the spouses of drunken men is perhaps no better illustrated than in a letter from the wife of a 41-year-old labourer, committed under warrant to Grangegorman in 1897. She asks for a visiting pass to see him and requests his discharge next board day:

> as I now there is noting wrong with him when I put him in it was between me self and me little boy and when he annoyed me I charged him Sir if you find anything wrong with him that he will be only humbuging himself to keep himself in for the hard Weather?
>
> (RMCB, 1905–1906, 85)

As I have noted earlier, the processes of admission and discharge are ones of negotiation, rather than unilateral decision by any one actor. So we find in the 1890s a 48-year-old married woman from the rural west of County Cork, admitted with melancholia and regarded as curable. Twice in 1894 and 1895 a relative, probably her sister (who had reported to the hospital that the probable cause of illness was the husband beating her and making her deaf) asked for her discharge: on the first occasion it was refused, on the second the medical superintendent wrote saying that they could take her at their own responsibility. The case book does not indicate why this never occurred. She remained in the asylum till her death in 1921. In her later years she is observed as a harmless chronic patient, but one who does good work around the hospital. Comments throughout the case notes record her being noisy and abusive (recalling the circumstances of her admission when she had been 'screaming and shouting on the public road') and perhaps explain the eventual reluctance of relatives to take her back (CFCB, 1894, fol. 31, 91/22/66/3).

Such a case points to the reality which dominated political and media perceptions of the asylum from 1850. This was the image of it as a place of resort for the hopelessly incurable. In a familiar rhetoric the Irish inspectors of lunatics had warned in 1851 that 'the uniform tendency of all asylums is to degenerate from their original object, that of being hospitals for the treatment of insanity, into domiciles for incurable lunatics' (5th Annual Report of Inspectors of Lunatics, 1851: 6). The examples I have just cited suggest the ambiguity of the status of long-term patients. We have clear evidence in them of decisions taken or avoided which are determined by the prospects, frequently dismal, of a viable life outside some institutional setting. Hence, a familiar pattern in the records is the frequency of discharge to the workhouse, as well as a reverse movement from the workhouse to the asylum. The asylum in this case was a refuge for the destitute, hovering uncertainly between the workhouse and the outside world which had little place for them.

Perhaps the most striking way to conclude this brief survey of the functions of the asylum as a refuge is to go back nearly one hundred years to a review at Grangegorman of the prospects of some female long-stay patients. The review of the register of patients was aided by Mrs Conlon, the Matron, who had been on the staff for thirty years. At least one of the patients called her 'Mamma' and her extensive knowledge of the inmate population proved indispensable to the doctor (probably Norman) who was conducting the review.

Here the evidence suggests the asylum as a place for the forgotten. The name and identity of one woman had to be reconstructed by deduction as it appeared from her case note that she would be 113 years old: it was concluded that she had been wrongly taken to be a patient who had died thirty years before. Two other inmates on the register, it is recorded, were 'probably dead'. Other inmates, it appeared, had long since lost contact with the outside world. For some, the memories of family were only that, since sons or daughters no longer visited them. Even after thirty or more years the circumstances of committals might be recalled by some as brutal and shocking – one woman recalling being taken by a brother to the police, her head shaved and sent to gaol, before being eventually transferred to Grangegorman. Another recalled that her mother asked for her discharge at one time but she (the patient) refused saying she would only put her back in; she 'feels contented as she has no place to go to out of this' (RFCB, 1852–1857, 45).

Self-perception by this time, thirty years after admission, might meld imperceptibly into an account of social context which was remarkably evocative of the reality of asylumdom for such people. Alongside those considered confused or rambling were those whose words summon up powerful images of the asylum. In their perspective the asylum is a place of separation from a world which cannot or will not own them. So, Rosanna, a single woman of 23 years had been admitted from the South Dublin workhouse in 1867; 'I was a cripple and I got resided,' she says in 1897. Resided, she explains, means 'not capable of being in the world to be exercised' (ibid., 81).

Jane, another long-term inmate who had been admitted with 'anxiety of mind' arising from 'reversal of circumstances' refers to the asylum as the 'camps and plains . . . a fenced, walled city for fallen nations' (ibid., 69).

CONCLUSION

The meanings and contexts of incarceration for insanity in nineteenth-century Ireland were many. Consistent patterns are, however, discernible as I hope to have shown in this chapter. They include the following;

1 The dominant mode of admission was through judicial warrant. This did not mean that there were more dangerous lunatics in Ireland than in other comparable societies. Rather, the magistrate's warrant was principally an administrative device. Its widespread use has to be understood against a background of substantial provision for accommodation of those deemed insane, a provision which was centrally administered and paid for in ways which provided powerful incentives to associates of the insane to shift the financial burden of their care to public agencies.

2　The widespread use of the Dangerous Lunatics Act did not always arise from the initiative of police: indeed, it is more likely that police responded to requests from other public officials and from families to take action. The importance of police in the procedure may nevertheless have laid the ground for more recent practice (Walsh, 1990: 5–11).

3　Admission to the asylum and discharge from it were procedures of sometimes complex social negotiation. In this process I have shown that asylum inmates themselves often played an active role. Case study evidence suggests that they might seek out the asylum as a refuge – in Wing's words, a 'haven for rest and a harbour from which to set out' (Wing, 1990: 822). Others arrived less willingly, but the circumstances of their committal suggest that the asylum could promise a respite from aggravated and sometimes violent social relations.

4　Discharge was similarly a process of negotiation. Here the unenviable social position of many inmates rendered them vulnerable to the whims of relatives, friends, medical judgement and the workhouse master. Most, after all, were poor or very poor. Few were admitted to the public asylum as paying patients. Even so, the evidence suggests that money was not the only consideration in this negotiation. Rest and recuperation had a meaning for relatives as well as for the inmates themselves. Once a respite had been obtained, familial obligations and desires played some role in seeking the return of incarcerated relatives.

From this perspective the asylum was an institution whose uses were moulded by a diversity of social forces. Only some of these were formally laid out by law and regulation. In fact, law provided no more than the mandate for actions whose intentions and motivations aggregated to serve ends which were quite different from the original objectives of the Dangerous Lunatics Act. For this reason it is the asylum as a refuge, as much as an agency of social control, which deserves continued historical inquiry.

NOTE

1　Statistical data is drawn from the tables in Finnane, 1981. The archival sources used and listed below include case books from the Richmond District Lunatic Asylum, which were inspected at their original location in St Brendan's Hospital, Grangegorman, Dublin, in 1976–1977, prior to their more recent removal to the National Archives.

REFERENCES

Annual Report of Inspectors of Lunatics in Ireland, *British Parliamentary Papers.*

CDLA – Cork District Lunatic Asylum, Committal papers, 91/22/65/3, Cork Archives Institute.

CFCB – Cork District Lunatic Asylum, Female Case-book, 1894, Cork Archives Institute.

CMCB – Cork District Lunatic Asylum, Male Case-book, 1892–1894, Cork Archives Institute.

CSORP – Chief Secretary's Office Registered Papers, National Archives, Dublin.

Finnane, M. (1981) *Insanity and the Insane in Post-Famine Ireland,* London: Croom Helm.

Journal of Mental Science.

Joyce, J. (1968) *Ulysses,* Penguin: Harmondsworth.

Mackenzie, C. (1985) 'Social factors in the admission, discharge, and continuing stay of patients at Ticehurst Asylum, 1845–1917', in Bynum, W.F., Porter, R. and Shepherd, M. (eds) *The Anatomy of Madness, vol. 2, Institutions and Society,* London: Tavistock.

Malcolm, E. (1989) *Swift's Hospital: A History of St Patrick's Hospital, Dublin, 1746–1989,* Dublin: Gill and Macmillan.

Medical Press and Circular.

ODHAR – Omagh District Hospital, Admission Register, Public Record Office of Northern Ireland, Belfast.

Prior, P. (1993) *Mental Health and Politics in Northern Ireland: A History of Service Development,* Aldershot: Avebury.

RFCB – Richmond District Lunatic Asylum, Female Case-book.

RMCB Richmond District Lunatic Asylum, Male Case-book.

Walsh, D. (1990) 'The future of psychiatric services in Ireland', *Irish Journal of Psychiatry,* Autumn: 5–11.

Walton, J.K. (1985) 'Casting out and bringing back in Victorian England: pauper lunatics, 1840–1870', in Bynum, W.F., Porter, R. and Shepherd, M. (eds) *The Anatomy of Madness, vol. 2, Institutions and Society,* London: Tavistock.

Wing, J.K. (1990) 'The functions of asylum', *British Journal of Psychiatry,* 157: 822–827.

Chapter 6

The refuge function of psychiatric hospitals

Dylan Tomlinson, John Carrier and James Oerton

In this chapter we are concerned with the question of whether psychiatric hospitals have provided refuge in any sense during the twentieth century. In 1990, as a result of our involvement in an evaluation of two large psychiatric hospital closures in the London region, Friern and Claybury, and of being able to obtain ready access to patients' case notes, we conceived a small-scale empirical study to address this question. We aimed to concentrate on two kinds of use of the hospitals as refuges, involving attempts to seek sanctuary in them, on the one hand, and attempts to withstand efforts to be resettled from them into the community on the other. In order to look at the latter kind of use in particular, we resolved at an early stage to focus on a small number of patients (twenty-three) who were quite remarkable in that they had each, at the time our study began, been continuously resident at one or other of the two hospitals for a staggering period of more than sixty years. We were interested in the experiences of this group because of our suspicion that these patients were more likely than any others to have used the hospital, at least after first becoming securely domiciled within it, as a place of refuge or sanctuary. This was on the grounds of our feeling that members of the group must have clung, at times almost tenaciously, to their hospital abodes, despite the best efforts of successive rehabilitators over the period from the 1930 Mental Treatment Act, which introduced voluntary admissions, to decarcerate patients and to resettle all those capable of being settled in the community. The sheer quantity of reviews of their status and prospects, as compared with patient groups having lesser lengths of stay and having been admitted more recently, seemed certain to provide an excellent source of data for empirical evaluation of the asylum function.

There were a number of reasons why we expected to find serious attempts to rehabilitate the patients in our sample to have been made throughout the period from 1930. For example, the 1940s' regional hospital surveys, which were carried out for the Ministry of Health would have had some effect on Friern and Claybury. These surveys appeared in the Domesday Book of the Hospital Service. According to Means and Harrison (1988), the surveyors stated that 'the reproach of the masses of undiagnosed and untreated cases of chronic type which litter our Public Assistance Insitutions must be removed'.

Those of our group resident at Claybury Hospital in particular could be expected to have been able to benefit from the most advanced psychiatric approaches during their residence in order to promote their rehabilitation. Dennis Martin (1955), as Claybury's Deputy Physician Superintendent, was one of the first to comment in learned journals on the fact that the admission of patients into hospital, in relieving them of their family and work responsibilities and in providing 'hotel' facilities, made it hard for those patients to motivate themselves to take up those responsibilities again. He noted how the 'well institutionalised' patient was considered a good patient and raised the question of how the attitudes of doctors and nurses might change in relation to these processes. The impetus from the therapeutic communities subsequently developed at Claybury on long-stay wards, which are described by Schoenberg (1972) must have been felt by the patients from Claybury in our sample. Equally, Sergeant (1976) reports on an initiative to resettle the long-stay patients in one of Friern Hospital's sectors during the early 1970s. Again, it must be expected that such efforts would have affected the patients from Friern in our sample.

There were, however, a number of attendant problems with the data set, and our first inclination in devising the study was to interview the patient group with which we were concerned (and possibly, with patients' permission, also to interview their family or friends) in order to gain some insight into the ways in which some of them may have used the hospital as a refuge. However, there were two problems for us in considering such a method of proceeding. The first was of an ethical nature. Potentially, as researchers, we would be attempting to draw out disclosures from patients about events in the past, either at admission or during their lives in hospital, which may have been experienced as very painful. Unless we were to act in concert with a patient support service or alternatively, some form of therapeutic programme oriented towards reminiscence, then we might, at least hypothetically, easily be responsible for the deterioration of some of our respondents. But second, even if such interviews could be ethically sound, there seemed to be little possibility of obtaining much information about the refuge issue from the chosen patient group, since a number of them were mute, and others were suffering from dementia.

We considered carrying out a series of informal and tentative unstructured interviews, of a non-probing nature, with those of the patients who were not mute, or suffering from dementia, and who wished to talk to us about the past. We felt it may have been possible to build a relationship with them over a period of time. But on exploring this possibility, in making initial contact with ten patients, we concluded that such a large amount of time would be involved in relationship building as to preclude any realistic possibility, within the compass of a modest project such as ours, of making an assessment of uses of asylum by this method.

We therefore fell back on the medical case notes with which we were familiar before conceiving the study. Our preliminary inspection of the notes, and our reading of key texts on asylum seeking, such as Finnane's important (1981) work on Ireland, suggested to us a number of categories for a content analysis, the most important of which were as follows:

1 The 'how and why' of admission according to the medical account.
2 The relatives' account of the troubles leading to admission.
3 Opportunities for leaving the hospital.
4 Community acceptance or rejection (if resettlement had been attempted).
5 Quality of family contact during the patient's hospital residence.
6 Factors which can be considered to have excluded the patient from being considered for resettlement – such as violent behaviour or asocial behaviour.

As was noted above, the sample of twenty-three patients we selected was an unusual one in that all its members had experienced such an extremely long period of residence in a psychiatric hospital. Having made a preliminary inspection of the range of records available for the sample, we decided to concentrate our analysis on the medical notes for fifteen patients, as these patients had all recently been comprehensively assessed as part of the clinical study of hospital closure with which one of us was closely engaged. We judged that the material available from the clinical survey could potentially help us to refine our conclusions from the content analysis.

But we also recognised that if this limited study of asylum seeking and retaining was to have more than a speculative value, we needed to consider the notes for groups of less remarkable patients who had been resident in either Friern or Claybury hospitals for long periods and had been first admitted at roughly the same time (i.e. the inter-war period) as the initial sample. In order to control for some of the effects of the extraordinariness of the 'remarkable' group, we were thus led to the case books for patients admitted in the inter-war period, who were their contemporaries, and to consider a group of fifteen patients with more conventional lengths of stay. It was thus that we identified a 'four plus' group, all relatively young (though we did not define an upper age limit, including one patient in his forties), who were all discharged during the inter-war period and who were all resident in hospital for more than four years. Our method in identifying these patients was to use one male and one female discharges register and to select any complete case history (some histories were continued from one volume to another) for a patient who had remained in hospital for more than four years. We simply started with surnames that began with the letter A, and worked through each book, until we had identified eight men and seven women. However, we did not include all those patients who fitted these criteria as we wished to ensure a balance between patients transferred to other hospitals and patients discharged home. Six of this 'four plus' group were transferred as 'not improved' to other hospitals, probably under arrangements to deal with the overcrowding of Friern. The remaining nine were discharged as recovered or relieved.

In identifying the case notes for this further sample, we used only the archives of Friern Hospital, and not those of Claybury, for reasons to do with ease of access. We felt that this was a valid way to proceed since the clinical survey referred to earlier had indicated that there were, at least at that time, in 1985, no differences between characteristics of the long-stay populations at Friern and Claybury.

By this stage in the study we had begun to draw some prelim-inary hypotheses about asylum or refuge seeking as we conceived it. We decided to study the case notes for a further thirty patients admitted to hospital during the inter-war period, fifteen men and fifteen women. In this instance we wished to focus on those with short stays and on such issues as the relative solitariness of patients, before admission, at admission and during their stay in hospital. We considered that it was important to get at least some indication of the experience of the patient before being admitted in order to deal with the problem that we were already encoun-tering of our hypotheses inevitably reflecting institutionalism in the hospital patient, rather than any asylum seeking or refuge seeking by that person. It was for the same reason that we wanted to focus on so called 'first admission' patients.

We were thus led to draw up quite tightly defined criteria for the short-stay patients, which were as follows:

1 They had no known psychiatric history (whether in their con-tact with general practitioners, local infirmaries or psychiatric hospitals).
2 Accounts of the circumstances leading to their admission given by relatives were entered in the case books.
3 Each patient was under 40 years old at admission.
4 Each patient's length of stay in hospital was less than four years.

Using these criteria, we were unable to identify more than thir-teen female patients' histories from one discharge register and so drew the remaining two that would make up half the sample of thirty from an additional discharge register. We should say at this point that we were struck by the fact that eight out of the fifteen male patients identified by this method were Jewish, with a further two being Italian, and that on further inspection we found that two out of three patients whose names were entered in the discharge register for the period which we perused were Jewish. Could this be accounted for by a lesser proportion that became very long-stay or died? Was this register unrepresentative of others for the period? Could admission recorded in it have been of people from predominantly 'Jewish' parishes in Whitechapel and Stepney? Did the mental stresses of racist attacks account for a higher rate of admissions from Jewish than from C. of E. and Catholic communities? Could the hospital have been used by some among the Jewish community to control their troublemakers? While we certainly found a number of Jewish patients in our case notes sample who could be said to have been troublemakers for their families, and while White's work points to the significance of what he calls the 'policy of class control exercised by the Anglo-Jewish bourgeoisie' (1980: 255) this is an issue that, in our view, clearly requires further research, and lies outside the scope of our modest project. Before we turn to our findings, we must first draw attention to the problems of accepting medical case notes at face value, and then comment briefly on the debate which gave rise to our study.

The more we read the case notes the more formulaic the entries began to appear. We draw attention to one in particular, 'accounting for oneself' later on in this chapter, but there were a number of others which regularly cropped up, such as 's/he is dull, solitary and introverted', 's/he lacks all ambition and interests' and 'there is marked psycho-motor retardation'. On first reading the notes, one imagines these entries in some sense to define the case. Hunter and Macalpine's (1974) work on the history of Friern however, suggests that we should be careful not to infer that the physicians of the period could have known the patient whose history they recorded. The stark fact is that there were nine physicians attending 2,000 patients in the 1920s (Hunter and Macalpine, 1974: 84). The physicians were making entries in the case books because they were required to do so by law. It is in such a context then that we make something of an interpretive leap in the dark.

As wholesale closure and resettlement plans for psychiatric hospitals in England and Wales began to be implemented in the 1980s, their ability to offer refuge, despite its inherent tendency to institutionalise the recipient, was, in a sense, rediscovered (Parry Jones, 1988). What was happening was rather like what happened when working-class back-to-back terraces were bulldozed for slum clearance in the 1960s and sociologists bewailed the disappearance of intimate, mutually supportive, working-class communities – a rediscovery, in Laslett's phrase, of the world we have lost (Young and Willmott, 1962). Whereas for an earlier generation of social scientists, the evils of want, ignorance, squalor, disease and idleness were the key social problems to be addressed, with adequate housing being a critical area of provision, some of the later generation could be seen as finding merit in squalor and want. The former at least forced neighbours to live in each other's pockets and to care about one another, the latter forced them to help each other out with the proverbial cups of sugar. Without squalor and want this good neighbouring would, it was hypothesised, disappear.

In the same way one can point to the earlier generation of clinicians, represented by Wing and Brown in their 1970 study of three psychiatric hospitals, considering a key issue for the mentally ill to be the link between institutionalism and schizophrenia. Wing and Brown suggested that environmental poverty – the lack of activities and contact with the outside world among long-stay patients, was associated with a 'clinical poverty syndrome ... compounded of social withdrawal, flatness of affect and poverty of speech'. (We shall return to this point later in discussing the 'unaccounted for' among our group of sixty inter-war patients.) They even went so far as to say that a 'substantial proportion, though by no means all, of the morbidity shown by long-stay schizophrenic patients in mental hospitals is a product of their environment' (Wing and Brown, 1970: 177)

As with sociologists, some of the later clinicians could be seen to find merit in environmental poverty and the separation of the mentally ill from society which was offered by mental hospitals. They began to raise the particular concern that chronic patients would, in their view, be in danger of being abused or otherwise interfered with in densely populated and potentially hostile urban neighbourhoods. They required psychological and personal space (Social Services Committee, 1985).

This debate led us to our principal concern. What is the evidence that a refuge function – psychological and personal space, freedom from abuse and intolerance, has ever been provided in psychiatric hospitals? We became aware that there was little, if any, empirical evidence available. Moreover, defining what refuge might consist of was going to prove a major problem, though there were a number of attempts at definition to guide us.

Parry Jones has perhaps written most specifically on the asylum function in historical perspective. He questions whether 'pure asylum' has ever been given in psychiatric hospitals. This is because 'the explicit provision of asylum, without the primary objective of treatment and possible cure, has not been customary, although *in practice* this often became the case' (our emphasis). Instead of pure asylum, Parry Jones suggests that in the nineteenth and early twentieth centuries, 'passive asylum' may have

Table 6.1 Original diagnoses

	60+	4+	Short-stay
adolescent insanity	1		
confusional insanity			6
congenital mental deficiency	3		2
dementia praecox	3		3
delusional insanity	3	4	
general paralysis of the insane			2
imbecility with epilepsy			1
insanity and epilepsy		1	
recent mania		1	3
manic depressive insanity		1	
melancholia		1	1
primary dementia	1		4
recent melancholia	1	4	5
recurrent melancholia		2	
schizophrenia	1		
stupor	1	1	3
thought disordered	1		

been granted, with historical research on clinical records indicating that: 'there has been an enduring body of mentally disordered people having basic needs for care, protection and shelter, who have proved resistant to the treatment of the day and whose behaviour was not tolerated in their contemporary society' (Parry Jones, 1988: 489).

Wing describes the functions of asylum as, first, the provision of refuge, shelter, retreat and sanctuary, including protection from cruelty, competition, pauperism, social and intellectual poverty and isolation, and from harm of self and others; second, the function of reparation, including diagnosis of social disablement, treatment, and rehabilitation and resettlement. These functions were able to be fulfilled by the best practice of psychiatric hospitals such as Netherne, in Surrey, in the 1950s and 1960s, which were usually able to provide places for patients requiring asylum rapidly in times of emergency (Wing, 1990: 824). These are rather wide definitions. They give few clues as to the specific attributes of the asylum that cannot be identified in other sorts of settings than psychiatric hospitals. From our reading of them they were rather too sweeping for us to be able to operationalise them in the study.

To return to the categories we generated by inspection of case notes for our content analysis, an important source of information was the admission card for each of the patients. On this card there are headings providing for a description of family history and the circumstances preceding the patient's presentation at the hospital, together with demographic and organic data from medical examination. As might be anticipated, the sixty plus group were diagnosed as suffering from predominantly schizophrenia-type illnesses at the time of this examination.

For the four plus group however, there is a much more even split between the 'melancholias' and 'manias'. This distribution might have been anticipated in the sense that the melancholias may be expected to have had a better outcome, and patients suffering from such illnesses to stay for shorter periods, regardless of the validity or otherwise of the diagnostic categories, than the manias.

For the short-stay group, over half were diagnosed as having a schizophrenia-type illness (N.B. assuming confusional insanity is such an illness). However, only three were seen as suffering from 'dementia praecox' and another four from 'primary dementia', with six patients being seen as 'melancholia' cases, perhaps suggesting a more even distribution of illnesses than might be at first supposed. Between the dementias and the melancholias, a group of six patients were given a diagnosis of 'confusional insanity', and smaller numbers were recorded as 'stuporose', or as having congenital mental disorder or general paralysis of the insane.

Our groups are too small to be able to make any sound generalisations from these findings about diagnoses. Nevertheless, the virtual absence of melancholia diagnoses among the sixty plus group is, on the face of it, noteworthy in comparison with a presence of such diagnoses among the other groups. But this has to be seen in the context of our case notes revealing that the long-stay patients' diagnoses were often changed on several occasions during their stays in hospital. It therefore seemed to us that it would be more fruitful to move on to our 'how and why' question in considering factors relevant to any hypothesised need for asylum.

From our study of the information given for the reception of the sixty plus group by the hospitals, we identified in the cases of thirteen of the fifteen patients, though at the risk of some over-simplification, that there appeared to be three 'dominant' reasons for their admission (as opposed to their mental illness): terror, trauma and troublemaking. The different causes of these dominant reasons are shown below.

Dominant reasons for admission (sixty plus group)

1 Terror/persecution

Pt 9 Strange behaviour (hiding) – thought someone was after him
Pt 13 Terrified by vivid visual hallucinations
Pt 15 Says food is poisoned
Pt 24 Wants to do himself in rather than let the gang get him

2 Trauma

Pt 1 Saw a girl killed in the road which gave her quite a shock
Pt 5 Depression and anti-social behaviour following loss of job
Pt 6 Took to brooding after desertion by husband
Pt 10 Agitated and despondent, thought she had been drugged and raped
Pt 12 Frightened by a dog, frightened by a drunken man
Pt 14 Had a shock: suspected to have been molested

3 Troublemaking

Pt 7 Attacks mother
Pt 16 Violent to father and mother
Pt 19 Attacks mother

A number of the group were in fear of people being 'out to get them', these making up the terrorised or persecuted sub-group. Others had experienced a traumatic event, such as rape or desertion, and these can be considered a sub-group for whom the trauma appears to play the greater part in the progression to being a 'case' of mental illness. Our third sub-group became violent, usually towards their parents, for no apparent reason, and this appeared to have been an important pressure which led towards admission.

The experiences of most of the four plus group can also be seen as falling into these broad categories. Six were terrorised, with a typical instance being of a patient seeking help because of her belief that people were plotting to kill her. Three had experienced traumas of abuse, unemployment and desertion respectively. A further three can be considered as belonging in the trauma category in that they believed themselves to have committed an unpardonable crime or unforgivable sin and possibly feared retribution. One patient seemed to be a 'troublemaker', having been very violent at admission and having assaulted an old lady prior to admission. Another patient was described as dangerous, lacking self-control, and wild and maniacal at reception.

For the short-stay patients chosen, as we have said, because of the family history given in the case notes, again, the broad categories we have defined appear to have some validity. If we look at the women to begin with, there are four cases of persecution. One patient, for example, believed that a lodger was spying on her, abusing her and threatening her. Ten case histories could be said to fall into various categories of trauma. One patient saw an accident and had a haemorrhage and then gave birth to a child prematurely. For a further three childbirth itself seems to have been the main traumatising factor. One was worried that the child would be born deformed and one did not appear to recognise the baby after giving birth. One woman was said to be chiefly troubled by money worries owing to the unemployment of her husband.

For the men, there is a different pattern again in terms of dominant reasons for admission. The largest group is the troublemaking group, with the number of Jewish patients in this group quite striking. One of them was said to have tried to attack his father several times before admission, another to have threatened to knife his mother, and another was described as giving trouble on account of his alcoholism. Three men were terrorised, one being thought to have been scared by a burglary while on holiday and believing there were people under the bed trying to do him injury. Three further patients were traumatised, and again unemployment appeared to be the dominant reason for admission in one instance.

What is the significance of terror, trauma and troublemaking in relation to the use of Friern or Claybury hospitals for refuge? Leaving aside for a moment the nature of the mental illnesses which they were suffering, and the treatment appropriate for them, we might suggest that those who were in a state of acute terror or feeling persecuted, would welcome an environment away from the thing or persons feared. Though admission may have been experienced as terrifying too, use of the hospital as a refuge by such patients subsequently, given its security, predictability and relative safety, may be plausibly argued to have occurred in some instances. Similarly, patients who had experienced shock or a major reversal of personal circumstances, who we tentatively suggested were admitted largely for reasons to do with trauma, may have been expected to welcome a setting where they could be relatively well protected from further shocks and reversals. Use of the hospital for this type of asylum could be plausibly argued to have taken place among the traumatised group. Troublemakers, on the other hand, could not be said, on the face of it, to be using the hospital for asylum, though the troublemaking may well have been associated with other fears and insecurities.

Our examination of 'dominant reasons' for admission thus gave us fairly strong grounds for thinking that we might be able to find some evidence from the case notes of the use of Friern and Claybury hospitals for refuge purposes by a proportion of patients. We therefore moved on to analyse the notes for evidence that any patients had actually sought admission, or that they appeared to be happy with admission, and that there were reasons for them to welcome the provision of the kind indicated above.

We pointed out earlier that we deliberately chose to study the sixty plus group because we wanted to examine what changes occurred in patients' lives after the 1930 Mental Treatment Act which we expected would have made for some pressure to decarcerate inmates. The sixty plus group were thus all compulsory admissions. Nevertheless, consistent with their experiences of terror and trauma indicating that there would be good cause for some patients to welcome reception into hospital, we found evidence that five of the fifteen in the group could be said, at some stage, to have used the hospital for refuge purposes. Thus one refused to leave hospital to live with his brother and refused to see relatives. Another sought admission herself and was later reported as happy on her ward. A third also applied for admission, in this instance owing to a 'trivial disagreement with her mother'.

Retreat?

Sixty plus group

Pt 1   Refuses to leave hospital care of brother, refuses to see relatives

Pt 2   (1934) 'Satisfied with the present position and no plans or desires for the future'
(1960) 'It's my home and I don't know anything else'

Pt 3   Seeks admission
'Quite happy on E2 and has no desire for a better ward'

Pt 4   (1951) Agitated that she may have to leave hospital when told she would be made a voluntary patient

Pt 5   Applies for admission because of trivial disagreement with her mother

Four plus group

Pt 1   'He wanted to be taken care of'
(at admission)
later, unwilling to be discharged

Pt 2   Noted as happy and fatuous

Pt 3   'Does not appear anxious to go home'
'Has no desire to leave'

Pt 4   Expresses no hope of getting well enough to leave hospital because he believes he will break down again

Pt 5   Quite happy in present environment

Pt 6   Thought she had been sent
(to the hospital)
by the Marquis of Northampton for a rest

Short-stay (women)

Pt 1   At admission she said she was no use in the world and wanted to be by herself. She said she wanted be taken care of as she could not trust herself

Pt 2   'Satisfied with her present lot'
'Smiles fatuously, lacks normal ambition and interests'

Short-stay (men)

Pt 1   At admission states that he is quite happy and strongly denies any suggestion otherwise

Pt 2   At admission 'appears happy and contented with his lot and is lacking in all ambition' later: 'fatuously contented'

Pt 3   At admission 'happy and contented with his surroundings' intends to buy the hospital and turn it into a factory

Pt 4   At admission is without ambition and 'appears happy and contented to remain here indefinitely'

For the four plus group, we can identify, admittedly on the basis of rather perfunctory entries in contemporary case books, seven patients who appear to have sought refuge. There were two striking cases recorded at admission, with one patient wanting to be taken care of and later being unwilling to be discharged on the grounds that he was happier in the hospital than he would be outside. The other patient was constantly approaching the police and asking to be arrested so as to escape the people plotting against her. There were also patients who, like the five sixty plus patients, were recorded as being happy and having no desire to leave hospital. Finally, one patient thought she had been sent to the hospital by the Marquis of Northampton for a rest.

Somewhat less convincing evidence is available of the short-stay patients having sought admission. Certainly one of them, on being certified to the local Infirmary, said she wanted to be taken care of as she could not trust herself. There were a further four men who appeared to have no desire other than to stay at the hospital at an early stage in their admission. Another of the women patients was recorded as being satisfied with her lot, but this was five months after admission.

At present then, we simply lack more than this rather superficial information to consider the provision of refuge within the asylum as a response to asylum seeking. However, it is clearly worth noting that a minority of patients, even in this period of certified admissions, apparently did seek to gain entry to the asylum, with this tendency being more marked among those who became long stay.

Busfield (1986) has coined the term 'curative individualism' to describe the way in which the patient was perceived in the asylums of the nineteenth and early twentieth century as an organism to be cured solipsistically. This notion helped us to understand an otherwise rather puzzling phrase which occurred repeatedly in the notes that we studied. A patient was often described as being 'unable to give an account of him/herself'. This note about accounting was often accompanied by comments to the effect that the patient showed no ambition and lacked interest in his or her surroundings. Such views are interesting in the context of eugenics and the widespread belief during the early twentieth century that certain groups in the population were genetically defective. This is especially so in that a number of patients were noted as being of low educational attainment. As Jones (1986: 33) comments of the setting up of such organisations as the National Council for Mental Hygiene in 1922 (Jones, 1986: 28): 'it was increasingly assumed that alcoholism, prostitution, vagrancy and to a large extent unemployment were a complex of problems with a single root – feeble-mindedness' (Jones, 1986: 33). We pictured the scene of the doctor's periodic clinical assessment which so often led to such a report being given as a sort of '11+' educational examination result. (11+ is shorthand for a national examination which used to be taken by all British primary school students at the age of eleven so that they could be graded for entry to streamed secondary schools.) The patient was being asked about what s/he had done the day before and what their plans were for the future, seemingly without any prompts and without the assistance of prompters. Patients were commonly asked to recite the Lord's Prayer, and to give the name of the Queen, or they might be asked the question 'How many shillings go to make up a pound?' One patient was said to be able to identify a sixpence, a two shilling piece and a pen.

These questions raised issues of culture and IQ testing for us in reading the record of the accounting process, especially in relation to Jewish patients, whose parents would probably have been first generation immigrants fleeing from Russian and Polish pogroms. Those without command of language and disoriented in terms of place of residence could have been little expected to comprehend the test. The issue of motivation is perhaps clearest in the case of the man who was stated as being 'unwilling to give much account of himself'. Of two Italian male patients, both said by relatives to be fluent in English, one would make no reply to questions or give any account of himself, and the other refused to give any account of himself. Of one female patient it was recorded that she could not be induced to speak or to give any account of herself.

We use the analogy with the '11+' exam because there was clearly a grade awarded in accord with the ability of the patient to give some sort of account. It was evident that those who could give an account would be candidates for discharge. The sixty plus group registered consistent failures at the accounting examination. The full list of the accounting is reproduced because of its significance in relation to refuge. It raises the question of whether the specific attribute of asylum which only the mental hospitals could provide, an attribute welcomed by many of the patients whose notes we examined, was that it provided a place where they were able to be 'unaccounted for'. They were able to not be cajoled or forced into giving an account of themselves while being able to be cared for.

Giving an account of oneself

- No coherent account
- Gives no reasonable account of herself
- Can only give a poor account of himself
- Incapable of giving a correct account of himself
- Can give no account of himself
- Unable to give a connected account of herself
- Unable to give any sort of account of herself
- Unable to give a coherent account of himself
- Unable to give any detailed account of her recent history
- Can give a good account of herself
- Cannot give a very good account of herself
- Unable to give an a/c of himself
- Gives a poor account of himself
- Cannot give any account of himself
- Unable to give any account of herself
- Can give only a poor and rambling account of himself

We mentioned that the members of the sixty plus group had evidently been able to demonstrate their need for refuge during various rehabilitation drives undertaken by hospital staff, especially those of the 1970s (Sergeant, 1976). This ties in closely with the perception that such patients are 'unmoveable' from the asylums because they are mute and withdrawn and, in essence, considered unsuitable for social life. Is the hypothesis that the long-stay residents who remain in psychiatric hospitals constitute asocial or anti-social isolates borne out for either our sixty plus group or for our four plus group? Though the groups are so small in size, in each case their members' case histories do provide some degree of support for this hypothesis.

Asocial groups?

Sixty plus

Pt 1   No constant friend, introverted type, does not mix
Pt 2   Constantly described as a social

Pt 3   Mute, manneristic, solitary, idiot
Pt 4   Solitary, resents interference
Pt 5   Quiet, solitary and withdrawn 'Asocial but helpful'
Pt 6   Mute and inaccessible
Pt 7   Mute and sits by herself all day
Pt 8   Sullen and asocial

Four plus

Pt 1   'Leads a solitary, asocial existence'
       'Now rather solitary and quiet'
       'Shy and solitary in his habits'
Pt 2   'Solitary and asocial, does not mix with the other patients
       very well'
Pt 3   'He is solitary and asocial'
Pt 4   'Solitary and uncommunicative'
       'Solitary, preoccupied and asocial'
Pt 5   'Solitary and despondent' at admission later 'very solitary
       and quite unoccupied'
Pt 6   Attempts to hide herself in her room
       'Always looking for a chance to hide, always looking for a
       chance to escape'
Pt 7   Described many times as 'asocial', 'withdrawn' and 'solitary'
Pt 8   'Depressed and solitary'
       'Solitary in her habits'

Short-stay patients (men)

Pt 1   Three months into admission 'solitary'
Pt 2   Noted at admission and after as never to speak, even to
       relatives visiting. Hence 'very solitary'
Pt 3   'Dull introverted and still solitary', some way into admission
Pt 4   Three days in, 'solitary and introverted'
Pt 5   At admission 'does not converse with other patients', months
       later 'still very dull, solitary and rarely speaks', later still,
       same
Pt 6   At admission 'lies in bed showing no desire to mix with
       other patients', later 'he is inclined to be solitary'

Short-stay patients (women)

Pt 1   Not speaking, no interest in her surroundings at admission,
       later, 'solitary, devoid of interest and of normal desires',
       'always solitary and inactive'

Pt 2   Early in stay refuses to sit with other patients at meal times, later doesn't associate with other patients

Pt 3   Very resistive to attention (secluded), later on is 'solitary'

Pt 4   At reception wanted to be by herself but later 'more cheerful and social'

Pt 5   Early in admission is 'still depressed, solitary and inactive'

Pt 6   Preoccupied and solitary – several other references to her being solitary

Pt 7   4/52 into admission noted as 'inclined to be still solitary', later 'solitary and silent habits'

Pt 8   Does not speak to anyone in hospital but talks to her husband when he visits, later on 'mute and inaccessible'

Pt 9   At admission 'no amount of persuasion will induce her to speak', later refuses to speak

Pt 10   At admission 'very solitary in her habits', many other references to her solitariness

Comments in the medical notes suggest that perhaps eight of the sixty plus and a further eight of the four plus were considered 'asocial' in nature. Whether they would have been considered asocial outside the artificial community created by the psychiatric hospital we shall never know. Even outside that context, however, it is clear that the possibility of 'unnatural' withdrawal from family or friends would be inevitably difficult to distinguish from a 'natural' proclivity for withdrawal. As noted earlier, Wing and Brown associate social withdrawal with the environmental poverty of institutions. Does the asocial behaviour noted by physicians for our groups fit in with that picture? For the sixty plus patients perhaps we can only again point to an evident tenacity in withdrawing exhibited through attempts to engage the group in activity during the rehabilitative drives to improve the institutional environment in Friern and Claybury. We can also draw attention to some patients being noted as solitary at admission.

When we turn to the short-stay patients, however, the thesis of long stays possibly being, to a certain extent, a consequence of determined social withdrawal, appears more debatable. Altogether sixteen of the thirty short-stay patients had at some stage been considered solitaries. Moreover, ten were noted as what we might call 'withdrawers' at or around the time of admission, and continued to be so during their stay in hospital. Their withdrawal was thus apparently not an effect of the institution. Thus one patient was reported as taking off for solitary walks in the small hours of the morning, prior to admission, while being noted in hospital as being 'solitary in habits'. Others were noted as having lost interest in their surroundings prior to admission. Some refused to speak, spent their time lying in bed and did not mix. Nevertheless, one female patient, who was noted as being mute and inaccessible some months into her admission did not speak to other patients but did speak to her husband, and clearly institutionalism would have played its part in such instances. The commonness of asocial behaviour among those being discharged relatively quickly suggests that its degree of association with refuge seeking is a topic worthy of further investigation. All that we can report at this stage then is that a significant proportion of all patients whose notes we examined, who were admitted to the psychiatric hospital in the inter-war period, were solitaries and were relatively isolated.

The picture is clearer however in relation to vulnerability. This can be considered a 'second-order' phenomenon to those which were of concern to hospital staff at admission, being rather, in our view, a creeping perception within the notes of the need to protect the sixty plus patients from exploitation, abuse or public censure. Three patients appear to have been constantly attacked by their co-residents, and two seem to have been sexually exploited.

Vulnerability

Pt 1   Occasional note of violence towards him by other patients
Pt 2   Constantly struck by other patients + self-injury
Pt 3   Inclined to promiscuity
          Patient said to be annoying men in the gardener's shed
Pt 4   Urinates in dustbins sometimes
Pt 5   Subject to abuse – testicles examined for tenderness
          Suspicion of sexual exploitation by another patient
Pt 6   Begs later in history

Others were deemed vulnerable to a lesser degree, for a variety of reasons, ranging from begging through masturbating in public, to urinating in dustbins. This theme of our group needing protection from abuse, arising at a relatively late stage in their institutional lives, is all the more significant given that our scanning of the entries in the notes could reveal only one of the fifteen to have been actively suicidal and another to have been suspected of suicidal intent.

For the four plus group, suicidal intent appears to have had much greater significance. Six of them are noted as having had such intent at various times, to a degree where special precautions were seen to have been worth taking. Two patients were recorded as having tried to strangle themselves while in hospital. Four patients were deemed to have been unable to take care of themselves unless supervised, though in each case this was after their having spent some years in hospital residence. Urinating and masturbating in public appear to have been almost absent as forms of antisocial behaviour among the four plus group, suggesting that it may be a product of longer stays in a particular hospital.

In line with our view of vulnerability being a second-order phenomenon, it is highly significant that for short-stay patients we could find very little suggestion of their vulnerability to attack or abuse by other patients. Only one of the male patients, who was only 11 years old at admission, and was said to be interfering with the others on his ward, was noted as being struck by his fellow patients. Another was arrested for begging prior to his admission. Eight of the thirty were actively suicidal, with one patient taking paraldehyde while in hospital.

If we exclude the issue of suicidal intent, the evidence we present here is a little thin for one to argue that a main function of the asylum for either of our groups could be said to have become one of protection on grounds of physicians' beliefs about their vulnerability to physical or sexual abuse or to public censure for unacceptable behaviour. It is worth noting that this relatively novel perceived function of the old asylums is somewhat removed from the idea of asylum as refuge or retreat from intolerable pressures. The perception of patients as vulnerable does, on the other hand, appear to be fairly clearly associated with institutionalism. We can perhaps thus tentatively remove the function of protection for the vulnerable from our list of possible characteristics of asylum as refuge for the patient sample whose notes we have examined. They did not, on the whole, appear to have perceived themselves as vulnerable to the general public, but rather as vulnerable to specific persecutors and others plotting against them.

THE TAPS CLINICAL DATA

At the beginning of this chapter we noted that we had chosen to focus on fifteen sets of case notes for the sixty plus group partly

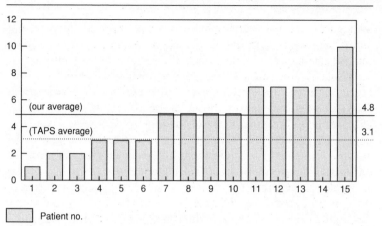

Figure 6.1 Number of severe problems for each patient

because the patients whose life histories we were concerned with had also been interviewed, together with their carers, by our colleagues from the Team for the Assessment of Psychiatric Services (TAPS) using a battery of clinical assessment instruments. At this point we can turn to the data derived from these assessment instruments to examine whether they reveal any of the concerns with specific kinds of vulnerability which we identified as distinctive of the later institutional lives of the sixty plus group.

Because of our specific concern with the vulnerability issue, we chose to focus exclusively, from the many assessment techniques employed by TAPS, on the Social Behaviour Schedule (SBS) a schedule devised by Sturt, Wykes and Creer, and subsequently developed for use within TAPS. This schedule seeks to identify problem areas in 'communication' and 'behaviour'. The SBS assesses patients in over twenty areas of 'competence' and they receive ratings from the most knowledgeable carer available to the interviewer. In addition there is also a category for this informant to choose what s/he believes to be the most 'difficult' problem for that patient. Once all the categories have been scored, the 'severe problem' categories (items afforded a score of 2 or more) are identified and summed to arrive at an overall SBS score. Whatever one's reservations about the external validity of such data, we considered that they were at least worth serious consideration.

Since TAPS began its baseline interviewing in 1986 (that is, interviewing of all long-stay residents of Friern and Claybury) over 1,000 SBS assessments had been conducted at the time our study began. It was against the backdrop of this large pool of data that we intended to examine the SBS data for our sixty plus group. Figure 6.1 shows the SBS scores as calculated for each of the fifteen patients in the sample (i.e. the number of severe problems). Also shown here is the average SBS score for the group as a whole, as well as the TAPS average for the entire study to date. As can be seen from the examination of this figure, the TAPS average at 3.1 is considerably lower than that shown for our sixty plus group, which is calculated at 4.8.

Having looked into the performance of our group in terms of their overall scores, we then decided to look more closely at the descriptive aspects of the schedule. Among other data, we examined the most commonly occurring problems among the group, which were revealed to be those of appearance and personal hygiene. This category of problems was found to be recorded for twelve of the fifteen patients assessed. When this finding is considered in the light of previous TAPS findings, which have shown that the same category is judged to be the most commonly occurring SBS problem throughout the entire interviewed long-stay population, occurring in more than 50 per cent of cases, then members of our group appear fairly unremarkable. The second and third most common problems, affecting just under half of the group, were socially unacceptable habits and problems in social mixing. The existence of the second most common problem thus appears to be consistent with the vulnerability perceptions which we identified in the notes and suspect to be of a secondary nature in relation to refuge seeking.

The members of our sixty plus group, assessed by means of the SBS, after each of them had spent a lifetime in hospital, thus appear to be untypical of the long-stay population only in relation to the number of social behaviour problems they were judged to have. From this clinical perspective, asylum for the sixty plus group has possibly, at least of late, been judged appropriate as much on the grounds of social vulnerability as on the grounds of mental health.

CONCLUSION

As was noted in the introduction to this book there were plenty of 'social' reasons why some patients might have welcomed admission to hospital, leaving on one side the nature of their mental illness. Wife beating and food adulteration, features of East End life commented on by Fishman (1988) in the latter part of the nineteenth century, could have provided two such reasons. Pressures on the second generation Jewish immigrant population discussed by White may have provided others. The level of aggressive competitiveness in the East End, which Hobbs points to, might have given good cause for those having to take part in the competition to be fearful of violence against them. The environment was clearly one stimulating to the febrile imagination.

We have speculated in this chapter, at the risk of some oversimplification, that there were three dominant reasons for the patients whose case notes we studied being admitted to hospital: terror, trauma and troublemaking. We have identified some evidence that a minority among all the patient groups either wanted to come into hospital or were happy to remain in hospital from an early stage in their residence there. We have further suggested that the perception of long-stay patients as being vulnerable to abuse or public censure appears to have been of relatively recent origin in terms of the case notes records. It can perhaps, we have indicated, be attributed, at least in part, to institutionalism.

We have drawn particular attention to the way in which our sixty plus group consistently failed to account for themselves when examined by hospital staff, and that the accounting process was evident in the case notes of all the groups of patients notes studied. We consider that it is this aspect of asylum which is perhaps distinctive to the mental hospital, i.e. that its staff 'allowed' patients to remain unable to give a coherent account of themselves for extended periods, evidently being content to make efforts to engage patients in such accounting rather infrequently. This feature of asylum bears closer examination if 'true' or active asylum is to be given in the community.

REFERENCES

Busfield, J. (1986) *Managing Madness*, London: Hutchinson.

Clifford, P., Charman, A., Webb, Y. and Best, S. (1991) 'Planning for community care: long-stay populations of hospitals scheduled for rundown or closure', *British Journal of Psychiatry*, 158: 190–196.

Finnane, M. (1981) *Insanity and the Insane in Post-Famine Ireland*, London: Croom Helm.

Fishman, W.J. (1988) *East End 1888: A Year in a London Borough among the Labouring Poor*, London: Duckworth.

Goffman, E. (1968) *Asylums*, Harmondsworth: Penguin.

Hobbs, D. (1989) *Doing the Business*, Oxford: Oxford University Press.

Hunter, R. and Macalpine, I. (1974) *Psychiatry for the Poor*, Folkestone: Wm Dawson and Sons Ltd.

Jones, G. (1986) *Social Hygiene in Twentieth Century Britain*, London: Croom Helm.

Laslett, P. (1971) *The World We Have Lost*, London: Methuen.

Martin, D. (1955) 'Institutionalization', *Lancet*, 185, 2: 1181–1191.

Means, R. and Harrison, L. (1988) *Community Care: Before and After the Griffiths Report*, Bristol: School for Advanced Urban Studies.

Parry Jones, W. L. (1988) 'Asylum for the mentally ill in historical perspective', *Bulletin of the Royal College of Psychiatrists*, 12, 10: 407–410.

Scull, A. (1977) *Decarceration*, Englewood Cliffs, New Jersey: Prentice Hall.

Sergeant, H. (1976) 'Rehabilitation of psychiatric patients who stayed in hospital more than one year', *Psychological Medicine*, 6: 493–504.

Schoenberg, E. (ed.) (1972) *A Hospital Looks at Itself: Essays from Claybury*, London: Bruno Cassirer.

Social Services Committee (1985) *Community Care with Special Reference to Adult Mentally Ill and Mentally Handicapped People*, London: HMSO.

Tomlinson, D.R. (1991) *Utopia, Community Care and the Retreat from the Asylums*, Buckingham: Open University Press.

White, J. (1980) *Rothschild Buildings*, History Workshop Series, London: Routledge and Kegan Paul.

Wing, J.K. (1990) 'The functions of asylum', *British Journal of Psychiatry*, 157: 822–827.

Wing, J.K. and Brown, G. (1970) *Institutionalism and Schizophrenia*, Cambridge: Cambridge University Press.

Wing, J. and Furlong, P. (1986) 'A haven for the severely disabled within the context of a comprehensive psychiatric community service', *British Journal of Psychiatry*, 149: 449–457.

Young, M and Willmott, P. (1962) *Family and Kinship in East London*, Harmondsworth: Penguin especially pages 197–199.

Chapter 7

Haven within or without the hospital gate
A reappraisal of asylum provision in theory and practice

Rosalind C.S. Furlong

INTRODUCTION

Care of the minority of mental illness sufferers who are unable to cope without help on a 24-hour basis has become an increasingly high profile issue during the last decade. In the press it has predominantly revolved around the need to contain people with disturbing behaviour. In the caring professions the debate has extended to the quality of life in different care settings (Wolfson, 1992). Central to this whole theme has been the loss of the old style 'asylum' care with the closure of the large mental hospitals.

When a decision was taken, in 1983, to close Friern Hospital, an opportunity was provided to plan a new style of asylum with progressive care, in the form of the Haven project (Wing and Furlong, 1986). The aim was to combine the advantages of non-hospital domestic-scale settings with the positive aspects of the hospital milieu. The project was adopted as part of the Friern 'reprovision' plan, but was abandoned for financial reasons and alternative reprovision plans were made for the forty-two patients originally expected to move into the Haven community. The destiny of these patients, in the absence of the Haven community coming to fruition, is reported and discussed in this chapter. This is followed by an analysis of the meaning of the term community for this group and the role of asylum in their care. Finally I discuss the implications for the future planning of services.

THE DEVELOPMENT OF THE HAVEN

Local mental health policy

In 1983, NETRHA decided to close Friern Hospital over a ten year period. Its resident patients were to be resettled into new community placements provided by the then four district health authorities who were responsible for their care: Bloomsbury, Hampstead, Haringey and Islington. These districts cover a wedge-shaped area of North London stretching from the River Thames to the North Circular Road, Friern being situated at its northern boundary, well served by public transport links which radiate from central London. All but the Haringey authority had, by 1983, established out-patient clinics, short-stay beds and day hospital services attached to their district general hospital services. Haringey's district psychiatric services had only been developed in the east of the borough at a local hospital in Tottenham (see Figure 7.1), whereas the west of the borough continued to be served by Friern, which, though conveniently situated for West Haringey patients, was actually just outside the borough boundary, in Barnet.

Historical issues

Friern Hospital had an auspicious beginning. In May 1849 the foundation stone was laid by the Prince Consort, dedicating the hospital to 'non-restraint, the pride and boast of our metropolitan county' (Winslow, cited in Hunter and Macalpine, 1972). Ten million bricks were laid in record time and the keys were handed over in November the following year – an incredible achievement, particularly in the light of our recent experience with more modest building projects. Akin to our own experience, however, the cost was almost double that estimated: £300,000, which made it the most expensive asylum ever built. It was planned to accommodate 1,250 people who had become socially unacceptable through 'lunacy', and to provide a healthy environment in the absence of available specific medical treatment and the presence of only two resident doctors. It was a largely self-supporting rural community, with its own farm, gas works, upholsterers, bakery and brewery, the latter two of which, for example, employed only two paid staff to supervise the patients working there.

Throughout its early years, Friern pioneered humanitarian care with a community focus. On sunny Sundays, large groups of patients were taken for walks in the surrounding countryside. Visitors were so numerous initially that they had to be restricted to two per patient in any one day. The chaplain, Rev. Henry Hawkins, campaigned for funds and in 1871 formed the

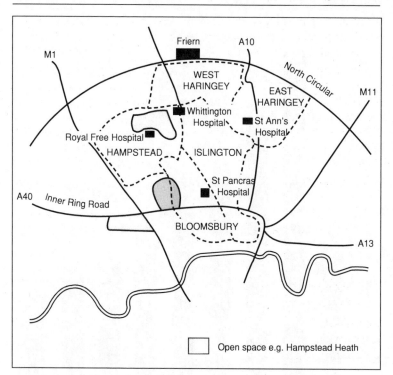

Figure 7.1 Map showing Friern, St. Ann's and the Haringey area

'Association for Aftercare of Poor and Friendless Convalescents on Leaving Asylums for the Insane', the forerunner of the Mental Aftercare Association which, to this day, enables many patients to be discharged from hospital into supportive settings.

Over the years the patient population grew steadily, and, although new building work took place, 'Colney Hatch' as it was then known became disastrously overcrowded. In 1937, when it held 2,700 patients, it was renamed 'Friern Mental Hospital' to remove old associations. However, the numbers continued to rise, despite the appointment of four consultant psychiatrists with the advent of the NHS in 1948, and by 1960 the patient population was at its numerical peak of 3,000.

After then, with a return to an emphasis on rehabilitation and increases in staff to facilitate it, the hospital population reduced. Numbers of residents fell by over 2,000 in the period leading up to the closure programme (see Figure 7.2). It is noteworthy that

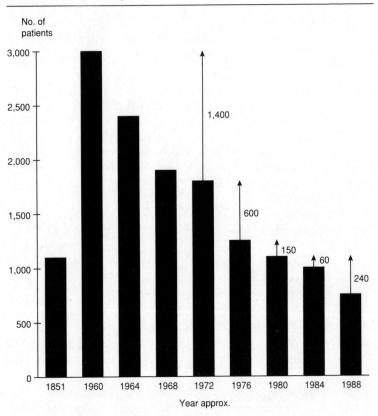

Figure 7.2 Number of patients discharged overall

the relocation of 120 of its short-stay beds on to general hospital sites in the 'feeder' districts referred to above occurred in the early 1970s, thus facilitating a large fall in patient numbers in that period. In 1983, when the closure decision was taken, 839 patients remained requiring placement.

Total Friern patient profile

In January 1983 a survey of all the then remaining Friern in-patients, comprising 392 males and 447 females, was organised by Dr Patrick Campbell and conducted by the medical staff of the hospital (Friern Medical Committee, 1983). This included 160 patients who had been admitted to short-stay wards for the under-65s, and a similar number admitted to wards provided for a category of patients known as the 'elderly severely mentally ill', or more commonly by the acronym, esmi. About half of this group had been recently admitted to the hospital with a primary diagnosis of dementia.

The presence of the short-stay residents under 65 and of the esmi patients accounted for the large number (246) who had been resident at Friern for less than one year.

However, the majority can be held to have been more representative of the type of asylum patients who tend to figure in the minds of the informed public. Thus there were 228 'new long-stay' patients – that is to say patients having been resident for more than one year but less than five years in the hospital – and 365 'old long-stay' patients – that is to say patients having resided more than five years at Friern.

Of the total population, short and long stay, twenty-five had various pre-senile dementiae and three suffered from neuroses. Other diagnoses included personality disorder, alcohol or drug addiction, mental retardation and epilepsy.

The majority of patients were elderly: only 39 per cent were under 60 years old, with 20 per cent being aged between 60 and 70, and the largest group, 41 per cent, being aged over 70. Significantly, only 5 per cent were detained under a section order of the Mental Health Act.

Most people were admitted because of a relapse in previously treated illness or because they needed long-term care. Around ninety of the old long-stay patients were people who had stayed in hospital because no effective treatment had been available at the time of their admission. Many more patients had been admitted to Friern on previous occasions to the spell of admission recorded at the time of the survey. For 300 patients, admission was necessary despite their already being resident in supervised accommodation outside the hospital, in a quarter of these cases because of non-compliance with medication. The extent of rehabilitation efforts with long-stay patients prior to the hospital closure decision is also demonstrated by the fact that ninety-seven patients had received hospital treatment for at least a year on a previous admission to Friern to that recorded at the time of the survey. A further seventy-eight had had more than one attempt at resettlement from the hospital.

Socially, overall, there was considerable deprivation. Only 30 per cent had a home address still theoretically available although, for many, negative attitudes of relatives prevented the possibility of returning to it. Only 13 per cent had a spouse or cohabitee still in contact, and of those admitted for more than five years, only 22 per cent had any contact with someone outside the hospital. Some 97 per cent were unemployed at the time of admission, although eight long-stay patients had regular employment outside the hospital.

Finally, the ongoing mental and physical health problems were of quite a serious nature in those who had been resident in hospital for more than one year, that is, the long-stay patients. One quarter suffered from physical illness or a physical disability. Nearly a fifth were judged to have impaired intellectual ability, and a third were still suffering from the symptoms of acute psychiatric illness. For many in a chronic phase of mental illness, behavioural problems had been preventing discharge e.g. physical aggression (17 per cent), actions which upset others like sexual disinhibition (22 per cent), incontinence of urine (18 per cent) and of faeces (13 per cent). The Medical Committee survey revealed that, in total, 428 (72 per cent) were considered to be in need of further hospital care, and a further 28 (5 per cent) in need of part III (local authority) old people's accommodation. The examination of the placement of the patients who were destined for the Haven which follows enables the accuracy of these survey predictions to be assessed.

Planning for Haringey patients in Friern

The main aim of the Friern closure programme was to provide a complete locally based district mental health service in each of the four districts served by Friern hospital. While it was planned that general hospital services would provide for acute (short-stay) patients, the intention was to provide accommodation away from the hospital sites in accordance with care in the community policy. This was to be funded in the long term by realising capital assets through the sale of the greater part of the Friern site, in order to finance the necessary acquisition of property and building refurbishment in the individual districts. At the time, the Regional Health Authority intended to also close Claybury Hospital, a large mental hospital situated, like Friern, in the outskirts of London, with closure to be achieved over the same ten-year period. Over a hundred patients either originating from Haringey or having become the responsibility of the DHA were resident in Claybury, which had traditionally offered services to the east part of the district, of which Tottenham formed a large part. The Haringey DHA therefore had to engage with two hospital closure processes in developing psychiatric services.

As was noted above, there were no psychiatric services in the western half of Haringey and its population was served by Friern. As the Friern site was conveniently situated in relation to the west of the borough, which lacked any viable local general hospital site, it was proposed to continue to provide services to the west of Haringey, after Friern's closure, from a base within a parcel of Friern land. This particular bit of land was in an attractive area, with pleasant views, shops and bus stops close at hand, and enjoying access to the parkland in front of the old hospital buildings, which was to be preserved as public open space.

A relatively modern building (25 years old), Halliwick House, was available on the proposed site which could have provided accommodation for West Haringey short-stay patients. It had been originally built as a psychotherapy in-patient unit, and was therefore well suited to house the short-stay (acute admission) wards, together with a day hospital, an out-patient suite and administrative departments. There was also an adjacent suitable plot on which a psychogeriatric unit was to be built with scope for the provision of a secure garden. Nearby, semi-wooded land provided a good location with independent road access on which was to be built the residential-style houses of the Haven community. This would have been home for forty-two of the most disabled long-stay patients. For the other side of the site, full plans had been drawn up for the medium secure unit (for patients usually detained in prisons or secure hospitals in the first instance and in the process of being rehabilitated). This was to be a forensic unit, replacing the interim secure unit in Friern Hospital, and would have included a free-standing gymnasium and occupational therapies complex which Haven residents could have used.

Lastly, a joint scheme was being planned with a local church, whose authority was going to build a community centre on an adjacent plot of land, part of which was to be a club room and coffee bar for the use of Haven residents and the local community.

Alongside these Friern proposals, a number of community reprovision schemes were being developed for Friern and Claybury patients from Haringey at locations away from the Halliwick and Tottenham hospital sites. For the elderly, twenty-two places were to be provided in mental health annexes to three existing local authority 'part III' care homes. A range of community provision was planned for the younger patients, mostly staffed to a higher level (numerically) than the corresponding provision in Friern. A twelve-place hostel was developed jointly by the health authority and the local authority, and another care home of eleven places was developed and staffed by the health authority. However the major part of the provision, a total of seventy places, was developed by the health authority working in conjunction with voluntary organisations and housing associations, with the authority not directly providing care itself. The seventy places included adult fostering schemes, supported flats and a number of care homes with a high staff/resident ratio. The placements were planned to be shared roughly equally between Friern and Claybury patients.

Decisions on appropriate placements for the Haringey long-stay patients, i.e. to Haven units on site or to community homes, were made by a multidisciplinary resettlement team including medical, nursing, occupational therapy and psychology staff, with advice from social workers when available. Each patient's care requirements were assessed, with the assessment including a consideration of the patient's social networks (i.e. friends and acquaintances in and outside the hospital). This was either carried out by asking the patients themselves or, in the case of those patients who were mute, by observing their non-verbal contacts. The assessment also took account of the location of patients' relatives and friends outside hospital, and considered their views where possible.

Final strategic outcome

In 1990, the plans for the Friern development were abandoned, not because of the cost of the Haven scheme itself but because Haringey Health Authority could not afford to continue to provide a 'split-site' service for its east and west sectors.

In the meantime, three other changes had taken place. First, the medium secure unit and its occupational therapies complex were no longer to be built on the Halliwick site (see above). This was because the neighbouring Enfield DHA had taken over responsibility from Haringey DHA for its development. Second the Regional Health Authority had changed the basis on which it calculated the numbers of Friern and Claybury patients for whom each feeder district health authority was notionally responsible, allocating some 'stateless' patients, (patients not originating from the catchment area of either hospital) whose care Haringey DHA had been planning for, to other DHAs. Third, the decision had been taken to delay the closure of Claybury Hospital, to concentrate efforts and resources on closing Friern Hospital on time.

The net result of these radical changes in planning assumptions was that the whole of the west Haringey acute admissions and esmi service was thenceforward planned to be relocated in refurbished wards in the Tottenham hospital already referred to, which was located in the south east of the district. This used up all of that site, and there was no scope, at that time, for the development of purpose-built houses or for the adaptation of suitable existing buildings at the hospital for a Haven complex. The concept of the Haven thus had to be set aside in all but philosophy. The forty-two patients that had been identified to live in it were to be resettled instead in a variety of types of facility to which the DHA had access, or which it managed, including a twenty-bed rehabilitation ward and a twelve-place intensive rehabilitation ward at the Tottenham site, the Haringey community homes already referred to (where Claybury patients' places had to be made available to those being resettled as a matter of more urgency from Friern), and a number of other care placements outside the Haringey district.

The multidisciplinary resettlement team reviewed each patient's needs and capabilities, referring all but the most disabled to the available community projects, taking account of social networks to refer groups whenever possible. This involved the team accepting that for some this would result in failure and readmission to hospital residence (probably at a rehabilitation ward moving from Friern to the St Ann's Tottenham hospital), while for others there would be inevitable relapses at times, with a need for temporary readmission or the imposition of a more restrictive lifestyle.

By March 1993, all Haringey patients at Friern had been resettled. Two short-stay (acute admission) wards and the two psychogeriatric wards provided for patients from the district were reprovided at St Ann's (although one of the latter has subsequently been closed). Some of the rehabilitation ward patients were also subject to an inter-hospital transfer by being moved to two St Ann's rehabilitation wards. For the majority of the older and some of the younger among this group, however, places were found in the homes making up the 104 community placements which were intended originally to house both Friern and Claybury long-stay patients.

The concept of the Haven

The aim of the Haven project was to provide a therapeutic environment, not only in medical aspects, but in social, occupational and recreational ways, for those whose mental illness was of sufficient chronicity and severity to prevent discharge within 3–6 months of admission, or who had been unsatisfactorily placed in the community and needed further preparation or an opportunity to restabilise.

It is becoming generally recognised (Wing and Furlong, 1986) that there are small groups of 'old' and 'new' long-stay patients for whom rehabilitation outside the hospital setting is either impracticable or undesirable in the short term. Such patients are those with the following problems:

1 Unresponsive schizophrenia who remain acutely disturbed in the early years of their illness and at risk of harming themselves or others.
2 Unpredictability of behaviour and tendency to relapse.
3 Low public acceptability because of behaviour problems e.g. verbally abusive without provocation, sexually disinhibited etc.
4 Lack of insight into their need for treatment.

The last group give rise to particular management problems when they relapse having refused medication. This is not an uncommon reason for admission as noted earlier and can have serious consequences, as it is known that some do not respond so well to medication in subsequent psychotic relapses and do not recover their previous level of functioning. When people are in hospital they usually accept medication more readily but can be maintained on it, if necessary, against their will. However, often such measures are unnecessary as is demonstrated by the very low number of patients detained in Friern under sections of the Mental Health Act.

The concept of the Haven project was to 'reprovide' for these people on a psychiatric hospital campus, retaining the helpful 'community' milieu of the large mental hospital but without the institutional aspects of care practice and building design.

A sheltered hostel and homes were to be grouped on the periphery of the hospital site, in non-stigmatising housing with private and peaceful outdoor space, accessible occupation and leisure activities, and proximity to the off-site club in the planned church community centre next door. Here, links could have been made by sharing facilities with the local people among whom a tolerant, understanding attitude had been built up over the years.

The houses were to be run with a flexible domestic regime to enable daily living skills to be retained when practicable, even though it was anticipated that there would be some fluctuations in residents' mental health. In the event of a relapse necessitating acute hospital care, the proximity to the acute wards would enable effective staff back-up, and, if admission proved necessary, contact could still be easily maintained with the staff of the home and with other residents.

The length of stay in the Haven would have varied with individual need. For some, it would have provided a short period of rehabilitation training and convalescence. Others could have stayed for several years during the acutely disturbed phase of their disorder, receiving active treatment. For the remainder, it would have been a home for life in the case, for example, of those suffering from pre-senile dementia with behavioural complications.

Key points in the philosophy were as follows:

1 Individuality of care package with self-care, occupation and leisure options.
2 Continuity of care personnel, despite the fluctuating needs of the patient.
3 Tolerance of surroundings to minimise interpersonal stress.

Key aims were as follows:

1 To encourage the highest level of functioning possible at any given time.
2 To provide gradual steps towards independence and integration with the non-hospital 'community'.

Planned Haven provision

The Haven community was to consist of six buildings: a core of three highly staffed units supporting a cluster of three lightly staffed ones. They were all to be built on a domestic scale and in a homely style, grouped as a cul-de-sac around an access road which linked them both to the hospital site and the entrance road. In order to make financial savings on this scheme, it was eventually decided to convert some existing staff accommodation for the smaller units and use the original medical superintendent's house nearby for the hospital hostel. These houses were located in semi-woodland which provided an effective screen from the other hospital buildings and the scope for natural-looking secure gardens for the first two units.

The buildings were planned as follows:

1 Haven One: a twelve-place hostel for the younger persistently disturbed.

   This would have been run along similar lines to the Maudesley Hospital Hostel, providing a flexible therapeutic programme of activities in a well-staffed environment with the aim of slow-stream rehabilitation. Such a hostel would provide for those who suffer from unresponsive, chronically acute illness (usually schizophrenia) and in whom there is an unpredictable risk of harm to the self or others, thus making necessary their containment to an extent. It would enable them to live in a more domestic style, maintaining their ability for self-care at times when their mental state allowed it, and to participate in decision-making where practicable.

2 Haven Two: a six-place house for those with organic disorders and pre-senile dementia.

   This was to provide for those patients under the age of 65 but seriously dementing. Often their need for heavy nursing care and containment (because of a tendency to wander and get lost) results in them being looked after on psychogeriatric wards alongside those with senile dementia whose nursing requirements are similar. Such arrangements are obviously undesirable, and against DoH guidelines. Alternatively, they are placed with less damaged rehabilitation patients, who can be both demoralised by their presence and seriously hampered in their rehabilitation programmes.

3 Haven Three: a six-place house for elderly active patients with behavioural disturbances and high nursing dependency.

   It is unsatisfactory to place some elderly patients with chronic schizophrenia with others of their age group in homes for the elderly. Their minds are often more alert and active but their delusional ideas can lead them to be disturbing to other frail elderly residents. They need more opportunities for physical exercise and diversional occupation than is usually available in homes for the elderly, as well as general nursing care.

4   Haven Four: A six-place house for active rehabilitation of those who have graduated from Haven One, acute patients in need of domestic skills assessment or training and those who have motivational problems.

This house was planned to link closely with the Haven One hostel, enabling people to graduate as they became less disturbed, prior to placement in community homes.

It was also to provide for those people with motivational problems who, with intensive domestic retraining, could become adequately self-sufficient to cope in community settings with social support and a minimum of practical help. This independence is encouraging for the individual once attained, but can be undermined by the availability of 'hotel' services in a hospital ward in which specialised occupational therapy is not available and where there is pressure to discharge sometimes hastily to a residential home rather than take time to rehabilitate and ascertain the patient's full potential.

5   Haven Five: a six-place house for slow-stream rehabilitation of those with personality problems who are difficult to place, or in whom there is a risk of relapse if off a hospital site.

There is a small group of patients for whom community placement is unsatisfactory because of the difficulty of living at close quarters with other potentially disturbed people. The group benefits from the wider aspects of an asylum-type situation. It includes people with repetitively demanding personalities who can be very wearing for other residents in the confines of a community home. Other patients resort to verbal or physical aggression in response to chronic paranoid psychotic experiences or frustration. This is usually aggravated by interpersonal pressure of a critical or hostile variety, often referred to as high expressed emotion, and a few generate this reaction in their carers and other residents. They benefit from the calming effects of a tolerant campus with open sheltered space in which to wander and let out aggression verbally if necessary.

Some patients persistently lack insight into their need for psychotropic medication and therefore frequently relapse out of hospital where no effective pressure can be applied to ensure continuity of treatment.

6 Haven Six: a six-place house including flatlet, providing a permanent home for older active patients and respite care of a short- or medium-term nature for those whose community placement has failed.

A few of the older long-stay patients with chronic schizophrenia were benefiting from the range of day occupation on site at Friern of a non-domestic variety, which would still have been available to Haven residents. They were very reluctant to move out of the hospital. As the alternative was community placement in homes which could not provide nearby day activities, it was decided to reprovide for them in a domestic-style Haven home.

As places became vacant, they were to be used for respite care for those already in the community. This sometimes becomes necessary when carers go away for a holiday or when a resident becomes acutely disturbed in a sheltered home due to a personality clash, or, indeed, an unhealthy attraction to a co-resident, and needs somewhere to stay while problems are resolved or an alternative placement is found. It is also useful to have a place in which those who have relapsed and were unsatisfactorily placed can stay while an alternative home is found.

Staffing

The hostel and the first two houses (i.e. Havens One, Two and Three) were to be staffed intensively as a core because of the heavy nursing needs of these patients, while the other homes (i.e. Havens Four, Five and Six) were to be a cluster, with individual key nurses responsible for day-to-day management of each home, but additional back-up being provided by the core nurses. The cluster homes were to have had full-time occupational therapy input and a psychologist based at the Haven One hostel assisting throughout the unit.

HAVEN PATIENT PROFILES AND PLACEMENT OUTCOME

Early on in the course of Haringey reprovision planning, long-stay patients were designated potentially for the Haven project. In this section I describe the individual patients in this 'Haven

Study Group', and their reprovision outcome five years after their designation for the project, at a point shortly before Friern closure. Later developments in their reprovision histories at the time of writing (i.e. after Friern closure) are also noted, where significant, and the question of whether a more beneficial outcome could have been achieved if the Haven had been developed as planned is considered.

The Haven One group

There were twelve patients identified for Haven One, all suffering from schizophrenia, and falling into three small groups. First, there were five young men, aged between 26 and 33, who had only been in hospital for two or three years. Four of them responded poorly to anti-psychotic medication, and one of the four presented the added complication for community placement of drug and alcohol abuse. The fifth member of the group had anti-social tendencies, namely towards stealing and fire-raising. All five were prone to physically aggressive outbursts, the first three at unpredictable times when responding to hallucinations. Their daily living skills were hampered by problems of motivation and fluctuated with mental state, day by day. All had family living locally with whom they were in contact, and were able to name some friends among other Friern patients, past and present, though not any originating from outside the hospital.

The reprovision outcome for three of them was treatment in the Intensive Rehabilitation Unit (IRU), a locked ward with a high staffing ratio, run along behavioural therapy lines, which was reprovided at St Ann's Hospital. Two of them have been discharged to sheltered accommodation since Friern closure, while one remains in the unit. The man with the substance abuse complication was still in hospital at the end of the study period, but has since been placed in sheltered accommodation. The fifth young man was placed in a 24-hour staffed hostel by the study period's end, but subsequently had a number of readmissions to hospital for aggressive behaviour, smoked very heavily, and died of acute viral pneumonia during his last brief hospital stay, at a time when the hostel staff thought they were unlikely to be able to have him back. For him, and for the man remaining in the intensive rehabilitation unit, the outcome could have been better if Haven One had been available with the intensive input and a domestic style of care.

The second small group identified for Haven One comprised three women and one man, aged between 44 and 50, and who had been in hospital for periods varying between seven and twenty-five years. They were less floridly disturbed, but were difficult to rehabilitate because of other complications, e.g. self-destructive behaviour, aggression and very poor self-care skills. None of these patients had contact with family or friends outside the hospital and were more generally isolated, possessing few friends.

For this second group, the reprovision outcome involved the man and one of the women being placed in community homes, another of the women dying before discharge of a physical disorder, and the third woman being taken into a ward by the resettlement workers of a neighbouring health authority (as a patient for whom they agreed to take responsibility as part of their reprovision group). Although one would have envisaged a similar outcome with or without the Haven for the first three of this group of four, the fourth person is now unfortunately permanently placed in an institutional setting.

The smallest, third group of Haven One patients consisted of three patients who were all seriously disabled but for whom it was hoped that the therapeutic opportunities of the hospital hostel would be beneficial. The youngest was aged 39, a man who was restless with very degraded behaviour, e.g. excessive drinking, including water out of the toilet if given the opportunity. He had a father living locally who visited regularly. The reprovision outcome for this patient was placement in the Intensive Rehabilitation Unit. After Friern closure, as he had not been making any progress, he was transferred to the rehabilitation ward where he needed special nursing care both for his own benefit and to protect the other patients from his pestering and stealing. He died unexpectedly there from heart failure.

The other man, aged 53, was quite socially isolated and had secondary dementia. He has remained in the rehabiliation ward environment and has changed very little, remaining socially isolated and often mute.

The last patient destined for Haven One was a 65-year-old woman who has been resident at Friern since her early twenties. She needed some nursing help and supervision, but was able to attend occupational therapy daily, and the hospital church service regularly on Sundays. She was, however, socially isolated with no friends or relatives and it was hoped that the opportunities for group activities within a smaller unit would have enabled her to foster links with others and facilitate her rehabilitation into the community. At the end of the study period she was still in a rehabilitation ward at Friern but was moved into a psychogeriatric ward at St Ann's at the point when Friern's doors finally closed.

Summarising the picture in relation to the outcome for the Haven One group, the outcome for the five people who it has been possible to settle into community homes at the time of writing would probably have been the same had Haven One come to fruition, though the Haven would have provided an easier transition between the hospital as the place of departure and the community home as the place of destination. Of the three patients who died, the first had been more relaxed when residing in hospital and so may not have sustained the same degree of smoker's lung damage were he to have been living in the sheltered environs of the Haven, and it can be conjectured that he might have survived the pneumonia. The third person would have had more supervision in Haven One, with its high staffing ratios, than he had on the rehabilitation ward, and this might have prevented him from doing something to himself to precipitate the heart failure, though again this suggestion is highly conjectural. Those four patients remaining on hospital wards would undoubtedly now be better off in a Haven domestic-style environment, and all the others would have enjoyed the more pleasant setting during their time in hospital.

The Haven Two group

This consisted of six patients who were all rated as highly dependent on nursing care and were all in their fifties. All had been in hospital over fifteen years except for one lady who had come in two years previously with pre-senile dementia. The other five were also suffering from dementia, but this was secondary to schizophrenia for four of them and to epilepsy in the case of the fifth. The woman with pre-senile dementia had no relatives but was visited by a local nun. She was placed in one of the mental health annexes to part III local authority homes for the elderly mentioned earlier, although at the time she was still under 60 years old.

Two of the group for Haven Two died before Friern closure, the man with epilepsy and one of the women. These were the only two in the group with relatives living locally who were visiting them.

Of the remaining three patients for the second Haven house, two were placed in psychogeriatric wards, one in Haringey, the other in Enfield, after one had his leg broken by a younger patient with schizophrenia whom he had annoyed. The other lady was eventually placed in a home near her relatives in Yorkshire.

Thus the placement outcome for the four patients in the group who survived at the time of Friern closure would clearly have been better with Haven Two available, affording them a less institutional style of care, particularly in the case of the younger woman placed on a psychogeriatric ward. Furthermore, it can be suggested that if he had been placed away from the younger acutely disturbed, it is likely that the man who had his leg broken would not have been involved in the incident responsible for this occurrence. The life expectancy of patients with organic disorders is considerably below average, so it is also clear that the existence of Haven Two would not have been likely to alter the outcome for those who died.

The Haven Three group

Haven Three was to be home for a group of elderly but physically active, behaviourally disturbed patients, made up of four men and two women. Their ages ranged from 64 to 88 years, and they were capable of very little communication. Four still had some contact with relatives, one being visited fortnightly by a nephew living nearby. This man (aged 88) used the gymnasium at Friern regularly and used to go to the Jewish club meetings although he spoke very little. Because of his Jewish links he was placed in a Hackney home run by the Jewish Welfare Board. One of the men was transferred to a Haringey psychogeriatric ward, and an 86-year-old woman was placed in a mental health annexe to a part III home, which was a little further away for her relatives to visit her than Friern had been. The other three in the group all died within the study period.

As with the group suffering from dementia who were identified for Haven Two, the existence of Haven Three would have been unlikely to have prolonged the life expectancy of the elderly patients who died. However, all but one of these patients could have had a more personal style of care in a six-place home, as would others who could have taken up any vacant places occurring and been taken in from larger settings for the elderly, in which these kind of patients with aggressive tendencies cause considerable disruption.

The Haven Four group

This was again a group of six patients, in this case aged between 44 and 61, and who were all suffering from schizophrenia with complications of personality or motivation. All were long-stay patients, although one had theoretically only been in hospital for two years since a brief unsuccessful placement in the community.

Of the three women, one was visited weekly by her brother-in-law, who had always been fond of her, one had a local boyfriend with whom she used to stay for long leaves quite frequently, and the third was totally in a world of her own. The reprovision outcome was that none of them had been very satisfactorily resettled. Two remained in the rehabilitation ward which transferred to St Ann's Hospital after several attempts at community placement, and the other discharged herself against medical advice to move into her boyfriend's bedsit. He is getting on in years, cannot cope with her financial demands or assist her with personal hygiene and has to sleep on the floor. She, on the other hand, frequently presents herself at St Ann's Hospital asking for admission but discharging herself again after a few days.

Two of the men were good friends and worked daily in a laundry two bus-rides away from Friern, having found the job while resident in hospital. One was detained on a Home Office order having been transferred from Broadmoor Hospital because of a serious offence while in a psychotic state. He had been well stabilised on anti-psychotic medication for some years but was reluctant to move out of Friern into sheltered accommodation because he would have had to give up more of his earnings. Both were moved together into a sheltered flat where initially they settled well. One remains happily settled, but a year later, the second man discontinued his medication, became acutely disturbed and was admitted to hospital for stabilisation. He was discharged back to the flat by the end of the study period, but subsequently had further problems with redundancy, disappointment with his Cypriot relatives and sexual disturbance (exposing himself and following girls in the street). After several further admissions (at his own request)

to St Ann's Hospital, following Friern closure, he died unexpectedly after jumping off the balcony of the hostel in which he had
been placed, although never having talked of suicide.

The last man in the group, aged 61, is intermittently aggressive
and has actively resisted any further attempts at rehabilitation.
He remained in hospital beyond the study period and transferred,
as a resident of Friern's remaining rehabilitation ward, to St Ann's
Hospital, where he is visited quite often by his twin brother.

If Haven Four had come into existence, with its domestic style
of care, it would almost certainly have provided a better home
and more scope for rehabilitation for the first three women and
possibly for the last man. The one who died needed the support
of a hospital setting, but one which could allow some independence and personal choice on a day-to-day basis, more
characteristic of hostel-style care. This form of asylum could have
been provided in Haven Four. Hopefully the outcome for the man
successfully resettled into the sheltered flat would have been the
same had Haven Four been available.

The Haven Five group

This group of six was the most diverse, and contained patients
for whom there was still hope of a suitable placement becoming
available in the community. They could be said to represent a
sample out of the large number of long-stay patients who were
identified as candidates for sheltered reprovision homes, some of
whom would prove to be in need of long-term asylum in the
Haven.

There were three women and three men in the group, whose
ages ranged from 39 to 72, four having primary diagnoses of schizophrenia and two having severe neuroses. The oldest patient was
a man with profound depressive obsessional neurosis for whom
rehabilitation attempts were unsuccessful during the study period.
He remains at the time of writing in the St Ann's rehabilitation
ward, still depressed and preoccupied with his bowels. One of the
women also transferred to St Ann's as a resident of the rehabilitation ward. She had previously been fit and well on a regular
dose of neuroleptic, leading a relatively independent life at Friern.
Her previous admissions to the hospital had been caused by
relapses as a result of non-compliance with medication, and this
pattern has continued despite her being placed for six months in

a 24-hour staffed sheltered flatlet scheme. Unfortunately she became paranoid again in this placement, refusing to take her medication and having to be re-admitted to hospital before the end of the study period because of fire risk and threatening behaviour. She had also begun to move the furniture into an adjacent coppice where she preferred to sleep.

Two of the Haven Five group, one man and one woman, successfully moved with other patients from Friern into a private residential care home. The woman, who was 39 years old and suffered from unpleasant tactile hallucinations, was motivated by having a close relationship with a more able male patient who had already moved into the home, and together they assist in practical tasks for the staff for which they receive some remuneration.

The other two patients making up the group both tried living in a reprovision sheltered home. One, with relapsing schizophrenia, returned to hospital after a short community stay and by the end of the study period had been taken into a hospital unit in the neighbouring Enfield district, as she has no links with Haringey. The other, a 59-year-old woman with depressive neurosis, was placed in a reprovision home but developed signs of dementia. After several years of the staff attempting to overcome her profound reluctance to attend to her personal needs in the home, she was referred on to a mental health annexe to a part III home, a year after Friern closure.

In summary, half of the group are, at the time of writing, living on a rehabilitation ward because, as anticipated, they are difficult to place in the community and might have made more progress in Haven Five. The outcome for the other three would probably have been similar. There are, however, other 'non-Haven' long-stay patients who, it was initially hoped, might be resettled in the community, but are now also in the rehabilitation ward which is unsatisfactory (see Section on p. 159). Haven Five would have been an ideal environment in which their potential could have been maximised through rehabilitation. Those needing a long term hospital home, such as the 51-year-old woman mentioned above, could have graduated on to Haven Six.

The Haven Six group

The Haven six group were all older patients, with ages ranging from 61 to 87. They were all suffering from chronic schizophrenia and were prone to aggressive outbursts at times. This had prevented previous rehabilitation being successful and they had, between them, an average length of hospital stay of forty years. They used opportunities for activity off the ward, some attending the gymnasium and others the industrial therapy workshop, and they had loose social networks, based mainly on non-verbal types of communication e.g. the exchange of cigarettes. Two had sisters living nearby but saw little of them, and one, a man with profound secondary dementia, had relatives who visited from Camden. The Camden (Hampstead Health Authority) team later took responsibility for placing this patient, with the Haringey team taking responsibility, by way of reciprocity, for a Camden patient with Haringey links. One other patient in the Haven Six group was placed by the Enfield Health Authority on one of its psychogeriatric wards.

The reprovision outcome for this group involved one of the women being settled into a home staffed by ex-Friern nurses and the other three being moved into a local authority part III home mental health annexe, where the eldest of them has since died.

Although the outcome for two of these patients was satisfactory without Haven Six, and could not have been particularly improved upon by being placed in it, the four who ended up in homes for the elderly would have benefited greatly from the daytime opportunities of the Haven development, the more familiar parkland setting and the freer style of care.

Summary of the patients' outcome

In conclusion, as can be seen from Figure 7.3, over half (twenty) of the surviving patients who were identified in Friern for the Haven (thirty-six) were still in hospital at the end of the reprovision resettlement programme for Haringey (as some were in hospital in other districts). Five, including one younger patient with pre-senile dementia, were placed in mental health annexes attached to part III local authority homes for the elderly, where the style of care is more institutional than the Haven would have been. However, nine people had been settled in sheltered homes and one, somewhat unsatisfactorily, in independent accommodation.

At the time of writing, the same number of people is in sheltered accommodation, some having been recently discharged from the hospital, thus counteracting losses in terms of the total

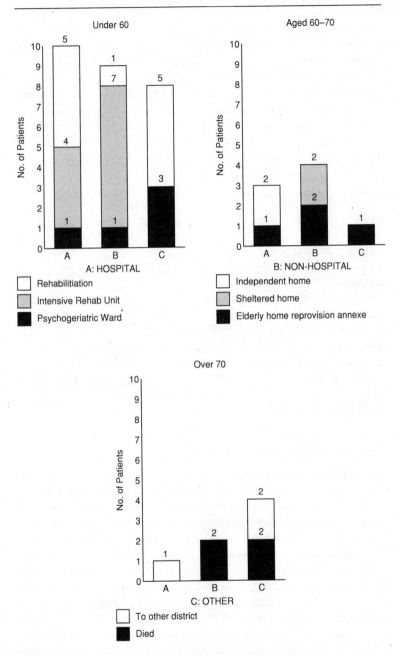

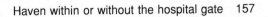

Figure 7.3 Reprovision outcome for Haven study group

number, from others dying or moving on to homes for the elderly. It is noteworthy that six of the ten deaths in the original Haven group have been in the under-60 age group, although only one is probably through suicide. This, together with the greater than expected number of suicides/unexpected deaths among potential long-stay patients in West Haringey during recent years obviously gives rise to some concern. The higher death rate might have been avoided were an environment available providing an acceptable form of asylum (see Section on p. 162).

Planned hospital provision

In addition to the Haven groups whose placement outcomes I have described above, there were four patients among the Haringey long-stay population at Friern who were considered too disturbed to be looked after in the Haven unit and were expected to continue living in the Intensive Rehabilitation Unit to be transferred from Friern to St Ann's. At that time, this unit was occupied by patients from three of the catchment area districts, an arrangement that was expected to continue after closure when the unit was relocated. In fact the unit was reprovided by Haringey HA at the St Ann's Hospital site in order for intensive care to be given to the chronically disturbed and to allow for behavioural regimes to be available for those who are unresponsive to ordinary treatment programmes.

Potential new long-stay provision

One of the most interesting findings from assessing the destination of Haringey patients in the Friern reprovision process is the large number of potentially 'new long-stay' patients requiring care. There are thirty-seven who had been in hospital for over six months during the study period. These patients represent quite a separate group to the original long-stay Haven candidates but might have benefited from its existence by taking up places freed when some of the original Haven occupants would have been effectively rehabilitated and moved on. The majority of those patients with stays of more than six months were relatively young homeless people suffering from schizophrenia. Most had been in hospital before their current admission, i.e. they were so called 'revolving door' patients, but had been unable to return to their previous address because of a deterioration in their level of functioning or because of carers at home being no longer able to cope. Nineteen of these patients were still in hospital at the end of the study period, twelve in a rehabilitation ward, three on acute admission wards because of their level of disturbance, and four receiving therapy in the Intensive Rehabilitation Unit.

Significantly, eighteen of these potentially new long-stay patients had been placed in reprovision homes which would not have been available for the revolving door group prior to the reprovision exercise. These places came from the pool originally intended for Claybury as well as for Friern patients but which was diverted to Friern usage only, in order to ensure that the latter hospital closed on time. There were also some places available through the failure to discharge some of the old long-stay patients. Using these reprovision places for this non-reprovision group enabled the remaining Haringey Friern patients to transfer into the available space in the new resource opened at St Ann's Hospital.

SERVICE IMPLICATIONS

There are two serious issues which have a bearing on service provision requirements. The first pertains to the quality of care. In general, as has already been noted, there was a sizeable number of patients who could not be settled in community homes despite all the efforts prior to Friern closure, and for whom asylum had to take the form of a hospital ward. For some, this hospital residence was in a homogeneous unit for older people or for the younger behaviourally disturbed, but for others it was in a mixed group on a rehabilitation ward.

Without a Haven-type range of smaller units with different styles of care and catering for different age groups, it is very difficult to provide a satisfactory standard of care for long-stay and potentially new long-stay patients who remain mixed together on a rehabilitation ward. It is demoralising for those younger patients who have been admitted from unsatisfactory community placements to be in a large ward with people suffering from unresponsive chronic schizophrenia and pre-senile dementia. Furthermore, staff attention is constantly absorbed by these latter groups, who need continuous observation and a lot of physical care, and staff are thus deflected in their efforts to rehabilitate potentially new long-stay patients, with disastrous consequences.

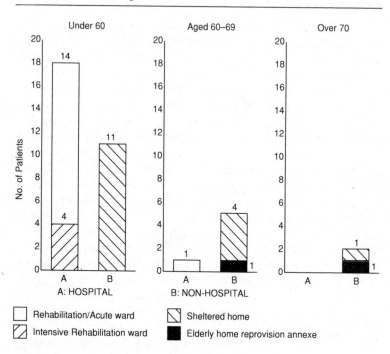

Figure 7.4 Placement of potentially new long-stay inpatients (i.e. six months plus) during five-year study period prior to closure

Some can become institutionalised, dependent on the 'hotel' services of the hospital and lose their confidence to make decisions. Others become more disturbed when demoralised and can enter a vicious circle of a deterioration in mental state which then reduces the scope for discharge.

The quality of care is equally unsatisfactory for the older more chronically disturbed patients. They can become unsettled by those in a more acute phase of illness and deteriorate themselves or even may be injured occasionally, for example when pestering a volatile younger person for cigarettes.

The second serious issue pertains to the quantity of care provided, in particular for the younger patients. The placement problem for potential new long-stay patients which I have highlighted has been masked by the Friern closure programme. This is demonstrated by the extent to which more recently admitted/readmitted younger patients, not in the original long-stay group, have been settled long term in reprovision homes (see Figure 7.4). In total, sixteen new long-stay patients occupied sheltered reprovision places, financed with uniquely available capital and revenue from the hospital closure.

This group includes people with unresponsive or fluctuating chronic disorder, for whom community placements tend to break down after a while and for whom readmissions can be lengthy while they restabilise and while efforts are made to find a new community placement for them. Some of these patients were therefore, in reality, the old long-stay of the recent past. However, the majority had illnesses of fairly recent onset.

At the time of Friern closure, eight patients under the age of 60, originally expected to be on the hospital site, either in the Haven or in the intensive rehabilitation unit, had been placed in the community, but there were still fifteen potentially new long-stay patients in Haringey non-acute beds for whom placements had to be found. Since then, an additional small, but significant number of new patients have accumulated for whom care cannot be provided by the local social services department, the voluntary sector or private care homes. This is sometimes not just because staffing levels are inadequate for their care needs, but for other reasons mentioned previously e.g. low public acceptability of behaviour or the patient lacking insight into the need to take medication reliably to prevent relapse. These patients have become new long-stay along with a few who have come back into hospital from reprovision homes because of persistent behavioural problems after several unsuccessful attempts to resettle them.

The time of Friern closure therefore represented a peak of community placement availability, since which there has been a gradual build-up of difficult to discharge patients. At the time of writing, this is contributing to an acute bed shortage not only in the Haringey District Unit but throughout the old catchment area of Friern, with all beds occupied not only in the NHS units but in the private sector also (from which DHAs are forced to buy places for acute admissions). Making savings through reproviding a reduced number of psychiatric beds is not only causing disruption to the service but is also in danger of proving to be a false economy.

A compromise solution would be to adapt buildings on a district hospital site into smaller functional units with specific roles and styles of care along Haven unit lines. Any domestic-style housing available can be of great value, especially as it is usually located on the periphery of the site, and adapting a ward can be a last resort to provide a separate location for the most disabled, i.e. Haven Two equivalent. This would enable staff to work more effectively with each group of patients. Those who could return to the community would make faster progress, releasing beds, while others could settle into a satisfactory lifestyle on site.

COMMUNITY AND THE ROLE OF ASYLUM

The power of terminology to influence public opinion in a misleading way is epitomised in the effect of the phrase 'community care'. Its current usage as a synonym for non-hospital-based support, in antithesis to the asylum care of the large mental hospital, inevitably gives rise to the notion that asylums are isolating places, devoid of a social structure in which the individual patient can find a valued role and feel a sense of community. In practice, the reverse often pertains, though not in every aspect.

A definition of 'community' is 'a body of individuals with awareness of some unifying trait' (Merriam-Webster, 1986). For the successful identification as part of a community to be a positive experience, certain criteria have to be fulfilled:

1 Recognition of a unifying trait e.g. the shared task of living with the disability of a mental health problem.
2 A sense of belonging and acceptability, without which the common ground can just be a source of frustration.
3 Continuity of relationships, which provides the context for belonging to a continuing network of supportive people.

The large mental hospital asylums, though having other serious disadvantages, did fulfil these prerequisites for providing a beneficial community more effectively in some ways than community care settings do. In terms of category 1 above, they provided a social setting in which people with similar disabilities were part of a large group. Mixing within this they could find others of a similar age group and attitude with whom they could form a stronger bond (even resulting in marriage occasionally). The much smaller groupings in community homes are more restrictive in this regard, and the less adventurous or unmotivated do not make the effort required to attend a day resource or community facility, particularly as a journey on public transport is often necessitated.

However, some prefer to ignore their disability, coping through the strategy of denial. For them, living in a mental hospital is inevitably unacceptable, and associated with an unwelcome stigma. Unfortunately, often group living in community settings with others suffering from mental illness is equally unacceptable for them and brings its own frustrations.

In terms of category 2 above, a sense of belonging and acceptability was one of the most positive characteristics of the asylums. Within their confines, tolerance existed of a much greater range of behaviour than would be acceptable in most places, and because of the historical context, this usually extended to the local environs as well, especially the shops. The staff also tended to form a friendly network, becoming very familiar with the patients and each other over the years. Finally, the social club and coffee bar were places where patients could feel part of a normal peer group, and a number of ex-patients would return regularly to meet up with their friends at the club.

For some, living in 'community homes' can increase stress. The close proximity of other non-handicapped people with no disability who have the scope for earning a living, buying a home and bringing up a family, can lead to a feeling of isolation, resentment and bitterness.

The public attitude to residents in any individual home covers a range of response. At one extreme it can be welcoming and positively supportive, if somewhat patronising, and at the other, rejecting and critical. For most, it is wary indifference.

For all, the stigma of mental illness hovers in the background, fed by fear and misunderstanding. It is powerfully associated with large mental hospital sites, but can hopefully be greatly reduced around single community homes. Sadly, it can create a barrier between any mental health resource and the surrounding population, which one day may be minimalised through public education.

In terms of category 3 above, continuity of positive relationships is a crucial part of an effective community. It is often overlooked that the patients in large asylums benefit from contact with a consistent group of the general public in the form of the staff, ancillary as well as nursing, who often spend most of their working lives in one hospital. The scale of the organisation and scope for rotation within it provide a measure of variety for the staff as well as patients, resulting in a settled, family-type atmosphere. Although this carries inherent risks of institutionalisation, which need to be specifically counteracted, it is greatly preferable to the rapid staff turnover occurring in many of our reprovision homes.

In these community homes, the day-to-day responsibility for ensuring that basic tasks of self-care are performed by a small unchanging group of people can be very wearing. Progress is often minimal and considerable effort is needed just to maintain the level of functioning. Contact with other colleagues is much lower than would occur in a hospital setting, and the staff involved usually have less training and more unrealistic expectations. It is therefore hardly surprising that few staff stay more than two years in one home and so the relationships that residents form with them are more intense but transient.

In summary, there is much that fostered an effective caring community on the old asylum sites, which was particularly of benefit to people with a high level of disability, and is often lacking in the smaller-scale community homes. The advantages were primarily due to the hospital size, and would still apply to a Haven-type of development which would provide a non-institutional style of care, encouraging individual choice in a less stigmatised group of domestic scale buildings.

RETREAT AND THE ROLE OF ASYLUM

Apart from a sense of belonging to a large flexible community, there are other subtle ways in which the asylums could meet psychological needs, some of which go unacknowledged and unrecognised, but which, in effect, can make the difference between satisfactory and unsatisfactory care in community homes. The lack of the asylum to meet psychological needs can result in those who leave it seeking to retreat back to hospital in order to escape the demands of the world at large. In this respect it is important to note the finding of Dayson and Sammut's (1992) study that there is a higher prevalence of anxiety among hospital leavers at a point two years after their discharge to sheltered accommodation than at the time of their leaving hospital. Explanations for this finding can be suggested as follows.

First, retreat can be needed from the general public who are in closer proximity when patients are resident outside hospital in a community home. This can increase anxiety through a subconscious fear of failure to cover up disability, or fear of rejection because of it. Sometimes this undermines rehabilitation attempts, particularly when the paranoid tendencies of schizophrenia increase susceptibility. The loss of the wider tolerant environs of the large mental hospital can take its toll in this way.

Second, anxiety may be gradually generated in a community residence, and retreat become increasingly necessary because of difficult relationships within the home. In practice the majority of people with chronic mental illness are suffering from schizophrenia. It is now well established that one of the key factors in maintaining a remission of this order is the avoidance of high expressed emotion relationships (i.e. relationships of a highly charged nature in which the sufferer is the butt of critical comment), or the limitation of time spent in face-to-face contact with anyone interacting with the sufferer in such a way. Yet such interactions have been noted by Kuipers (1992) between staff members and one or two residents in 42 per cent of the community homes in which Friern and Claybury patients have been resettled. These strained relationships can easily build up in the limited confines of a small home, for the reasons already mentioned to do with the lack of a large network of staff and patients to interact with that the hospital was able to provide. In the early stages, the strain can manifest itself as anxiety, and, if persisting, can lead to retreat into the less intensive atmosphere of the larger more anonymous pool of the hospital ward.

Third, hospital asylum often provides an obvious type of retreat in that admission allows an escape from the responsibilities of adult life. This goes beyond the practical aspect of provision of 'hotel' services, to include the psychological aspect of the parenting role often assumed by the staff. At its worst this takes the form of a patronising dominance, but at its best it can give an ego-affirming framework in which emotional development can take place, previously stunted by the interlinked effect of mental illness and rejection by those who were nearest and dearest. Initially, dependency needs emerge and regression occurs, but in a supporting structured environment, emotional growth can follow gradually as an inner sense of security is fostered. Although this can also take place in any home with a therapeutic milieu, the initial regressive behaviour cannot readily be tolerated in a sheltered home unless well provided with psychotherapeutically experienced staff. Hence anxiety is likely to show itself in relation to the lack of willingness of home staff to tolerate regressive behaviour.

It is thus important to note that lesser degrees of practical regression do occur at times when ex-patients have minor relapses, or become intolerant of the continued effort of having to carry out day-to-day chores. Brief periods of respite care or extra help can prevent these developing into a more serious relapse. For a few, persistent symptoms can lead to chronic emotional dependency and a further resistance to discharge from the safe, womb-like environment of the hospital asylum.

Finally, there is one last sense in which anxiety in the community may be related to the loss of retreat in the asylum. The hospital asylum did permit an avoidance of the potential reality of incurability. The simple fact of being in a hospital is a tacit acknowledgement that illness continues, that efforts to treat it are still being made and that the sufferer has not become 'well' enough to be expected to live outside hospital indefinitely on their current treatment and at their level of disability. It has been noteworthy that, despite preferring their community home to hospital, a little while after discharge several patients have begun to talk of suicide and become very negative about the future, and one has died under circumstance of deliberate self-harm. Hope for the future is precious for those who are essentially healthy, but for people coping with unpleasant psychiatric symptoms it is of profound importance, especially for those in early adulthood. It is of great importance that the step out of hospital asylum does not become a step away from active care and that access to new therapeutic options is emphasised both for the present and the future.

CONCLUSION: PLANNING RECOMMENDATIONS

In studying the practical outcome of the Friern Hospital closure for the patients whose resettlement was the responsibility of the Haringey Health Authority, a number of important issues have arisen. These are likely not only to have relevance for similar urban areas, but have significance for the closure plans of other large psychiatric hospitals and, hopefully, for the development of better services in the future for those suffering from chronic mental illness.

To summarise the service planning implications, there is a clear need for a range of domestic-scale units providing specifically for the diverse needs of those for whom sheltered accommodation in the community is impracticable (e.g. those with pre-senile dementia and young people with unresponsive schizophrenia who are persistently disturbed). These units would be most effectively provided if clustered at the periphery of a hospital site, but in suitably adapted accommodation and with individualised care programmes.

There is also a need for adequate resources off the hospital site to be made available for the care of the younger potentially new long-stay patients in the medium term, who have recently been occupying community placements which were intended primarily for the care of the so-called old long-stay population.

In considering 'community' and the role of asylum, I have raised two specific planning issues. First, the advantages of contact with a wide group of people with similar health needs was noted, to increase the sense of belonging and acceptance, and to reduce the potential for interpersonal conflict. This could be aided by developing a varied range of daytime occupations with good transport links of a flexible variety.

Second the acknowledgement of the strain on staff in small homes is important, and the need for a career structure that enables them to have a change of client group without totally losing contact with those currently in their care. This could be achieved by developing rotational links with other homes in the district.

Finally I have highlighted a further two issues in discussing the role of retreat. There are particular ways in which the pattern of life in sheltered accommodation imposes a strain, particularly on those who suffer from schizophrenia. It is clearly important to have flexible respite care available, to provide a break from the practical and emotional demands of living in a small community home.

Last, but by no means least, the important need emerged for an active continued input after discharge from hospital, both to review ongoing health care problems and to consider recent developments in treatment availability, in order to help each patient view the future with some hope and self-respect. This, ultimately, has to be the aim of any pattern of care.

REFERENCES

Dayson, D. and Sammut, R. (1992) 'Long-stay patients two years after discharge from hospital', *Seventh Annual Conference of TAPS, Summary of Proceedings*, London: North East Thames Regional Health Authority.

Friern Hospital Medical Committee (1983) In-patient survey.

Hunter, R. and Macalpine, I. (1974) *Psychiatry for the Poor*, Folkestone: Dawsons.

Kuipers, E. (1992) 'Expressed emotion in staff: implications for optimum care practices in persistent mental illness', *Seventh Annual Conference of TAPS, Summary of Proceedings,* London: North East Thames Regional Health Authority.

Merriam-Webster (1986) *Webster's Third New International Dictionary*, Volume A to G, London: Encyclopaedia Britannica.

Wing, J.K. and Furlong, R. (1986) 'A haven for the severely disabled within the context of a comprehensive psychiatric service', *British Journal of Psychiatry*, 149: 449–457.

Winslow, F. (1849) 'The new county asylum for Middlesex', *Journal for Psychological Medicine and Mental Pathology*, 490.

Wolfson, P. (1992) 'New measures for new environments', *Seventh Annual Conference of TAPS, Summary of Proceedings*, London: North East Thames Regional Health Authority.

Chapter 8

The American, Flemish and British cases of asylum in the community

Dylan Tomlinson

To what extent have attempts been made in Europe and America to establish asylum in the community? Asking this question presupposes that asylum is a desirable facility. As Scull points out in Chapter One, the term asylum has become associated with images of containment and social control, and not with images of relief from cruelty, personal crisis or persecution. Even Parry Jones' (1988) notion of 'passive asylum' suggests that while patients gave some form of latent agreement or tacit consent to an admission and detention in hospital there was nothing volitional about this form of asylum.

THE AMERICAN CASE

In the context of the USA, the fact that these negative images are associated with asylum has led to a situation where almost any argument in favour of asylum is dismissed as a summons for the return of psychiatric institutions. Zipple, for example, argues that 'asylum is not a useful concept' being 'extremely vague' and having 'defied any description that does not make it seem like the kinds of institutions we abandoned, although belatedly, long ago' (Zipple *et al.*, 1987: 540). Thus, in Zipple's view, though proponents of asylum routinely disclaim their calling for a return to psychiatric hospitals, they are unable to offer any definition of an asylum service which can clearly distinguish it from the structured, tolerant and supervised facilities provided by such hospitals.

Lamb (1988) provides the boldest argument for asylum from a clinician working in the American context. He argues that there is a need for asylum in two forms, those of structure, in order that the client be engaged in a level of activity, and protection, so as to prevent the client becoming a victim of self-neglect. For these two conditions of asylum to be met, the daily living situation must, ordinarily, be supervised by co-resident carers. Asylum could therefore, in this respect, be given in 'family' homes, or in board with care homes, just as it could be given in some psychiatric institutions, depending on the degree of nurturing required to engage and protect the client.

Those who are critical of the belief held by Lamb and others that asylum is a property of supervised living situations argue that this demonstrates quite clearly that its advocates are not in favour of non-institutional solutions that would allow independent living for long-term sufferers of mental illness. The implication of arguments for asylum is thus that those clients who are guided by staff visiting, rather than living in their own homes, cannot receive asylum.

Since asylum is held to be inimical to the goal of achieving independent living in this way, it is rejected altogether by many clinicians in the USA, and it does not have a place in official policy. Schroeder (1987), for example, as Director of a county mental health system, explicitly states that his Wisconsin-based system does not provide asylum. Instead, non-institutional mental health services in the USA are being developed through the adoption of 'community support systems' (CSS). The CSS approach represents the programme for addressing long-term mental health problems which is promoted by the government's National Institute for Mental Health (NIMH). Its main aim is to keep people who suffer from such problems *in situ* i.e. domiciled in the their own homes rather than in care homes or hospitals.

The construction of CSS as a policy conceived in opposition to that of asylum is illustrated in Parrish's highlighting of what she calls the *mission* of the movement which is to 'help people with severe mental disorders succeed in living in their own homes in the community alongside other citizens' (Parrish, 1989). Sheltered living situations are regarded as transitional in the system and are to be succeeded by independence.

CSS consists of twelve elements (Anthony and Blanch, 1989):

1   Client identification and outreach – finding clients, informing them about services and 'engaging' them with those services.
2   Mental health treatment – chemotherapy and psychotherapy.
3   Health and dental services – general medical and dental care.

4 Crisis response services – family crisis therapy, walk-in crisis services, crisis residential programmes.

5 Housing – transitional sheltered living and help to achieve permanent housing.

6 Income support and entitlements – welfare rights assistance.

7 Peer support – towards improving the social networks of service users.

8 Family and community support – educational and self- and advocacy initiatives.

9 Rehabilitation services to develop the skills of users in the community – especially employment skills.

10 Protection and advocacy – to heighten patients' awareness of and ability to take action on their rights both individually and collectively.

11 Case management – to improve outcome and lessen the drop-out rate from programmes.

12 Systems integration – pursuing a legislative and inter-agency framework in local states to improve service delivery.

This system is thus based on a rejection of the structure and protection by co-resident carers which Lamb deems to be key components of asylum. Zipple again, for example, argues that 'controlled, protective, isolated long-term settings' cannot be helpful for people with severe mental illness (1987: 541). In CSS, any structure and protection are to be supplied, pre-packaged, by care managers operating from community bases, and not by the process of relocating the sufferer to a structured and protected environment. In a booklet prepared for NIMH for those delivering and consuming CSS, no mention is made of the word asylum (NIMH, 1988).

CSS does, however, in addition to its recognition of the role played by 'transitional sheltered living', allow that in some instances there will be a need for clients to have access to care homes into which they can be received at certain times. These institutional solutions, albeit of limited duration, form part of CSS' 'crisis assistance'. This is 'conceptualised as a range of responses to be used in crisis situations', with it being anticipated that crisis residential services will be required for a certain proportion of clients. Such residential settings are, nevertheless, to be of a limited kind in relation to the possible use of them for asylum. They are to be provided for a short term only and to be 'non-hospital' in nature.

It is interesting that in an earlier NIMH prospectus Clark Turner and Shifren (1979) do include explicit provision for asylum in the array of CSS components to be provided. These authors refer to the need for a range of options, 'including twenty-four hour emergency telephone services, trained personnel able to visit the client's home or work place and places in the community that offer treatment of emergent psychiatric symptoms or at least *asylum from unendurable stress*' (1979: 4) (my emphasis). Where intensive care is required, crisis hostels, crisis foster homes (with trained mental health back-up), community treatment programmes, and halfway houses are required 'as alternatives to hospitalisation' (ibid.: 5).

The missionary nature of CSS then, is clearly linked to the way in which the notion of asylum is so bitterly contested in the USA. To advocate asylum is to advocate for the undermining of clients' self-esteem (by assuming schizophrenics do not get better); to support vested interests (the unions of hospital workers who wish to preserve their institutional bases); to put profit above client interests (by preferring board with care and nursing homes to outreach programmes); and to encourage family disownership of kin who become ill (by preferring clients to be treated outside the family) (Parrish, 1989). The bitterness of the conflict reflects the difficulty which has been experienced by proponents of CSS is wresting a greater share of the resources spent on services for mentally ill from the government subsidies given to hospitals and residential care homes through grants and insurance. Rejection of asylum is linked to rejection of private nursing homes as a failed element of the deinstitutionalisation programme (Brown, 1985), a solution which should not be endorsed in programmes for community services advocated by informed practitioners and planners (Clark-Turner and Ten Hoor, 1978).

On one level, the American debate suggests that any form of supervised residential care cannot meet the requirements for a minimum level of social rights, or citizenship in Marshall's (1963) terms to be granted to the sufferer, that is, the possession of a sufficient income, of adequate and secure shelter and the benefit of protection from exploitation or abuse in order for he or she to enjoy full participation in the community. Sufficient income for the leisure and recreation opportunities enjoyed by the 'average citizen' is obviously not consistent with the provision of social security to meet minimum needs that will constitute the entitlement of most. Adequate and secure shelter is inconsistent with the encouragement of owner occupation in USA and UK policy, which form of housing tenure is in turn dependent on the occupier being in stable, well-paid employment. Most long-term sufferers will not achieve such an employment situation. Protection from exploitation and abuse, historically, would seem a function ill-suited to many forms of residential care (Martin, 1984).

The wider context of USA social policy, and the contamination by its principles of, or the leaking out of its principles into, British and European systems in which social class, as a form of social solidarity has historically been more important, cannot be ignored. Its support for competitive individualism (Ginsburg, 1992) as opposed to social solidarity, and anti-statism (Friedman, 1962) are of obvious importance for the liberal revolution by which one can almost suggest that a policy of society without the state, in relation to welfare, is being pursued. The corollary of such principles is clearly that it will be hard for any County or State authority to justify more than temporary protection from competitive individualism for clients of the mental health service. As Scull comments in Chapter One of this volume, the mentally ill are unlikely to benefit, in this sense from being cared for by health services rather than social care services. State structuring of the ill person's life by medical services will not be deemed appropriate for more than an extremely limited period. By definition therefore it is difficult to see how the giving of asylum, as relief from poverty, persecution, or inadequate accounting for oneself (see Chapter 6) can be sanctioned for more than recurring temporary periods. Such asylum, inevitably, will be granted under increasingly stringent conditions.

Family care, in this context, perhaps offers the only feasible kind of provision within which longer-term asylum can be granted. Family protection and structuring are sanctioned on the basis of its higher moral authority and higher caring ability than any other sector of the care economy.

THE FLEMISH CASE

In this respect, 'Europe's first therapeutic community' in Geel (Roosens, 1979) is worthy of study. It was developed in a skeletal form over 700 years ago, when pilgrims seeking a cure for their 'Haughtiness' or 'Impurity', to which mental illness was at the time attributed, as one Belgian historian has it, came to the town in praise of St Dympna. The legend of St Dympna was based on Dympna choosing to be killed by her father rather than submit to his incestuousness towards her, and, in such an act of sacrifice curing her father of his rage and impurity. The pilgrims to Geel were lodged by local townspeople and, in this way, a tradition of lodging for the mentally ill developed, and subsequently, family care in association with the Geel psychiatric hospital. By 1979, more than 1,300 patients of the hospital were lodged among the 30,000 residents of the town.

While the town is noted as being a town of charity, the extensive study carried out by Roosens and his colleagues indicates that, as the origin of the lodging of the mentally ill suggests, charity or brotherly/sisterly love was not the main motive of the residents. Indeed, in more than a thousand interviews with heads of host families, only once was charity mentioned spontaneously as the motive for a lodger from the Rijkscolonie (the psychiatric hospital) being taken in. The need for money was the most common reason for taking in a lodger, and Roosens notes that in the more affluent times in which his study was undertaken, it had become a mark of social status not to have a patient lodging in one's home.

In what respects does the Geel system provide for asylum seeking and asylum retaining? Boarding out at Geel can be usefully examined, in this respect, in relation to three questions:

1 How do patients get into family care?
2 Which patients are excluded from family care?
3 What demands of the patient are made by family care in relation to patients' propensity to seek privacy and withdrawal from society?

Taking the first two questions together, Roosens' work and the publication of the Flemish Ministry indicate that arrangements for entry to the town's board with care scheme do not differ from those pertaining to adult fostering arrangements elsewhere. Patients are referred to the 'Centre for Family Care', which co-ordinates out-patient services and host family placements on behalf of the hospital. The Centre has a number of requirements that a patient should meet. Firstly, the patient must be Dutch-speaking. Second, the patient must be able to cope with crisis situations that occur in the family (with the hospital taking an IQ of 70 or above as a rough guide to a patient possessing such ability). Third, mobility is necessary. Fourth, pronounced person-ality disorder or paranoia is a 'counter-indication' to placement. Fifth, committed patients are not considered suitable for family care. Finally 'extreme "uncontrollable" patients are not placed in the families. Experience seems to have demonstrated that, for these people, life is not possible in an open, normal environment' (Roosens, 1979: 34).

Many 'chronic patients' are thus well able to meet the require-ments of boarding out. In relation to their hypothesised need to cling on to asylum-as-retreat, which is a focus of this book, it is worth noting that a small minority of the 1,300 boarders in Roosens' study (4.7 per cent) do not speak at all to their host families. A further 5.5 per cent are noted as occasionally mumbling a little, and another 21.2 per cent to answer when spoken to. Thus, about a third of boarders show some similarity, at least in rela-tion to verbal communication, with those long-stay patients who were recorded as being 'unable to give an account of themselves' whilst resident in Friern and Claybury hospitals (Chapter 6).

Nevertheless, a further layer of selection criteria was encoun-tered by Roosens' team in its interviews with townspeople. In the town, host families drew a distinction between a 'good' patient, who was valued and who they wanted to keep, and a 'bad' patient who they did not value and who would be returned to hospital if too bad for the family. A good patient was one who worked well, either in carrying out light domestic chores or in assisting on the farms where many boarders were traditionally placed. A good one was also someone who was relatively placid in demeanour and pliant in behaviour and able to perceive the environment and events in it accurately, at least to certain degree. A bad one, by contrast, was someone who did not work or assist the family, was disturbed in demeanour and anti-social in behaviour. Historically, all kinds of 'bad' and aggressive patients were sent to Geel, with some having to be put in irons and physically restrained in other ways (Roosens, 1979: 29).

Even in the contemporary period, the distinction drawn by Geelians between the 'good' and the 'bad' has not resulted in the exclusion of bad boarders altogether. In this respect, again one can conjecture that, transported to Geel, some of the more hostile of the 'unaccounted for' in the Friern and Claybury study would have been accepted for placement, even if only between spells of return to hospital. For example, a 'bad one' is described in

Roosens' study, whose behaviour was characterised by obstinate and domineering actions towards the family, and who refused to work. She would shout when asked to do something, though at other times hardly speaking, and bang her fists on the table. She was described as being incontinent 'from sheer stubbornness', each time putting her soiled linen in the closet and not allowing the host mother to take it out of her room for cleaning. While this patient returned to hospital eventually, another 'bad one' is described by Roosens who was tolerated for a long time and eventually became a 'good one'. Even so transformed the patient still got his 'whims', having become enraged, for instance, that his bed was too narrow and having not been satisfied until he got a new one. As a 'good one', the same patient could still not bear to have any men in the house and, tellingly, for the theme of asylum, only when left alone in the house did he feel in control.

A third patient, from Roosens' sample, an epileptic, was also tolerated by the host family who were happy for her to stay with them even though they experienced her as 'primarily someone who is difficult to live with' (Roosens, 1979: 42). This patient's placement is also significant in terms of hypothesised needs for asylum, in that she did not like to be with people, and was very unsociable when the family had visitors, though eavesdropping on their conversations. She was described by her host family as being troublesome when menstruating and to be prone to having tantrums which the family tried to ignore. The epilepsy itself seems to have been the least of the difficulties from the family's perspective.

The ability of host families to provide an accepting environment in these situations is confirmed by the Ministry of the Flemish Community (1990: 16) which asserts that the only difference between such families and 'the average family in the area' is that 'they have learned from childhood to live naturally with mentally handicapped people'. 'Because of this,' the Ministry continues, 'the concept of "fear" has retreated well into the background', with 'a higher level of tolerance of certain types of behaviour' having developed among foster families.

Moving on to the third question raised above, concerning the demands of the patient made by the family care system, perhaps the most important requirement is that the boarder remains a patient and can be recalled to hospital at any time. This status, in a sense, condemns the boarder to be regarded as someone of diminished responsibility and who cannot be an equal of non-boarders.

The difference in status is maintained in both overt and covert ways. Overtly, each patient is collected by bus and taken every fortnight to 'hygienic inspections' at the 'de Werft sanitary bath installation'. Despite the regimentation of such an arrangement, most patients are said to enjoy these occasions for their social opportunities. According to Roosens, beer is prohibited by the Rijkskolonie, although the prohibition is apparently nowhere respected. Patients are all but excluded from being members of voluntary organisations in the town, on the grounds that, belonging to a 'special class of people' they cannot be taken seriously, and thus that they would not qualify as members of an association (Roosens, 1979: 151).

Other ways in which patients' social life is restricted in Geel are apparent in the fashion in which their status as a 'special class of people' leads to them being refused as potential partners of the townspeople. In the town's bars, people who engage in conversation with patients do so in a tone which is either 'jocular or benevolent and condescending'. As Roosens goes on to explain:

> Provoking patients a little on the dance floor seems to be tolerated without evoking any reaction from the public. He can be laughed at to his face, he can be refused several dances in a humiliating manner, all without provoking any social response. Everyone accepts that one relates to patients in a different way than to ordinary human beings. The patient's social inferiority is taken for granted, because he is one from 'under the high trees' – a euphemism for the psychiatric hospital.
>
> (Roosens, 1979: 137)

THE BRITISH CASE

In 1984, the case for asylum was examined by the House of Commons Social Services Committee. Members of the committee felt that there had been a change among 'informed opinion' about whether the provision of asylum was necessary or not. Whereas in the years following the 1959 Mental Health Act community care had been pitted against institutional care on account of the disabling effects of the latter, by the 1980s some of the virtues of institutional care were being rediscovered. The Committee thus noted the 'growing recognition that "institutions" – meaning primarily hospitals – may have fulfilled at least one function which has to be replicated should they be replaced: that of "asylum", by which is meant the *provision of shelter and refuge*' (House of Commons Social Services Committee, 1985) (my emphasis). Informed opinion had given up the idea of the massive reductions in the need for long-term care being achieved by the switch of services and accommodation to community settings, and was 'returning to the idea that there will always be a substantial number of mentally disabled people who are entitled to some sort of protection and support, *which may involve their partial withdrawal from the rest of the community*' (ibid.: para 25) (my emphasis).

The Committee went on to point out that the lessons from enquiries in abuses in hospitals (see for instance Martin, 1984) should nevertheless be taken account of by informed opinion in its 'rediscovering' of the asylum function of psychiatric hospitals. The concept of asylum, the Committee maintained, had 'nothing inherently to do with large or isolated institutions'. Asylum could be provided, its members argued: 'in a physical and psychological sense in the middle of a normal residential community: traditionally indeed in the midst of a busy church. We must face the fact that some people need asylum' (ibid.: para 26).

In their visits around the country, and to mental health centres in the USA, the Committee had particularly taken up the issue of asylum for the so called 'new long stay' – 'those people suffering from chronic but fluctuating mental illness'. It seemed to the Committee that hospital hostels offered facilities to care for those who either would not or could not live in the community. Such hostels were able to 'provide some of the functions of asylum which larger institutions did without the attendant drawbacks' (ibid.: para 74). The Committee cited the view of a psychiatrist in support of its case for the hostels that: 'For a not inconsiderable number, asylums are still life-saving places, although everybody would agree they should be much smaller places to avoid the nasty, non-productive nursing and medical politics that thrive in large bureaucracies'(ibid.: para 74).

To conclude its suggestions on the issue of asylum, the Committee made two specific recommendations to the government. The first was that resources being spent on services for those with the most severe mental disabilities should continue to be devoted to that purpose in the future. The second was that the Department of Health should: 'draw on the experience of the

existing hospital hostels with a view to producing practical guidance to authorities on the lessons to be drawn for future provision
of asylum care' (ibid.: Recommendation 32).

In response (DHSS, 1985), the government agreed to evaluate
experience with the hostels, but did not commit itself to producing
guidance on the lessons to be drawn on the future of asylum care.
More importantly, the government agreed with the Committee
that 'positive asylum' was a necessary component of mental health
services:

> providing for those who need it, at a particular time in their
> lives or for life, a place of refuge and belonging, with personal
> space, that they have not been able to create for themselves
> through family ties and their roles at work and at home.
>
> (DHSS, 1985: para 46)

Hospital hostels, in the government's view, were only one means
of providing such positive asylum, with 'sheltered communities,
or residential or day centres with a high level of tolerance and
appropriate structure' providing 'other forms of asylum'. Some
'small home from home schemes in ordinary houses, flats and
bungalows' were also held to provide asylum, described in this
form as 'a balance of opportunity and shelter of which even the
casual visitor is aware' (ibid.: para 46).

The Social Services Committee examined community care for
the mentally ill again in 1989. Though it welcomed the recognition by government that some form of asylum service was
required, it recommended that government should 'give further
and detailed consideration to what is meant by the term "asylum",
(and to) who this type of service is for, and how it can be best
provided and financed' (DoH, 1991: para 105). Significantly, the
government rejected the idea that it should give further consideration to the meaning of the term asylum. This was because it
regarded the meaning of the term as already well understood by
providers of services. The government thus stated itself to be of
the view that: 'the need for *long-term residential care for some
people with a mental illness, often referred to as asylum* is well
recognised by health and social services authorities' (my
emphasis).

> The form this should take locally, its nomenclature, the extent
> to which it is needed, and the particular patients for whom it

is appropriate, are matters best decided at local level, within
the context of the overall assessment of service provision appropriate to that locality.

(ibid.: para 25)

In its previous pronouncements, the government had indicated
that positive asylum could be provided in a wide range of placements, including what it referred to as a 'home from home'
scheme. In its 1989 statement, however, asylum as long-term residential care appeared to be the approved form. In responding to
the Social Services Committee's enquiry as to how it intended to
monitor the adequacy of discharge programmes from long-stay
hospitals, the government gave a further indication as to its belief
that asylum was suitably provided in such form.

Indicating as before that there was no package of service which
could be applied to all localities as an alternative to the service
previously provided by psychiatric hospitals, the government did,
nevertheless, outline 'common components' (ibid.: para 16) which
would be included in the packages adopted locally. These were
itemised as:

1 An in-patient facility for assessment and short-term treatment.
2 Provision for longer-term asylum care.
3 Day care facilities.
4 Community-based psychiatric teams to support patients in the
   community.
5 A whole range of social care services (to be supported with a
   dedicated Mental Illness Specific Grant for local authority-
   funded services).

Given the identification of these five elements, and the distinction drawn implicitly between health care and social care within
them, what the government would appear to be requiring in relation to asylum is long-term residential health care. In fine, it is
exactly the area of asylum care so explicitly rejected by the
community support system model of the United States.

In summary then, the government in Britain has formally
defined asylum broadly as a place in which one has privacy and
a sense of belonging, and where some form of structured psychiatric regime is provided. Indirectly it has, at the same time, offered
a definition of asylum in narrower terms as a place of residential
health care. Notwithstanding these indications as to the nature of

asylum approved of, it has refused to commit itself to any model of asylum in the community.[1]

In 1987 a three-day 'forum' on 'the need for asylum in society for the mentally ill or infirm' was held in London, with experts in the psychiatric field presenting evidence to a panel of people distinguished in public life. The forum produced a 'consensus statement' at the end of the proceedings which, in common with the pronouncements of government, did not specify forms of service necessary to fulfil the agreed requirement for asylum. This requirement would be met by services ranging from those intended to provide a response to short-term crises to those intended to provide for long-term residence.

The panel worked from a definition of asylum as: 'a safe place of refuge or shelter, providing protection and support which may or may not involve total or partial withdrawal or removal from the rest of society. It may or may not involve treatment.' Like the government again, the panel appeared to be placing some emphasis on asylum as long-term residential care, particularly in relation to some sufferers of schizophrenia and dementia. The statement thus points to the need for help, in terms of 'accept-able accommodation and support' for those suffering schizophrenia who are unable to look after themselves in relation to diet, clothing and heating and who may be at risk of petty infringement of the law and occasionally of committing serious crime or self-injury. The panel also, like Lamb in the USA, laid some emphasis on supervision, stating that asylum was 'likely always to involve "treatment" or care', where this included 'nursing, habilitation and rehabilitation in the widest definition'.

Abrahamson criticises the consensus statement for making 'only passing reference' to the need to take into account the views of patients residing in long-stay hospitals for their future placement and for making no reference at all 'to involving them in choices during what may otherwise be a painful transition period; as if they will be magically and painlessly transmuted from hospital to ideal asylum in the community' (1988: 76). Abrahamson argues that the possibilities which Fulbourn hospital discloses, of devel-oping existing hospital sites to enable patients to have a wider range of choices, should have been considered by the consensus conference.

The possibilities of the Fulbourn model referred to by Abrahamson have been set out by Shepherd (1987) for the consensus conference in a paper entitled 'Need in the community – a district model'. In it, he adopts the official DHSS line of argument that asylum can take many forms. He goes on to propose that the solution to the problem of meeting this need lies in providing combinations of what he terms 'partial asylum', such as sheltered accommodation and sheltered daytime activities. Shepherd argues that a good quality of care can be provided in a 'segregated setting', though achieving such quality is more difficult than in a non-segregated setting. 'Patients do have a right,' he suggests, 'to be with other patients sometimes, just as they have a right to be with so-called "normal" people.' The problem, Shepherd continues, is one of 'how to give them these opportunities without either imprisoning them in the sick role, or denying their disabilities' (1987: 9).

Again, following the broad view of asylum formally espoused by the British government, Shepherd and his colleagues estimated that there were between 400 and 450 people living in the Cambridge Health district who required 'some sort of asylum due to the effects of long-term mental illness' (1987: 1). This population was made up of long-stay patients remaining in Fulbourn hospital on the one hand and long-term community clients of the Rehabilitation Service on the other. A range of sheltered accommodation was provided for the latter population, from permanent places in group homes to transitional places in hostels. With regard to hospital residents, a hospital hostel described as a ward in a house, and situated in the hospital grounds, had recently been added to the range of residential accommodation and further staffed houses in the hospital had been planned. A number of day care facilities, offering sheltered work, work placement schemes and social support, provided a further form of partial asylum available both to the long-term community clients and long-stay patient groups, with a 'Fountain House' club facility about to be opened.

Shepherd reports that the Fulbourn asylum service was being developed on the basis of a choice to 'retain a fairly substantial proportion of our asylum provision on the hospital site – at least in the medium term future'. He argues 'that this is justifiable given the needs of these patients in terms of day activities, medical and nursing care and the relatively good accessibility of the hospital to the community' (1987: 7). Interestingly, the Cambridge service he describes also includes an acute admission ward mainly for 'long-term patients from the community who are suffering acute relapses', which is run by the Rehabilitation service. Thus the crisis type of asylum, the only type endorsed by the USA's CSS model, is also provided, in addition to long-term nursing care by the Cambridge authorities.

Renshaw (1987) offers perhaps the clearest British discussion of asylum in a GPMH publication, albeit one eschewing, once again, definition of asylum services and consideration of for whom they are suitable. 'True asylum', she believes, fulfils two quite separate functions. The first is a 'retreat or haven where it is possible to escape the pressures and anxieties of everyday life'. The second function is 'protection from harm or danger'. Renshaw argues that the nature of asylum will be different for each person and that the solution should not be sought in service solutions, contrary to Shepherd's assumptions. Rather, research into user views had indicated that the first function was already being provided for in a variety of forms of psychiatric facilities. Thus 'acceptance in a pressure free setting', judged important for many people by Renshaw, was found in day care by some of those interviewed in a study by Davis which she cites. With regard to the second function, Renshaw departs radically from the conceptualisations of asylum considered thus far. In effect, this function has two parts to it. On the one hand, protection from exploitation and abuse needs to be secured by setting some limits to the freedom of the sufferer to engage in activities unsupervised and unsupported. This part of protection from harm is of a similar nature to that defined by the government. The other part, however, takes the form of professionals deciding when to detain those 'who are deemed to constitute a danger to themselves or others'. In this respect, compulsory admittance to a psychiatric facility can be a form of asylum. To sum up then, true asylum for Renshaw can be seen as 'asylum from one's troubled self'. On the one hand, it is asylum from the enforced loneliness which exclusion by the community entails. The person seeks to save their isolated self and to bring it into a community. On the other hand, it is asylum from one's vulnerable self, either in terms of self-harm/propensity to exploitation or in terms of dangerousness to others.

Possible ways to provide true asylum are numerous in Renshaw's view and can include: 'houses and flats with supervision, small crisis units which provide a breathing space free of responsibility with high support, day and leisure facilities which make few demands, and intensive domiciliary help'.

CONCLUSION

The concept of asylum has traditionally been associated with mental hospital care and with the removal from society, often compulsorily, of those placed within such institutions. The Geel system of asylum in the community, though it pre-dates the development of mental hospitals, is clearly imbued with the care and control exerted by the psychiatric hospital with which it has become associated. It can be suggested that because, on the one hand, the idea of withdrawal to a place of asylum for any length of time is felt, by many writers on the subject, to involve an infringement of the person's social or civil rights, and, on the other, that day facilities do not ensure sufficient protection *vis à vis* diet, heating etc. for those unable to attend to such basic needs at home, that, at the time of writing there are no model forms of asylum in the community identifiable. Possibly, a Geel system in which boarders were discharged from patienthood, had more control over placements, and had the support of advocates, would attract some support as a regime of care which would allow sufferers to remain unaccounted for though being continued to be given every opportunity for social engagement.

NOTES

1   In 1994 the House of Commons Health Committee (paras. 9–11) endorsed the view of its predecessor Social Services Committee, reporting ten years earlier, that asylum be provided as an element of services for those suffering serious mental illness. The provision of asylum by psychiatric hospitals was again acknowledged and, though the Committee did not undertake any detailed examination of the concept, its members suggested that 'asylum as refuge and protection from the public' should be provided as a discrete component of community services.

The reference for this report is: House of Commons Health Committee (1994) *Better Off in the Community? The care of people who are seriously mentally ill*, London, HMSO.

REFERENCES

Abrahamson, D. (1988) 'Comment', *Bulletin of the Royal College of Psychiatrists*, vol. 12.
Anthony, W.A. and Blanch, A. (1989) 'Research on community support

services: what we have learned', *Psychosocial Rehabilitation Journal*, 12: 3.

Brown, P. (1985) *The Transfer of Care*, London: Routledge and Kegan Paul.

Clark Turner, J.E. and Shifren, I. (1979) 'Community support systems: how comprehensive?', *New Directions for Mental Health Services*, no. 2.

Clark Turner, J.E. and TenHoor, W.J. (1978) 'The NIMH community support program: pilot approach to a needed social reform', *Schizophrenia Bulletin*, 4, 3: 322.

Department of Health (DoH) (1991) *Community Care: Services for People with a Mental Handicap and People with a Mental Illness*, London: HMSO (CM1522).

Department of Health and Social Security (DHSS) (1985) *Government Response to the Second Report from the Social Services Committee, 1984–1985 Session*, London: HMSO (CMND9674).

Friedman, M. (1962) *Capitalism and Freedom*, Chicago: University of Chicago Press.

Ginsburg, N. (1992) *Division of Welfare: a Critical Introduction to Comparative Social Policy*, London: Sage.

House of Commons Social Services Committee (1985) *Community Care, with Special Reference to Adult Mentally Ill and Mentally Handicapped People*, London: HMSO.

Lamb, H.R. (1988) 'When the chronically mentally ill need acute hospitalization: maximising its benefits', *Psychiatric Annals*, 18: 7.

Marshall, T.H. (1963) *Sociology at the Crossroads*, London: Heinemann.

Martin, J.P. (1984) *Hospitals in Trouble*, Oxford: Blackwell.

Ministry of the Flemish Communities (1990) information pamphlet in English on Family Care in Geel, Geel Psychiatric Family Care Organisation.

National Institute for Mental Health (NIMH) (1988) *Community Support Systems for Persons with Long Term Mental Illness: Questions and Answers*, Maryland: NIMH Community Support Program.

Parrish, J. (1989) 'The long journey home: accomplishing the mission of the community support movement', *Psychosocial Rehabilitation Journal*, 12, 3; 112–115.

Parry Jones, W.L. (1988) 'Asylum for the mentally ill in historical perspective', *Bulletin of the Royal College of Psychiatrists*, 12, 10: 407–410.

Renshaw, J. (1987) *The Asylum Trap: What Does It Mean for Mental Healthcare Today?*, London: Good Practices in Mental Health.

Roosens, E. (1979) *Mental Patients in Town Life: Geel – Europe's First Therapeutic Community*, Beverley Hills: Sage.

Schroeder, M.R. (1987) 'Escape from asylum – response to Wasow', *Schizophrenia Bulletin*, 13: 4.

Shepherd, G. (1987) 'Need in the community: a district model', paper presented to the Third Kings Fund Forum on 'The need for asylum in society for the mentally ill or infirm', London: Kings Fund Centre.

Zipple, A.M., Carling, P.J. and McDonald, J. (1987) 'A rehabilitation response to the call for asylum', *Schizophrenia Bulletin*, 13, 4.

Chapter 9

Some models of asylum and help in times of crisis

Jan Wallcraft

INTRODUCTION – A NEW DIALOGUE BETWEEN SANITY AND MADNESS

'Asylum' is a term which, according to the dictionary definition, means 'a place of refuge or protection.' As Judy Renshaw (1987) has pointed out, the use of the word 'asylum' as a place to contain people regarded as 'mad' has given an alternative, more pejorative meaning to the word. Renshaw speaks of the concept of 'asylum' as having two aspects – that of 'function' and 'place' – the function being conceived as 'escape from pressure' and 'protection from harm'.

Yet madness, like death is something most people prefer to see in its most mythical and sensational forms in literature and at the cinema rather than confront in reality. Asylum as escape from pressure or protection from harm has thus featured little in the popular imagination. As Foucault (1965) put it:

> In the serene world of mental illness, modern man no longer communicates with the madman ... As for a common language, there is no such thing; or rather, there is no such thing any longer ... the constitution of madness as mental illness, at the end of the eighteenth century, affords the evidence of a broken dialogue.

The policy of community care means that the dialogue between sanity and madness is re-opening, and the 'mad' this time have a seat in the debating chamber. No longer constituted solely as a social problem, or as passive recipients of treatments varying from the humane but disempowering to the frankly abusive, they are rediscovering their citizenship, finding a collective voice.

The inclusion of the voice of service users raises a number of important questions about the medical paradigm or model which has dominated debates about mental health for the past 200 years. For instance, could the closure of the large asylums mean something beyond a cynical cost-saving exercise? Could it also be an opportunity for the replacement of the illness model in psychiatry with a social model of the causation and solutions of madness and emotional distress, as radical psychiatrists such as Ronald Laing (1970), Thomas Szasz (1974) and Peter Breggin (1993) have argued for? If so, what would be the place of treatments such as psychotropic medication and ECT? Do the physical treatments still have a central role in the new community-based services and the small in-patient units, or by clinging to the medical model of psychiatric treatment, are we in danger of merely transferring psychiatry unchanged into community mental health centres and resource centres and missing a historic opportunity to transform it?

What, if any, will be the need for asylum – in its functional sense as escape from pressure and protection from harm? What kind of place could provide this function, without repeating past mistakes and recreating the total institution?

There are many people who term themselves 'survivors' of psychiatry, among whom I number myself, working through the various national and local mental health user groups, and through charities such as MIND, who are asking these and other related questions. A growing number are building links with the disability movement recognising that, they, like disabled people, face social discrimination which exacerbates their problems and often causes more hardship and suffering than the problem itself. Many consider that the psychiatric treatment they received did them more harm than good, and are campaigning individually and collectively for alternative, non-medical forms of help for people in emotional distress.

Despite the large numbers of people who are deeply critical of the psychiatric services they have received (note, for example, the abortive 'class action' against the manufacturers of Ativan and Valium, which at one point numbered 2,376 people claiming that these drugs had ruined their lives (Sunday Mirror, 1993)) mental patients have not yet had the public impact that, for instance, the Thalidomide victims and their families had. The ascription of the term 'mental patient' seems to render people invisible and to silence their voices. Self-advocacy in mental health rarely makes national or even local news, being vastly outweighed in publicity terms by negative stories about the actions of 'schizophrenics' in the community.

Yet, despite centuries of stigmatisation, the voice of psychiatric survivors is making itself heard in debating chambers, conference halls and training and education establishments. The conscious-ness-raising and educative work that they are doing, by valuing their own and each other's experience, are making the unthink-able possible. People who had been written off by the medical profession and society, people with labels of schizophrenia and manic depression, and people who have been institutionalised and regarded as unemployable are finding new roles as mental health educators, advocates, organisers of self-help services and consul-tants to purchasing authorities. Government, professional and voluntary sector bodies are consulting self-advocacy groups and reporting their findings, often commissioning survivors to do the research and writing. For the first time in history, current and former mental patients are breaking their isolation and silence, and speaking out collectively and individually. A recent impor-tant milestone in the recognition of the voice of service users was the Task Force User Conference in Derby, a two-day event spon-sored and supported by the Department of Health's Mental Health Task Force (1994), and run by psychiatric service user consultants, at which 200 service users, selected to represent as fairly as possible the many user groups across the country, came together for two days to discuss and endorse the two-year programme of consultation work which a group of user consul-tants had carried out on behalf of the Task Force.

One of the demands made at that conference, and one which surfaces again and again in consultations with psychiatric service users is for the provision of non-medical asylum or crisis care (OpenMind, 1993/4).

ASYLUM AND CRISIS HOUSES

One way of fighting back against oppression is for oppressed groups to redefine language which they believe has been misused in relation to them. For instance, feminists have argued that the term 'history' in practice means 'his story', and have set them-selves the task of writing 'her story'. 'Asylum' is a term which, when used in relation to mental patients, loses its general meaning of 'a place of safety' and transmutes into a deeply stigmatised place of incarceration and forcible treatment. Users, recipients and survivors of psychiatric services have collectively begun to reclaim the term 'asylum' and to redefine its meaning for them as a place of refuge and safety in their own terms.

Asylum for people in mental distress, as defined by mental health system survivor groups, can have a number of practical meanings, on a spectrum from informal to formal. At the informal end of the spectrum it can mean a safe house among friends where someone who has escaped from hospital while held under a section of the Mental Health Act, or who is afraid of being sectioned, can stay and recover in their own way in their own time. At the other end of the spectrum, it can mean the use by someone in mental distress of formal psychiatric services but on their own terms, for instance, being able to self-refer to an acute psychiatric unit, with confidence that no unwanted treatment will be forced on the person and that prior agreements about the person's needs and preferences will be respected.

In between the formal and informal methods of providing asylum, survivors have identified a third set of possible services, such as 'crisis houses' or 'stay-out services'. These would provide a combination of formal and informal support. For instance, a crisis house would have a set of operational policies in keeping with survivor demands for freedom of choice, freedom to self-refer, and come and go at will, respect for individuality, and a homely, supportive atmosphere with availability of counselling, advice and information. However, the house would be staffed mainly by full-time, paid workers, probably a mixture of people with professional mental health training, such as nursing or social work, and people with a background of working in voluntary mental health services, including people who had been service users. Another important feature of such a service would be the monitoring process by which the views of service users were fed back into constant improvements of the service, to ensure that it continued to meet the user-identified criteria for genuine asylum. This in itself would differentiate such a service from mainstream psychiatric services, which do not see themselves as primarily accountable to a user-identified agenda of needs. A stay-out service, or crisis intervention service, would provide similar support without necessarily focusing on a building, so that intensive support could be given by trained staff in the person's own home if that were preferred by the person in need.

Many service users and survivor organisations believe that a combination of these formal and informal and mixed crisis services, plus ongoing community network-building and individual support for people who have been through a crisis, would help to minimise periods of crisis and enable most people who would in the past have been identified as 'mentally ill' and hospitalised for long periods to live satisfactory lives in the community.

CRISIS, BREAKDOWN OR MENTAL ILLNESS?

Many survivors now use the term 'crisis' in place of the popular term 'nervous breakdown', or the medical term, 'acute mental illness'. Crisis services and crisis intervention are terms used by a growing number of psychiatric professionals. But are these uses of the word 'crisis' identical, and how far are they a replacement for the concept of 'mental illness'? This chapter will examine some of the meanings of the term 'crisis' in mental health, and some of the current crisis services on offer or being planned.

The term 'crisis' is seen as more positive than 'breakdown' or 'mental illness' by many psychiatric survivors. A crisis can be seen as an opportunity for change and growth, as well as a catastrophe. It is a point of transition, a point at which all the previous assumptions about one's life may be open to question and radical changes, maybe for the better, can be made. The psychiatrist Gerald Caplan (1964) has built on the work of the psychoanalyst Erikson (1950) on developmental life crises. Caplan views a crisis as a turning point, which, if resolved well, can lead to psychological growth, increased maturity and strengthening of the personality. Since the 1960s, there has been a gradual development of crisis intervention work by mental health professionals, often taking Caplan's work on crisis theory as a starting point. Caplan, though undoubtedly innovative, was tactful in his approach to mainstream psychiatry, choosing to emphasise the valuable preventive role psychiatrists could have rather than condemning outright the conventional containment and treatment focus of most psychiatry, as more outspoken psychiatrists such as Szasz and Breggin have done. In taking this line, Caplan carved a respectable niche for crisis theory within psychiatry, which has led to finance being available for the setting up of numerous crisis intervention projects, a few residential crisis services, and some theoretical research.

The crisis theory approach to service provision was also taken up from the 1960s onwards by radical therapists and psychiatrists outside the mainstream. Linking crisis theory with a left-wing, libertarian, anti-authority stance, they set up small, innovative projects such as the Andover Crisis House, and the Arbours Centre in North London.

Over the past ten years, there have been numerous attempts by groups of psychiatric survivors along with voluntary organisations and community mental health workers to obtain funding for small local non-medical crisis houses and crisis phone lines, some of which projects have had limited success.

The concept of 'mental illness' itself was at first meant as a humane attempt to remove blame from those who could not help themselves behaving in ways unacceptable to society, replacing the warehousing of 'lunatics' by asylums offering medical treatment, at least for those whom doctors regarded as 'curable'. However, this project was doomed from the start. Psychiatric 'treatments' were often no less cruel than the punishments formerly given to terrorise and quieten the inmates. Many psychiatric survivors claim that little has changed today. The treatments may appear to be more humane, but the medical model of psychiatry still serves to shut away and silence those who make society uncomfortable by expressing their feelings too strongly or in socially unacceptable ways. It sweeps pain and distress and difference under the carpet and tries to make it disappear.

Crisis theory is at least an attempt to restore emotional distress to the realm of normal human reactions to intolerable stress, and to avoid using an 'illness' label. As such, it represents a challenge to orthodox psychiatry, though currently in a limited way, as in many cases, crisis intervention has become another branch of psychiatry, with many of psychiatry's old methods and assumptions left intact. Caplan, though a psychiatrist himself, warned against the wholesale transporting of psychiatric attitudes into crisis services. He pointed out that a wide range of professions may in fact deal with people in crisis, and that if the ways in which psychological and psychiatric professions perceive, assess and handle crisis problems were transferred unchanged to other professions 'this might not be to their advantage'. He posited the idea of standardising the kind of preventive work that needed to be done to help people in crisis towards mental health in the context of each profession, while continuing to accomplish the basic goals of that profession, 'all of which gifted workers are already accomplishing on the basis of their own human qualities' (Caplan, 1964: 52).

In order to show the different perspectives on crisis as clearly as possible I shall outline the three main ways of looking at severe emotional distress and the practical alternatives each of these three perspectives incur.

I would characterise these three perspectives as those of:

1 The conventional psychiatric practitioner.
2 The professional 'crisis intervention' worker.
3 The psychiatric survivor/community group.

There may be great variations within these groups, and certainly not all survivors of psychiatry have a common view on how to deal with psychological or emotional crisis, but I think that these categories have some heuristic value in separating out the range of opinions and models which exist.

I will look at how each of these groups views the process of 'going mad' or having a breakdown or crisis (the terminology of different groups will reflect their perspective on what they think is happening to the individual in crisis), and how each believes that crises should be dealt with. Then I will go on to look at some of the examples of crisis provision which differ from the familiar mainstream psychiatric hospital model. I will talk about the philosophy behind them, how they work and what can be learned from them. Finally, I will draw some conclusions about the choices that exist for the future of mental health services.

The conventional psychiatric practitioner

According to the view of the typical psychiatrist, the following obtains. People who go into a state of crisis, and are brought to the attention of a psychiatrist, can generally be put into one of three main categories:

(a)   neurotic;
(b)   psychotic;
(c)   personality disordered.

People who are neurotic may respond well to minor tranquillisers, anti-depressants and ECT, with psychotherapy also a useful option.

Psychotics, on the other hand, are felt to need stronger medication, such as the major tranquillisers, and to be securely hospitalised until their symptoms are under control. The control of symptoms in some cases may necessitate forcible treatment. As the *Oxford Textbook of Psychiatry* (1983) puts it,

> If, having obtained the necessary legal authority, a calming injection is required, the Doctor should assemble enough helpers to restrain the patient effectively. They should act in a swift and determined way to secure the patient; half measures are likely to make him more aggressive.

People with personality disorders are basically just difficult people, and there is not much that anyone can do with them, except perhaps to offer behaviour therapy if they are not too awkward to co-operate with it.

According to the conventional psychiatric view, even though a crisis may be precipitated by an actual life-event, such as a bereavement, the patient shows abnormality in not being able to deal with it in the way that psychiatric opinion, as laid down in the Diagnostic and Statistical Manual (DSM) (1987), classes as 'normal'. For instance, the 'normal' period of grieving after a bereavement is specified in the DSM, and someone continuing to grieve after this period could be diagnosed by a psychiatrist as having a mental illness, such as endogenous depression. The cause of the abnormality may be hereditary, biochemical or to do with a personality defect. The psychiatrist may have a particular leaning towards one of these as the prime cause of psychiatric problems, or may regard each case as having a mixture of causes. S/he may not believe that medication will cure the patient's illness, but will expect that the medication will calm the patient and make them more amenable to hospital routine, behaviour therapy, occupational therapy etc., or that it will lift a life-threatening depression.

The conventional psychiatrist believes that the best way to proceed with someone in crisis is early identification of symptoms, rapid admission, diagnosis and treatment, in order to bring down mania, lift depression or suppress the imaginary sights and sounds that the person experiences in psychosis. In this way, most people in crisis can be made to function less disturbingly in a fairly short time.

The professional 'crisis intervention' worker

The view I am characterising as the 'crisis intervention worker' and which I will now outline, is largely consistent with Crisis Theory though with some later modifications.

Crisis Theory comes from the work of two American psychiatrists, Lindemann (1944) and Caplan (1964), who worked with fire victims in Boston during World War 2 and went on to develop a theory about the ways in which people dealt with extreme stress. Caplan says that under certain extreme or prolonged stressful or traumatic situations, a person's emotional equilibrium can be upset. Their normal ability to solve problems proves inadequate to cope with the current situation, and they go into a state of tension. If the problem remains insoluble, the tension is not resolved, and a state of disorganisation results, in which the person becomes unable to cope any longer. At this point, the person in crisis may be regarded by those around her or him to be having a nervous breakdown or becoming psychotic. In fact, Caplan says, this is the precise moment when the right kind of help is crucial in order to ensure that the crisis is resolved in a healthy way, and mental disorder is avoided. If that help is not available, the crisis may have an unhealthy resolution. The person may become a mental patient, with all the stigma this entails, or may turn to other unhealthy solutions such as alcohol or drugs, or may commit suicide.

This is the theory, in various different forms, which is the basis for most of the existing crisis services in this country. It has also been extensively used in recent years for victims of disasters, such as the Kings Cross Fire and the Zeebrugge disaster.

Some of the practical problems with this theory arise once a person has become a mental patient. Crisis theory seems to suggest that from then on it is too late. The damage has been done, and crisis intervention cannot be of much help if a further crisis arises. A whole subsidiary theory of 'furore' has been invented to explain the recurring crises which some people experience.

In fact, some crisis centres specifically refuse to help anyone with a psychiatric diagnosis. This means that people in crisis must first be filtered through a standard psychiatric admission procedure, to decide whether they are in a genuine crisis, relating to a crisis-causing life situation or are in fact suffering from a mental illness.

In this way, crisis theory can be adapted to fit well within and alongside normal psychiatry. The language used by crisis theorists is often as professionally distanced from the client's perspective and as objectifying as that of mainstream psychiatry.

The concept of 'furore' as an extension of crisis theory was the creation of Tom Farewell (1976) of the Napsbury Crisis team. He described the way in which some people, whose original crisis was resolved in an unhealthy way, go through repeated crises, which are not based on current events, but on past unresolved problems. The concept of 'furore' has more negative connotations than 'crisis'. There are suggestions in the description of this concept that the person concerned is putting on a kind of performance, and is behaving in a manipulative fashion. 'Containment', rather than 'change' is all that can be looked for, once a pattern of 'furore' has been established, with the hope that one day the client can be helped to face the problem and change their unhealthy way of coping.

Much depends in practice on how each crisis service sees its role (also, from whence it receives its funding), and the version of theory and the practical limitations it operates within. While some crisis services do see their role as radically different from that of mainstream psychiatry, others seem to see their main function as reducing the pressure on hospital beds, or as reducing the number of needless admissions by weeding out those who are not really 'mentally ill'. This will be explored further when we look at the examples.

Professional crisis intervention lends itself to statistical evaluation, and studies such as the evaluations of the Napsbury (Ratna, 1981) and the Coventry crisis services (Cantley, 1990) have shown favourable results, in reducing hospital admissions and suicides, and in greater satisfaction expressed by clients and their families. Crisis intervention, with all its imperfections, does appear to be a cheaper and more effective way of treating people.

The psychiatric survivor/community group

Survivor-led groups, or survivors as individuals, often go several steps further than the crisis theory approach, or in fact start from a very different place. Like the radical psychiatrist, Thomas Szasz, this group tends to dispense altogether with 'mental illness' as a concept, except perhaps for those with an actual physical degeneration of the brain, such as Alzheimer's disease.

The following is an ideal type of survivor perspective, which not all survivors would subscribe to in every detail, but which characterises the starting point for many of those who reject the medical model in its entirety and seek a different paradigm.

If we dispense with the concept of mental illness, then everyone entering a crisis is in fact trying to deal with emotional distress or trauma, whether the cause is recent or immediate, such as a bereavement, shock or loss of some kind, or whether the original experience of hurt happened before conscious memory or even in the womb. In fact, it is very hard for us, from babyhood onward, to heal our emotional and physical pain, because our culture does not like to be confronted with pain. Children are discouraged from talking about incest, racial or sexual abuse, and disbelieved or told to forget it. Even minor hurts, such as rejection by a friend fail to heal properly if the grief and anger are repressed and hidden away.

Crying, shaking, shouting and laughing are natural ways in which to deal with grief, fear, pain, anger and embarrassment, but children are so often hushed and so rarely encouraged to express their feelings naturally, that it becomes second nature eventually to repress one's feelings. Men probably suffer most from having to repress sadness and grief, because in our culture, crying is seen as 'unmanly', while women suffer most from having to repress 'unfeminine' anger. Both sexes are harmed by this process and everyone carries a lot of unhealed distress because of it. The former psychoanalyst, Alice Miller (1987) has well described the process of repression built into most pedagogical principles:

> If there is absolutely no possibility of reacting appropriately to hurt, humiliation, and coercion, then these experiences cannot be integrated into the personality; the feelings they evoke are repressed, and the need to articulate them remains unsatisfied, without any hope of being fulfilled. It is this lack of hope of ever being able to express repressed traumata by means of relevant feelings that most often causes severe psychological problems.

Black people, whether born in this country or not, have been told a great number of hurtful and untrue things about themselves, which it is unlikely they have had the space and safety to deal with completely:

If I went to the zoo they would make jokes at me saying that monkeys were my relatives. When they saw other Black people on the street, they would say, 'There goes your uncle'. I did not understand it, but I knew it hurt ... My anger is a feeling that stirs my guts and points swords towards me ... I was forced to hold this anger inside me for fear of being punished, and to pretend I was all right. In doing this I would silence myself for long periods of time, going deep inside myself, locking the pain in and people out. Like a door with an inside key, I learned a powerful way of shutting out those people hurting me, and punishing them.

(McNeill et al., 1986)

White people are also hurt by racism, which separates us from black people and creates artificial barriers between us.

Working-class and middle-class people are subjected to different sets of conditioning and prohibitions, which all take their toll on our ability to deal with the problems life sets us.

All in all, it is hardly surprising that as we enter the adulthood, or pass through the various transitions in our lives, we are often unable to handle that 'last straw'. The natural resourcefulness and adaptability that we were born with have been whittled away and replaced by innumerable unresolved 'hurts', which we are desperately trying to keep the lid on.

It is almost a matter of chance which of us goes into crisis. This will depend to some extent on the amount of unresolved hurts that a person is carrying. Some people, particularly those who have been badly abused as children and have not been allowed to express their pain, are likely to be more vulnerable to crisis than others. But much will depend on current events and the availability of support. Something, maybe quite minor in itself, can trigger painful memories that become overwhelming, so that the repressed pain comes to the surface all at once.

However, according to this view, there is a great deal of hope in a crisis. The person in crisis may feel terrified and unable to control the explosion of emotion, but in fact he or she is actually attempting to be heard, and at last to get some attention for the submerged distress. If that attention is given, then the crisis will become less frightening, and perhaps the buried distress can be brought to consciousness and gradually let go.

If the person gets into the hands of the psychiatric system, it is very likely that their expression of pain, rather than the pain itself, is once again mistaken for the real problem. Psychiatric treatments are aimed at quieting, suppressing, hiding and masking the symptoms of emotional distress. The patient, of course, may feel relief at having their pain suppressed by medication. Alcohol and street drugs serve a similar purpose for many, including professional mental health workers themselves. But all that happens is that the crisis is again postponed, or put off indefinitely at the cost of addiction to psychotropic medication, and even brain damage in the long term for many recipients of major tranquillisers (the brain damage is achieved more quickly in the case of Electro-Convulsive Therapy (Breggin, 1979)).

EXAMPLES OF CRISIS SERVICES BASED ON THE FIRST TWO PERSPECTIVES

1 The mainstream psychiatric 'acute' service

This relies mainly on early intervention, removal to a place of safety, which may be a police cell in emergency, admission to hospital either voluntarily or under a Section of the Mental Health Act 1983 if necessary, and rapid commencement of the prescribed medication. This may be convenient for society, at least in the short term, but often achieves little for the person concerned. It is open to abuse and injustice, as is shown by the overuse of Section 136 on young black men, and the number of deaths from overmedication (estimated by Professor Malcolm Lader (Open-Mind, 1994/5) of the Institute of Psychiatry to be more than one a week).

2 Crisis intervention services and crisis houses

Most of the alternatives to the 'mainstream model' of acute services come under this heading. Crisis intervention needs funding and staffing, and at present only qualified psychiatrists have sufficient credibility and legal status to be able to provide a full crisis service. However, there is much to be learned from looking at some examples of existing crisis services. I will briefly describe a few of these:

Napsbury Hospital was home to a pioneering service in crisis intervention which was set up to provide a round-the-clock service, in 1970. It aims to be able to provide treatment for people in their own homes within two hours of referral. Referral is usually from a GP or a general hospital. However, known patients can sometimes refer themselves when necessary. Napsbury owes some of its theoretical grounding to Dr Laing, who believed that often the person in a family who is regarded as 'sick' by the others is merely a scapegoat in a network of unhealthy relationships.

The Napsbury administration aims to get the team of psychiatrist, nurse and social worker on to the scene as quickly as possible, and to help the person in their own home, by talking through the crisis in the context of the family situation. The teams are able to offer skilled family therapy, marital therapy and referral to other groups and resources in the catchment area of Barnet and Edgware. There does not seem to be any commitment to avoid the use of medication, in fact, the issue of medication is rarely mentioned in the literature about the service, except to say that medication at home is monitored by the Community Psychiatric Nursing service. However, a theoretical paper on crisis intervention, published by Napsbury Hospital (Ratna, 1981) states that there is dispute over the emergency use of psychotropic medication in crisis events, on the grounds that the premature removal of symptoms may prevent the patient from undergoing a maturational experience. However, it goes on to say that in the case of someone suffering from sleep deprivation, for instance, medication may be necessary. 'The timing of the use of drugs and the manner of their prescription constitute one of the finer skills in crisis management.'

Hospital admissions in the areas covered by Napsbury are at least 30 per cent lower than the average for the region. Dr Ratna, one of the original members of the Napsbury crisis team, has become a leading spokesman on crisis intervention, and expresses very radical, almost 'anti-psychiatry' views.

Tower Hamlets and Lewisham are two other London boroughs which have set up crisis intervention services. Lewisham's service seems to have a deliberately pragmatic, untheoretical style (Renshaw, 1989). It is run as part of a range of psychiatric services, rather than having been set up as a radical alternative. The crisis service is most often called upon to deal with young, male African-Caribbeans suffering from schizophrenia, and its objectives are to provide a rapid response for evaluating and beginning treatment of disturbed and severely distressed clients. There is an emphasis on helping the family to understand the nature of the disturbance or illness. Where possible, the family is helped to cope, otherwise hospital admission or other care is arranged.

Tower Hamlets has a similar service (ibid., 1989) with some emphasis on the availability of teams able to communicate with people who do not speak English, as there is a large Asian and Chinese population, and on trying to avoid hospitalisation at least initially, using family-based crisis theory where appropriate. The response is relatively quick (within 24 hours) and short term (up to three months). It is multi-disciplinary and home-based where possible.

Though these three services are called 'crisis intervention', it appears from reading about them that they consider only a small percentage of the people they deal with to fit into the classic 'crisis theory' model – i.e. people who have suddenly and recently become unable to cope because of their circumstances and life events. The impression given by the papers on Tower Hamlets and Lewisham's crisis services is that crisis theory probably has in practice little more weight than mainstream psychiatric theory in treatment decisions. The pressures on the workers in these boroughs are, on the one hand, to keep people out of hospital, because of the gradual run-down of the large hospitals, and on the other hand, to consider the family's ability to cope. Under these practical pressures, there may be little room to maintain an ideal. The papers give little evidence of a commitment to prioritise the needs of the individual with a crisis to resolve. Because of operational pressures and lack of ideological commitment to crisis theory, such a service may well resort to the use of psychotropic medication as a quick and convenient solution, becoming little more than a rapid medication service.

From the early 1970s onwards, another form of alternative provision of acute services was the crisis house. Two of these, the Arbours Centre in North London, and the Andover Crisis House, were set up, like Napsbury Crisis Intervention service with a strong Laingian influence.

Arbours is an independent mental health charity. It is an ordinary house, in a residential area. People using it are called 'guests', not patients, and are helped by psychotherapy and support. Medication is neither encouraged nor banned, though as Arbours is a non-medical facility, the therapists would not be in the position of prescribing medication. Arbours uses a combination of crisis theory and 'radical' psychotherapy to help people to live through crisis in a calm and supportive atmosphere (Arbours leaflet). However, because Arbours is costly to run, 'guests' must either pay for their places or be placed by the local social services (usually for a strictly time-limited period of up to two weeks). Arbours do not have a crisis phone-line, but do provide a low-cost sliding scale psychotherapy service.

The Andover Crisis Centre, is, like Arbours, a private venture, but until recently had sufficient funding to provide a free community service. From its origin in the early 1970s until the mid-1980s, Andover provided 24-hour, 7-day-a-week counselling and advice with short-term accommodation. However, due to increased financial pressures in the 1980s the service had to take the decision only to offer its short-term accommodation to homeless women in need of emergency support. It also had to cut down its drop-in and telephone counselling service hours (Andover leaflets).

Nevertheless, Andover still aims to deal with 'any person with any problem', and most people refer themselves to the service. It has six full-time staff and volunteers (some are Community Service Volunteers). The majority of people seeking help go there because of relationship problems or want help in finding accommodation. The help offered is described as 'a listening ear, and non-judgmental, non-directive counselling, along with practical help once they have made a decision about their lives'. There is a strict policy of respecting client confidentiality which is much emphasised.

Crisis centres were set up in the 1980s in Coventry and Leeds (the Coventry service has since closed). The Coventry project chose to avoid the dilemmas of a service such as Tower Hamlets and Lewisham, by screening out anyone who is diagnosed as mentally ill. This means that clients could not self-refer and prospective clients had to go through a standard psychiatric assessment before being referred to the centre. The service was intended for those with problems of grief, loss, anxiety and depression. Sticking closely to Caplan's description of crisis theory, the staff regarded anyone whose initial crisis was resolved in an 'unhealthy' fashion and who had therefore acquired a 'mental illness' label as beyond help by their service. They concentrated their efforts on primary prevention – aiming to prevent those who were assessed as mentally well but emotionally distressed from acquiring a mental illness label. As there were no psychiatrists on the staff team, they explained, at a MIND seminar on crisis services which I attended, that they could not take responsibility for people suffering from psychosis. As a service funded by the Health Authority and Social Services, undoubtedly this proviso would have been a condition imposed in the funding agreement.

The Coventry Crisis Centre served the whole of Coventry, and it was calculated that during its first year, it kept eighty people out of hospital (Cantley, 1987). People were given intensive support at the centre over a short period, usually not more than two or three weeks, and the service was 7-day-a-week and 24-hour. Care was taken that men or women could see a counsellor of the same sex if they preferred. Many of the clients were referred to the centre following an overdose. They were encouraged to realise that their grief and distress were related to real life problems, and helped to find ways to organise their lives in the long term. The service was set up as an experiment, and the Social Service research referred to in the notes showed a high level of satisfaction with the service. According to the client satisfaction survey, users of the service appreciated the time to talk and be heard by people who were professional but still human and approachable. Some said that they had been able to explore their problems and get to the root of them. The atmosphere was described as pleasant and informal, and the availability of personal contact with staff on a 24-hour basis was seen as very important. There were complaints about the lack of self-referral, which for some meant that they could not get assistance until after the crisis point instead of when they needed it most.

The Leeds Crisis Centre was set up in June 1989, by Leeds City Council Social Services (Annual Report, 1992). Its aim, like Coventry's, is to reduce admissions to psychiatric hospital by offering rapid crisis intervention. At first, the centre opened only from 11 a.m. to 7 p.m. After a programme of research confirmed the centre's success, it expanded its services, opening from 10.00 a.m. to 10.30 p.m. every day of the year, and now has a few beds available. Though most referrals are from professionals, some self-referrals are accepted. Twice as many women use the service as men. The report, like the Coventry study, shows a high level of user satisfaction with the service.

However, the report says nothing about involving survivors in the planning and monitoring of the service, despite the fact that there has been a strong, active local survivor group in Leeds since about 1987.

It may be different with the planned Islington crisis services. There have been campaign groups working for alternative, survivor-led non-medical crisis services in Islington since about 1985, and funding has now been agreed for two crisis houses to be set up. One, The Sanctuary Project, is funded by the local Health Authority and is to be for women only. The other, The Haven Project, is for men and women, and is funded jointly by Health and Social Services. The planning for the Haven project has been a community affair. The responsibility for designing and commissioning the service has been given to Islington MIND, who are working closely with the survivor-led Islington Forum and a steering group of local survivor activists and voluntary mental health workers. The Haven Steering Group is ideologically committed to a position more closely resembling the third perspective listed above – the psychiatric survivor/community group approach, than to classic Crisis Theory. The group does not make a distinction between people who are labelled and those who are not, though it remains to be seen how the members will respond to pressures from the founders, who are requesting tight definitions of the target client group phrased in medical language (Haven Steering Group minutes, 1995).

Though, as yet, there are no comprehensive survivor-run crisis services in the country, survivors and their friends and allies continue to support each other informally through crises as they have done for many years, without applying diagnostic labels or asking whether the person is experiencing a genuine 'crisis' or only a 'furore'. For a person in distress, being believed, respected and cared about are often more important than the application of professional labels and categories.

Survivor initiatives are growing in their scope and confidence – for instance, the national Hearing Voices Network challenges the orthodox medical explanations of hearing voices as a symptom of schizophrenia, offering instead a variety of different frameworks in which voice-hearing can have a psychological, spiritual or religious meaning, and can be coped with in a number of non-medical ways (Romme and Escher, 1993). Survivors are training professionals and organising conferences to share their perspectives on issues such as self-harm and eating distress (Pembroke, 1993 and 1994), and undertaking commissions to carry out research for organisations such as the Sainsbury Centre for Mental Health (Beeforth et al., 1994) and write training publications for organisations such as UNISON and the Mental Health Task Force (Reid and Wallcraft, 1992 and 1994; Graley *et al.*, 1994).

Survivors and users of psychiatric services are repeatedly challenging the medical model's long domination of mental health services, saying that they do not feel properly listened to, responded to or treated by the statutory services or by professional mental health workers. There are problems inherent in any expertly defined model of mental distress, however humane its intentions, if it is imposed uniformly on people suffering distress by those with professional training but no personal experience of coping with similar experiences, and without building in a way for the clients' needs, wishes and responses to the service to be fully heard and to feed back into adjustments to service provision. Total belief systems or paradigms in mental illness have for the past 200 years blinded practitioners to the recipients of their services. In medical terms, complaints about treatment have been dismissed as paranoia, delusions or symptoms of mental illness. In psychotherapeutic terms, dissatisfaction has been put down to 'lack of insight' or 'resistance'.

A radical survivor-led model would build upwards from the expressed needs of people in crisis or those who have survived crisis, rather than downwards from legal requirements and state policy. The only guarantee that a service was continuing to meet the needs of its users would be from continual feedback from service users and monitoring on quality criteria decided by consultation with service users and former users. People who had themselves survived crises would potentially have an important contribution to make as consultants, trainers and voluntary or paid service providers in such a service. Though proper training and support would be needed, people with personal experience of crisis would have advantages in being able to empathise with the distress of others, and perhaps would be less fearful, puzzled or alienated by the behaviour of people going through crisis than those without personal experience.

Politically, crisis intervention is an idea whose time has come. With the pressure on hospitals to admit less people and to shorten their stays, many health service commissioners are looking for community alternatives to admission. Crisis intervention teams may seem to be the obvious answer, and also offer a way to redeploy psychiatric consultants no longer needed in the hospitals. However, if the main concern of such a service is one of reducing pressure on beds, they could become merely mobile medication units rather than offering a genuine alternative to the traditional medical model of psychiatry.

Genuine user involvement is the only way to ensure that the past inhumanities of the asylum system are not repeated in the community services of the twenty-first century. Psychotherapy is often put forward as an alternative to physical treatments in psychiatry, but even psychotherapy can be abusive, as Jeffrey Masson has argued recently (Masson, 1990). Therapists often hide their practices in a professional mystique, and client's views on what makes good therapy are rarely sought, as Nona Ephraim writes (Ephraim, 1994). More psychotherapy instead of psychiatry, if the role of experts is not subjected to critical review by service users, may amount to no more than the substitution of one tier of experts by another.

It is economically wasteful as well as unnecessary and morally repugnant to keep on locking people away in asylums or in their own homes, trapped there by stigma, social attitudes, employment discrimination and treatments which debilitate physical energy and damage self-image. Psychiatric survivors, ex-patients and service users could be seen as a resource, of mutual support, self-help, consciousness-raising, awareness training and service planning, provision and monitoring, as well as people who have a considerable amount to offer to the mainstream job market if discrimination were removed. Psychiatric survivors and their allies are challenging the dominant medical model of mental illness, which has for the past two centuries blinded us to these possibilities.

REFERENCES:

American Psychiatric Association (1987) *Diagnostic and Statistical Manual of Mental Disorders*, third edition, revised, Washington, DC: American Psychiatric Association.

Beeforth, M., Conlan, E. and Graley, R. (1994) *Have We Got Views for You: User Evaluation of Case Management*, London: Sainsbury Centre for Mental Health.

Breggin, P. (1979) *Electroshock: Its Brain-Disabling Effects*, New York: Springer.

—— (1993) *Toxic Psychiatry* London: Collins.

Cantley C. (1987) *Coventry Mental Health Crisis Intervention Team: the views of clients and their families*, Birmingham: Social Administration Dept., University of Birmingham.

—— (1990) 'Crisis intervention: users' views of a community mental health service', *Research, Policy and Planning*, 8, 1.

Caplan, G. (1964) *Principles of Preventive Psychiatry*, New York: Tavistock.
Davis, A., Newton, S. and Smith, D. (1985) 'Coventry Crisis Intervention Team: The consumer's view', *Social Services Research*, vol. 14, no. 1.
Ephraim, N. (1994) 'Talking about therapy' OPENMIND no. 71 Oct/Nov.
Erikson E.H. (1950) *Childhood and Society*, New York: Norton.
Farewell, T. (1976) 'Crisis Intervention', *Nursing Mirror*, 2 September, 69–70.
Foucault, M. (1965) *Madness and Civilization*, New York: Pantheon.
Gelder, M., Guth, D. and Mayou, R. (1983) *Oxford Textbook of Psychiatry*, Oxford; Oxford University Press.
Graley, R., Nettle, M. and Wallcraft, J. (1994) *Building on Experience: Training Pack*, London: NHS Executive.
Haven Steering Group (1995) minutes.
Laing, R.D. (1970) *The Politics of Experience*, Harmondsworth: Penguin.
Leeds Crisis Centre (1992) *Annual Report*.
Lindemann, E. (1944) 'Symptomatology and management of acute grief', *American Journal of Psychiatry*, 101: 141–148.
McNeill, P., McShea, M. and Parmar, P. (eds) (1986), 'Through the break – women in personal struggle', *Sheba*, pp. 15–16.
Masson, J. (1990) *Against Therapy*, London: Collins.
Mental Health Task Force (1994) *Grassroots*, no. 26, 29th November.
Miller, A. (1987) *For Your Own Good: The Roots of Violence in Child-Rearing*, London: Virago, p. 7.
OpenMind (1993/4) *Crisis Services: Where are They?* no. 66, Dec./Jan.
OpenMind (1994/5) Comment, no. 72 Dec/Jan: 3.
Pembroke, L. (ed.) (1993) *Eating Distress: Perspectives from Personal Experience*, London: Survivors Speak Out.
—— (ed.) (1994) *Self-Harm: Perspectives from Personal Experience*, London: Survivors Speak Out.
Ratna, L. (1981) *The Practice of Psychiatric Crisis Intervention*, London: Napsbury Hospital League of Friends.
Reid, J. and Wallcraft, J. (1992) *Guidelines for Empowering Users of Mental Health Services*, London: COHSE.
—— (1994) *Guidelines on Advocacy for Mental Health Workers*, London: UNISON.
Renshaw, J. (1987) *Asylum Trap: What Does It Mean for Mental Health Care Today?* London: Good Practices in Mental Health.
—— (ed.) (1989) *The Good Practices in Mental Health (GPMH) Crisis Intervention Information Pack*, London: Good Practices in Mental Health.
Riley, T. (1988) 'A brief description of the Napsbury Community Crisis Intervention Service', *Community Psychiatry: Its Practice and Management*, August.
Romme, Prof. M. and Escher, S. (1993) *Accepting Voices*, London: MIND.
Sunday Mirror (1993) 28 February.
Szasz, T. (1974) *The Myth of Mental Illness*, New York: Harper and Row.
Wood, S. (1989) 'Crisis intervention in an integrated psychiatric service: the Lewisham Mental Health Advice Centre', in J. Renshaw (ed.) *The Good Practices in Mental Health (GPMH) Crisis Information Pack*, London: Good Practice in Mental Health.

Chapter 10

The Sanctuary project[1]

Geraldine Huka

BACKGROUND

The development of African-Caribbean Mental Health Association's (ACMHA) concern with the Sanctuary project has been ably described by Okezie (1992), in an issue of the journal *Black Housing*. His description provides a good basis from which to understand its 'background'. ACMHA was set up in 1982 because of the concern of members of the black community about over-representation of black people in the psychiatric network – police, hospitals, prisons, etc. ACMHA's experience since its founding has, as Okezie puts it:

> undoubtedly led us to believe that over-representation of black people in the mental health service is largely a product of mis-diagnosis and faulty decision making by psychiatrists and related professionals. Black people appear to have been treated more on the basis of their skin colour than their presenting illness and distress.
>
> (ibid.: 6)

ACMHA's three principal objectives are: first, to further understand about black people's mental health and to assist with the development of more appropriate methods to deal with their distress; second, to prevent the unnecessary hospitalisation of black people; and finally, to prevent further damage being done to black people in the psychiatric system and to explore ways of improving services and treatment.

It is in the furtherance of these objectives that ACMHA aims to provide services which range from psychotherapy to research, and among which the development of residential care is of a high priority. The Sanctuary project marks a very significant step for ACMHA toward achievement of its objectives.

The opportunity to develop the Sanctuary arose in October 1992 when a joint planning initiative was taken between voluntary organisations (including ACMHA), the statutory sector and users groups and carers groups active in West Lambeth. This initiative led to the production of an outline plan for the sanctuary being drawn up by the local authority and the West Lambeth Community Care Trust (WLCCT, 1992). This document outlined its four key aims to be as follows:

1 To provide 'a preventative diversionary programme of therapeutic and socially based activities for 6 to 8 clients'.
2 To offer an environment 'responsive to the immediate and self-defined needs of the individual ... which is non-coercive, but staffed by workers who are professionally trained and skilled in providing services which are culturally specific and comprehensive', (such services to include art, music, relaxation, counselling and advocacy).
3 To provide a suitable environment for the assessment and social and clinical support on a day care basis of 'a number of black mental health clients whose reception into (care) is usually a negative experience'.
4 To develop packages of care 'in collaboration with other agencies, significant individuals and the black user, particularly those with long-term mental health difficulties who often are vulnerable to "falling through the net" of statutory service provision'.

In July 1994, ACMHA opened two houses in South London in order to fulfil these aims. One house was purpose-built and one was purchased from the local authority. Together, the two houses form the Sanctuary project. The purpose-built house (Coburg) is for those who are seriously ill, and provides 24-hour care. Coburg is recognised by referring authorities and the funding organisations as being for disturbed people. A lot of Section 37 patients will be discharged into this place. The other house is for people who are recognised to be vulnerable but who can be sustained in the community with adequate support. An ACMHA housing officer is responsible for this house and visits residents daily. This second house has a preventative emphasis. It is for those, for instance, whom GPs and others are considering placing under a section of the Mental Health Act.

The Sanctuary project has what one might call a symbiotic relationship with the conventional statutory services. Psychiatrists and probation officers refer patients for assessment by the project. Cumbria provides an alternative to acute admissions, and, as it is funded by the South London mental health care purchasing agency, SELHA, together with the provider hospital Trusts and the local authority, a collaborative relationship is a fundamental requirement. The housing associations which manage the housing element of the project also have a right to refer people, in the event that they identify suitable candidates in their accommodation. Some of the more progressive psychiatrists from the referring agencies come and talk to our residents about the side-effects of medication. The relationship with the statutory services is thus a multifaceted and developing one.

WHY THE NEED FOR AN AFRICAN-CARIBBEAN SANCTUARY?

ACMHA had always recognised that the psychiatric system had not worked for black people. It was therefore thought a good idea to have a place of reception exclusively for black people, as reception into an accepting and friendly place is therapeutic in itself. However, we did not want a black hospital. This was for two reasons. The first was that we did not want to prejudge the needs of those coming to the sanctuary by using medical or nursing regimes as our primary means of response to the situation the sufferer found himself or herself in. The second reason was to do with the isolation from family and community support that removal to hospital entails. But it was not just the bare fact of a hospital being objectionable, and that we desired non-hospital care in order to be able to offer something non-medical and non-clinical. On the face of it, the hospital is there to normalise those who are deemed to be mad, and as such is not an institution that one has any objection to. But how can you normalise in an abnormal situation? It is because the hospital is irretrievably an abnormal situation that we feel there must be an alternative sanctuary which is not a hospital.

It is often the situation with Section 37 patients (Mental Health Act, 1983) that they are taken to hospital under force, in order to be helped. They are placed in psychiatric hospital as an alternative to prison. Most of the males who are on Section 37 or 41 are automatically in a place where they do not want to be. The question then arises of whether you should force people to be helped, and if that in itself is not injurious to one's health. Under common law that would be an assault. This is why ACMHA feels that there has got to be an alternative. The hospital does not work if the expectation is that it makes people better on the basis of forced treatment. The racism involved in the degree to which treatment is forced on black people has to be addressed. Clearly there will be more likelihood of Section 37 patients agreeing to a care regime if it is being offered by people whom they trust to be supportive, and consequently of responding to that regime. The Sanctuary can therefore, in many instances, avoid the recourse to forced treatment.

One of the things that Mental Health Tribunals look at when patients are being discharged is whether or not the patient is likely to reoffend. Often the Tribunal looks at whether the patient concerned has been fighting on the ward on which he has been placed. But if there is hostility in the ward, which is to be expected given the circumstances of admission and confinement, then clearly the Tribunal's measure of potential for reoffending by looking at violence on the ward is not realistic. Psychiatrists do not have a crystal ball any more than any one else does who is involved in assessing the situation. At ACMHA we will want to look more closely at the circumstances in which violence may have taken place. We want to take account of the aggravating factors in assessing whether a person is suitable for the Sanctuary project.

That assaults on staff take place in the hospital ward situation can certainly be attributed in part to their lack of training in alternative methods of dealing with hostility from patients. This is something we feel it is important to recognise and to address, since the system has not addressed the management of violence at all successfully. Leiba (1992) cites the findings of Wallace *et al.*, (1973) and Rice *et al.*, (1985) that when staff are given short courses in verbal and physical methods for preventing violence and injury, assaults on them become less frequent and the injuries they sustain are reduced. Leiba also notes that the majority of those attending workshops he organised on the management of aggression and violence

> felt that they used their common sense and managed somehow, but felt they had to rely too much on drugs, force, seclusion and the police. It appeared from the 'Case Reports' (of incidents of violence described by participants) that resolution was seen in terms of the client/patient being removed.

Despite this, Leiba notes, his participants generally 'felt the resolution which took place was unsatisfactory'.

The norm of removing troublesome patients simply reinforces
the abnormality of the ward situation, as I noted above, one of
the reasons for ACMHA choosing not to have a black hospital.
Removal of the aggressor is clearly not an option in ordinary situations which have given rise to the expression of anger and
hostility, and in the domestic or residential setting the parties
involved usually have to find ways of coping with the situations.
Alternatives for patients who are in this unnatural, abnormal situation should therefore be based on realistic living situations, which
are not hospital-based. That is our conception of Sanctuary.
Therefore residents of Coburg are taught how to live with other
people in a social setting, and how to exist in the outside world
knowing that other people matter as well. This is in addition to
giving them help with the more routine 'rehabilitation' type tasks
of managing money. The house is a place where residents are
asked to do the practical things for themselves as far as practicable, such as cooking, cleaning and gardening. There is an
expectation that they will do their own shopping. Not only, therefore, do we feel it important for staff to have experience in
managing conflict but they must be able to use their knowledge
to educate residents about, for example, ways in which they can
be assertive without being aggressive in expressing their needs.

The side-effects of much of the medication used for ACMHA
'sectioned' clients are such that they look more psychotic than
they often actually are. This is a further factor which adds to the
abnormality of the hospital situation. Any possibility of achieving
a reduction in medication is therefore most important from this
point of view. Moreover, by making residents appear less odd,
reductions in medication improve their sense of self-esteem and
give a more favourable impression of them. Then there is the
issue of whether people should be forced to take medication.
There is an ACMHA patients group in which people talk about
the effects of medication and talk about survival strategies. It is
fairly well known that patients get more help regarding medication issues from each other than from any professional. In this
respect though, the situation is changing in psychiatry, and for the
better. As I mentioned above, we have a psychiatrist who visits
to talk to our residents about what is known about the effects of
medication, for example.

For ACMHA, it is important that our residents should not be in a place where they have to get up for medication, where they are there to suit the agency's needs and method of organisation. We want Coburg to be a home in the sense of a family situation. There are no medical rounds or ward rounds, and there is no compulsory attendance at groups, or prescribed occupational therapy or other forms of the conventional day care offered in the psychiatric system.

More importantly in relation to a 'family' situation, residents also have a significant role in the management of the Sanctuary project. They are thus given some control over what is happening to them. One resident from each house sits on the ACMHA Management Committee. That obviously could make life difficult for me on occasion, when I was the Director of ACMHA, but it is a very important principle for the project as it gives autonomy to people who live in it. The residents are on the management committee both to give them a say in how the project is run and to represent the concerns of their co-residents.

In Coburg House, each resident has a key worker. It is part of the key worker's job to befriend the resident and to find out what that person's various interests are. To fulfil those interests, it is the aim that the resident use the facilities that everybody else uses. If people use a day centre, we would feel that the project had failed.

When potential residents are assessed for their suitability for Coburg we ask about hobbies and what they did before they entered psychiatric institutions. We approached the local College for the Gardener, and we also made arrangements for training with the local Sports Centre in Brixton. In this way the project seeks to continue to engage the resident in the networks and inter-ests which they found supportive and stimulating in their living situation prior to experiencing profound mental distress. This is in contrast to the prevailing hospital approach of making such efforts long after the initial crisis has passed.

IS THE SANCTUARY A RETREAT?

The project does provide sanctuary from forced treatment, and from lack of acceptance and hostility from people working in the psychiatric system. But our residential care is not intended to provide sheltered housing where people retreat from society and stay in such a retreat permanently. On the contrary, we have an explicit objective to 'help foster an atmosphere where genuine social contact and relationship with others both within the project and as part of a wider community' can take place. We have set a maximum period of two years for a resident to stay. We are thus, in a sense, forcing people to get back into society. While we are providing a sanctuary from racism in terms of the isolation, neglect and disadvantage which are commonly experienced by black people, including those who become mentally ill, it is clear to us that the black community in which the sufferer is involved will be the first place in which support to resist racism can be offered rather than in any project such as ours. We do not, in general, regard the black community or networks as the source of the sufferer's problems.

Nevertheless, it may be the case though, that in some instances residents of Coburg will 'graduate' to the other supported house, forming part of the project for those who are not suffering from serious illness. In this way, a few may be able to retreat for a longer period in our accepting environment, if that is their wish and if assessment of their needs indicates that such shelter is in their best interests.

It would not be possible to get people back into society without adequate housing, however, and this is where ACMHA has struck a very important deal with the local authority. The Community Mental Health Team has given ACMHA a guarantee that residents will be resettled into accommodation of at least as good a standard as the accommodation they were living in before they became ill. This is of great significance since it offers the prospect of a defence against the kinds of self-neglect and vulnerability so often found where people who are discharged from care are placed in temporary accommodation, or bed and breakfast hotels. It means that after residents leave they should be able to live in accommodation where they can receive guests without embarrassment and where they are secure.

A NORMAL ENVIRONMENT WHERE NORMAL PROBLEMS WILL BE EXPERIENCED

Of course there are problems in the domestic situation which is nurtured in our houses, just as there are for families in general. Residents who have come from hostile and often unaccepting hospital environments are clearly going to arrive with low tolerance levels. Yet we somehow expect them to have higher tolerance levels than most people. What happens when a resident wants to bring his girlfriend to stay? This is a common cause of problems of shared accommodation, so it would be surprising if it were not so for us. There are difficulties in relationships between people at the Sanctuary. But the difference is that such problems are encountered and coped with in a friendly and accepting environment for black people.

We all meet difficult and objectionable people in the course of our social and business encounters. There are clearly certain levels of such difficulty that will upset relationships in the Sanctuary so much that the project cannot be open to all-comers, and to all those who would like to be placed there. There has to be some form of assessment for suitability in this respect.

The provision of the sanctuary is not the end of the story for African-Caribbean people. A range of housing is needed to suit varying preferences and ways of life. In the general hospital sector there are obviously various kinds of hospitals with different traditions, offering different services to people suffering the commonest major illnesses. There are public, private and voluntary sector care homes and hospices. In those sectors it is not assumed that there is just one hospital or home into which everyone with a certain illness has to go. Similarly we need a range of types of community-based housing to provide sanctuary for people with mental health problems. Some of it will be more of the same, some of it will be different. Funding bodies can't say that there will be just one house for a particular area to serve a particular client group. There is clearly also the important issue of how other significant ethnic minority groups in our area of South London will be provided for.

THE PROJECT AND THE LOCAL COMMUNITY

As far as relations with the local community go, the project provides a resource for black people living across a wide area of South London. Its catchment area extends from Lambeth to Lewisham. In that sense it would not be accurate to describe it as a neighbourhood resource: if an African-Caribbean person living locally were to be considered for residence it would be because of their suitability in terms of Sections of the Mental

Health Act, vulnerability and so on, and not the fact that the person was living in the locality. Indeed, we refuse to let local residents in to view the project. The houses are homes and we cannot afford to get into a situation where people are referring themselves in 'off the street' so to speak. Before ACMHA residents moved in, however, we did go round the local neighbourhood to reassure local people.

Is the project a success?

There are those who are waiting for the project to fail, who were happy for it to be funded in order for this to happen and to be able to say 'I told you so', so we are wary of making large claims for its success. Every six months we will review residents' admission records. If we can show that for two years a resident has stayed out of psychiatric hospital then that will be one measure of success. And so far, at the time of writing (October 1994), we have not had anyone return to hospital. For many residents we negotiate around medication. In some cases they are medication-free. This is another measure of the project's success. It is related to our commitment to using alternative therapies. For example, we have a psychotherapist who practices acupressure. We are also trying African herbal remedies. We have a roof garden at Coburg and herbs are grown there. Another important aspect of the project in terms of its alternative therapeutic effects lies in the design of Coburg. The use of a circular room shape was planned on an African model to have a therapeutic effect, and this is a highly unusual feature of any purpose-built psychiatric services project.

CONCLUSION

The development of the Sanctuary project is an important step for ACMHA toward the realisation of its objectives. It offers the potential for the misdiagnoses and racist perceptions of black people which are encountered in hospital services to be addressed in a comprehensive way. The Sanctuary thus provides a source of support in relation to racism as much as in relation to the specific mental health problems being experienced by any resident. One of its key features is that it aims to maintain and strengthen the contact between the sufferer and his or her friends and supporters in the black community throughout the period of illness. As I have stressed, the Sanctuary should not be perceived as a project where all black people who are on Sections of the Mental Health Act get referred. It provides one part of a wider framework of facilities which still require to be developed.

NOTES

1 The views expressed in this chapter are those of the author alone and are not presented as necessarily those of ACMHA.

REFERENCES

Leiba, P.A. (1992) 'Learning from incidents of violence in health care. An investigation of "Case Reports" as a basis for staff development and organisational change', *Nurse Education Today*, 12: 116–21.

Okezie, P. (1992) 'Mental health, housing and community care', *Black Housing*, 8: 3.

Rice, M.E., Helzel, M.F., Varney, G.W. and Quinsey, V.L. (1985) 'Crisis prevention and training for psychiatric staff', *American Journal of Community Psychology*, 13, 3: 289–304.

Wallace, C.J., Teigen, J.R., Lieberman, R.P. and Baker, V. (1973) 'Destructive Behaviour Treated by Contingency Contracts and Assertive Training: A Case Study, *Journal of Behaviour Therapy and Experimental Psycychiatry*, 4: 273–374.

West Lambeth Community Care NHS Trust (WLCCT) (1992) *Developing an Alternative to Hospital for Black People in the West Lambeth District*, London: West Lambeth Community Care NHS Trust.

Conclusion

Dylan Tomlinson and John Carrier

The concept of asylum has been considered from a number of perspectives in this volume. The case notes and archival evidence examined in Ireland and England indicate that mental hospitals have to some extent been regarded as places of safety by the mentally ill and their families. However, it is also clear that for the majority of their residents they can be considered to have given relief in the form of passive asylum, as Parry Jones has termed it, at best. The development of user organisations presents the attractive possibility of active asylum coming more into play. This would enable facilities to be created which address needs on both a more democratic and a more effective basis, harnessing the experience of patients and their supporters to clinical knowledge.

Nevertheless, we feel it important to point out, without, we hope, appearing to sound a sour note, that the evolution of 'user perspectives' may risk leaving out of consideration the view of patients or clients who do not wish to identify themselves as users. It may also risk leaving out the wider public, members of which may at any point become users of the services. Even if we are wrong about this, to implement users' demands for specific forms of crisis houses could still lead to the continuation of passive asylum, since those coming to the facilities may be expected to be as terrified and traumatised (and therefore unable to speak cogently for themselves) as those coming to traditional psychiatric facilities.

By definition crisis houses cannot give long-term relief from the too-close critical scrutiny and questioning by others that residents may be expected to be shielded from in short-term stays and the abatement of the 'furore'. The development of the community support system in the USA, moreover, and its endorsement by

.the NIMH, appear to effectively rule out the concept of long-term asylum in that country. As has been suggested in Chapter 8, this is principally for three reasons: its prohibitive cost; its granting of permission for the sufferer to be dependent and not be obliged to provide for himself or herself; and its association with abuses of care, especially in private nursing and board-with-care homes.

But can any form of active asylum, be it short- or long-term, rather than passive and partial variants of it, be provided for those who remain inaccessible in terms of being able to suggest to staff that they can orient themselves to their past and to their future? As a senior figure in the field of British social psychiatry recently commented to us, he could not recall any of his patients ever having asked to come into hospital during their bouts of florid schizophrenia.

It is thus difficult to see how active asylum can be provided given the consequences of acute mental distress for the person experiencing it. Semi-active asylum, in terms of a response to the wishes of close friends and supporters of the person, and of a response to collective user demand, does, however, appear to be achievable.

To demonstrate that psychiatric hospitals have been used for asylum is one thing, but the flight to replicating them which such a finding tends to hasten is quite another. Furlong, alone among our contributors, has provided a persuasive argument for some degree of replication. Her view that a valued role of the hospitals has been to provide a tolerant environment for odd behaviour, and one in which there were no great expectations for improvement in the more impaired groups of patients, while giving them opportunities for undemanding activities, is obviously worth serious consideration.

Furlong has also argued, on the basis of her considerable experience in the field, that community homes put unacceptable pressure on the long-term mentally ill to participate in shared activities and to be sociable. Whilst a problem with the view she has expressed is that it comes from the top-down perspective of the clinician rather than from the bottom-up perspective of patients and their relatives and friends, it does give cause for some concern.

Furlong's account of the Haven project indicates, moreover, that British mental health services run the risk of going down the

American road where the level of political, professional and financial investment in community care systems becomes so great that alternatives are unthinkable. American society cannot afford for mental patients to remain ill in hospitals or hospital-like settings for any length of time. Parrish's reference to the mission of the Community Support System (CSS) in the USA, outlined in Chapter 8, is highly revealing in this respect. If the patient is not saved by CSS from his or her possession by madness then the patient is damned by CSS to remain under its purgative regimes until saved.

The family boarding system offered in Geel appears, like the care of the natural family in Spain, to be able to grant the sufferer the right not to account for himself or herself and to behave in an anti-social way while continuing to be cared for over the long-term. This is a system which actually predates the psychiatric hospitals, and in that sense is perhaps the oldest form of asylum in the community. Its clinical regimentation and unfreedom would tend to lead to its rejection by many user organisations, but would a Geel system, run by and for users and their supporters (including their professional supporters) not have some merit? Given the contemporary diversity of family households, within which lone parents and 'reconstituted' families are as important as the traditional 'nuclear' unit, such a system, on the face of it, should not become so prone to familial dependency and subjection to authority.

For a large proportion of those suffering mental illness or going through enduring emotional crises, the family, however, is not the preferred setting and asylum through independent housing would be required. This makes Shepherd's proposal for combinations of partial asylum (such as sheltered accommodation and day care) to be provided worth some consideration *vis-à-vis* asylum in the community. Such combinations would promise their recipients opportunities both for participation in activities with other users and participation in the wider society, without, on the one hand 'imprisoning them in their sick role' as he puts it, or, on the other, denying that they have needs. There does not seem to be any inherent contradiction, in relation to this proposal, between independent housing and the provision of a level of consistent care and support to its occupants from adjacent locations. But even so, to counter professional arrogance and the evident tendencies towards scientific domination in the idea of partial asylum, there would surely need to be some form of democratic control by users and their advocates over the running of the facilities provided.

For those users who are domiciled in the family home with carers, in situations where both parties wish asylum to be given there rather than in any discrete location, the situation in Spain offers prospects which are important to consider. Respite services, and support at home for the vocational and recreational needs of the sufferer, could not only give space to everyone in the household, but also alleviate the oppression of women connected to their familial obligations in this and other societies.

Respite care has featured in many programmes of community care which are designed to assist elderly relatives of people suffering Alzheimer's disease to have a break from caring. However, such services have not figured in programmes for the long-term mentally ill domiciled in a family setting. The lack of investment in facilities of this kind for community care seems surprising given the general commitment to the policy. It can be explained partly by the fact that until relatively recently families tended to be blamed for the illness of the relatives in their midst who were suffering from mental illness. The lack of involvement of families in the formal care management of the patient (Jones, 1993) means that their role in community care has not been valued in the same way as the roles of 'normal' families caring for the physically frail or impaired. It can also be explained by the process Martínez Azumendi discusses in his chapter, whereby the guilt of the family about the admission to hospital of the ill person begins to ease off after the first encounters with hospitals have been overcome. This obviously has inclined families towards seeing hospital admission as respite and relief from the burden of care. In the UK, the lack of respite services can also be explained by the relative availability, until the late 1980s, of single person's accommodation within public housing. This allowed the option of residential independence from the family to be taken up for those suffering long-term or recurrent mental illness.

Services offering practical support to carers rather than the traditional family therapeutic interventions are, however, unproven and their effectivness is largely untested in this specific field. But given the pressing desire of families for relief from the burden of care, then help from professionals in supporting the user's personal development, through he or she taking up desired vocational and recreational activities, would seem to offer the

possibility for the emotional intenseness of household relationships, which Furlong warns against, to be lessened.

A question we raised at the beginning of this book was whether
there was any empirical evidence to show that psychiatric hospitals have ever provided true asylum. The review of the evidence
presented in Finanne's chapter illustrates very clearly that patients
and their families negotiated the use of mental hospitals as places
of retreat. Prior, at the same time, in examining the contrary view,
that mental hospitals have been imposed on the population as a
means of social control, found the nature of admissions to the
hospitals to indicate quite clearly that the respectable were as well
represented in terms of numbers of patients as the unrespectable.
Prior has compared popular Irish belief in, and recourse to, ideas
about lunacy to explain bizarre behaviour with the belief in, and
recourse to, witchcraft of the Azande. This comparison indicates
the way in which mental hospitals were as accepted among the
Irish population as churches were. While Prior is unusual among
sociologists in the mental health field in taking this view, the scope
and depth of his scholarship suggest that it should point us well
away from the social control thesis and towards more of an appreciation of the various forms of asylum which were to be found in
mental hospitals.

In our own research we have indicated that there appears to
have been a minority of long-term patients who tried to get into
hospital, while others were recorded as being 'fatuously happy'
at an early stage of their admission, before institutionalisation
could have been presumed to have settled in. We have also pointed
out that there were plenty of social reasons for our sample to
have wanted to seek the sanctuary of the mental hospital whether
they were seriously mentally ill or not.

But if these aspects of true asylum in mental hospitals do require
to be reproduced, one is brought to an abrupt halt in any delib-
erations about the need for such reproduction by Raftery's
research. If there is something, in historical terms, which makes
the generation of inter-war patients who became long-term asylum
residents unusual, or if there were unusual social pressures in that
period, then perhaps the investigation of asylum should be looking
at more recent periods of mental hospital history.

Raftery also makes us aware that the mental hospital has far
from disappeared from the landscape at the time of writing: in
1994 only three out of ten hospitals which were open in 1960 had

actually closed (Audit Commission, 1994). In the meantime, as Furlong's narrative on Friern indicates, rehabilitation wards have been developed on district general hospital sites, indicating that DGH asylums-in-miniature may, at least in some regions, become the main providers of long-term refuge in the future, whether this was their objective or not.

The development of DGH services, itself an institutional solution dating back to the 1962 Hospital Plan for England and Wales, and to the period of the late Harold Wilson's white heat of technology, illustrates how much scope remains for asylum to be reconceptualised and redesigned. Forms of partial asylum encompassing crisis houses, the respite care offered from the Fulbourn asylum-in-miniature, and home care asylum are surely achievable in the twenty-first century. The continuing evolution of the user/survivor movement holds out the prospect of mental health services finally moving on from the white heat of technology model which, for all its other life-saving merits, is so plainly inappropriate for those remaining relatively inaccessible to society as a result of their mental illness.

At the same time, Wallcraft has provided a cogent argument in this volume for alternative forms of asylum to the acute admission facilities provided by psychiatric and general hospitals. This argument needs to be considered in the light of Raftery's finding that there are more short-term hospital places available in the contemporary period than at any previous period in history. It seems likely that the clinical models followed in hospital reception facilities will be viewed as inadequate to meet the needs for support which the growing literature on users' views identifies. The potential for shifting resources away from hospital to community in relation to short-term admissions therefore also seems to be eminently feasible, although it has not been our principal concern in this book.

Neither Wallcraft not Huka anticipate that those suffering from acute forms of distress are likely to require long-term asylum, contrary to what appears to be the official British policy. Their view is that the crisis or emotional disturbance should be resolved in a 'healthy' way, in a situation where the person is able to display their emotions and be with people whom they can trust and confide in. Provided a sufficient range of places and caring people for crisis resolution are provided, the need for long-term asylum should not be necessary. Wallcraft's contribution thus suggests to us that by taking long-term care as our focus we may be destroying the possibility of asylum in the community before it has been realised. We may be unwittingly helping advocates of institutional care to fit the concept of asylum firmly back inside the psychiatric ward because of our accepting that significant numbers of patients are going to remain inaccessible to treatment and unresponsive to care regimes for lengthy periods. This may be tantamount to a denial that alternatives to hospitals can work.

If one takes the pessimistic view that there will always be some among those suffering mental illness or an enduring emotional crisis who do not respond to treatment or support, then long-term asylum seems very important to secure. As Europeans we would argue that long-term asylum in the community, outside the mental hospital and democratically controlled, where residents or attenders may remain inaccessible for extended periods, is an essential part of future mental health services.

REFERENCES

Audit Commission (1994) *Finding a Place*, London: HMSO.
Jones, D. (1993) Professional carers and the families of people suffering mental illness, in Jones, D., Ramon, S. and Tomlinson, D. (eds) *Opening up the Dialogue, Informal and Professional Carers in Mental Health*, papers from a conference held by the Team for the Assessment of Psychiatric Services (TAPS) and the London School of Economics, January 1992.

Index